More Praise for *Passages in Caregiving*

"As a longtime champion for family caregivers, I am delighted that Gail Sheehy has brought this passage vividly to life from her own long experience and that of many others. This is one of those rare books that can drastically lighten even the heaviest of loads."

—Rosalynn Carter, President of the
Rosalynn Carter Institute for Caregiving

"I expect *Passages in Caregiving* to be the manual for caregivers for generations to come. Gail Sheehy has addressed every possible situation in an engaging, timely, and easy-to-follow manner."

—Gary Small, MD, UCLA Professor of Psychiatry and Aging

"In this insightful book that combines a moving firsthand account of her own journey and valuable strategies for navigating the labyrinth of caregiving, Gail Sheehy takes the mystery out of what can be a baffling, heart-rending experience. A must-read for anyone who gets the Call."

—Hugh Delehanty, Editor in Chief of AARP Publications

"Through her touching personal story, Gail Sheehy has captured the anxiety, the beauty, and the overwhelming experience of facing the end of life with someone you love. She offers hope, insight, and wisdom to the millions who walk this same emotional journey every day. This book will, at long last, shine a light on the tremendous needs of caregivers and empower all of us to create a humane and loving experience in the final phases of life."

—Carolyn Cassin, President and CEO of National Hospice Work Group

"No longer will you have to blindly navigate the murky corridors of caregiving. You have an easy-to-read road map right here." —Judith Orloff, MD

D0954816

"More and more people are left to deal with late-stage health care on their own. Gail Sheehy's masterfully researched and written book comes at a perfect time, when people need it most."   —Robert N. Butler, MD,
Founding Director of the National Institute on Aging

"I learned when producing my PBS series on death and dying that caregiving is among the most universal and least understood experiences that we humans have in common. Gail Sheehy has given us a gift with this moving account of her own journey to that place of love and suffering where most of us are headed."   —Bill Moyers

"Sheehy offers an empathetic, well-researched guide to an unfamiliar, often scary role to which boomers are being initiated, outlining eight stages of caregiving. . . . Sheehy contends caregivers are in desperate need of knowledge and support, and this resourceful manifesto provides it, including practical steps to take, strategies for each point of care, likely obstacles for both patient and caregiver, and a lucid explanation of what's to come: 'My intention is to illuminate the challenges and rewards inherent in the caregiving passage—to identify universal patterns in the chaos and give the journey a form that makes sense.' Sheehy achieves her goal ably, providing a steady beacon during a time of great sadness and overwhelming responsibility."   —*Publishers Weekly*

"Supportive and reassuring, Sheehy provides encouraging and practical information for both patient and caregiver in one of the most comprehensive and trustworthy resources a family can ask for when facing one of life's most disheartening challenges."   —*Booklist*

PASSAGES IN CAREGIVING

PASSAGES IN CAREGIVING

TURNING CHAOS INTO CONFIDENCE

GAIL SHEEHY

HARPER

NEW YORK · LONDON · TORONTO · SYDNEY

HARPER

A hardcover edition of this book was published in 2010 by William Morrow, an imprint of HarperCollins Publishers.

FIRST HARPER PAPERBACK PUBLISHED 2011.

The Library of Congress has catalogued the hardcover edition as follows:
Sheehy, Gail.
Passages in caregiving : turning chaos into confidence / Gail Sheehy.—1st ed.
p. cm.
ISBN 978-0-06-166120-4
1. Caregivers. 2. Chronically ill—Care—Psychological aspects. 3. Chronically ill—Family relationships. 4. Home nursing. I. Title.
RA645.3.S49 2010
362'.0425—dc22

2009042533

ISBN 978-0-06-166121-1 (pbk.)

11 12 13 14 15   WBC/RRD   10 9 8 7 6 5 4 3 2 1

To Clay Felker (October 2, 1925–July 1, 2008)

CONTENTS

FIRST TURNING:
SHOCK AND MOBILIZATION   53

THIRD TURNING: BOOMERANG   113

Fourth Turning: Playing God   157

FIFTH TURNING:
"I CAN'T DO THIS ANYMORE!" 203

INTRODUCTION

This book was inspired by my journey as a caregiver for my husband, Clay Felker. The story of how we survived and even thrived over the last seventeen years of Clay's life is threaded throughout these pages, along with the stories of many other inventive caregivers and the helpful strategies that we have all learned the hard way. But before we begin, I need to give a little context.

When people grow older, get sick and die, their formerly robust lives are often forgotten. To be forgotten is something we all fear. It's why we make an effort to leave a legacy. Obituaries that celebrated Clay as a "journalistic giant" and "magazine pioneer" and "legendary editor" all stopped before the rich final period of his life. It was not a period of public celebrity, but one of quiet celebration. To appreciate the challenges we faced in those years, readers unfamiliar with Clay's history should know something about the man in his prime.

Clay was born in 1925 in a racially segregated border state, Missouri, and his insatiable curiosity always led him to cross boundaries. Not content to be cosseted in the safe white suburb of Webster Groves, he ventured into the black neighborhood of St. Louis, hungry for the jazz music of Duke Ellington and Ella Fitzgerald. He found jukebox vendors who sold "race records" for five cents apiece. Jazz became the sound track to Clay's life.

He was always in love with New York, from the time he first read *The New Yorker* and *Esquire* as a shy, skinny preteen. He imagined the urbane editors of such magazines dressed in black tie, ready to slide into limousines at the drop of an invitation to the dinner tables of the city's power brokers. Editing the student newspaper at Duke University and the base newspaper during his three years in the navy was a mere out-of-town tryout. Two seasons of traveling the country as a sportswriter covering the baseball Giants exposed him to America's big-league towns. But to his mind, he was still a rube until he learned how to be an editor in America's premier City of Ambition, New York.

He came close during the late 1950s and early 1960s, when he was one of three young turks at *Esquire,* vying for the paternal nod to become editor in chief. Every week, for several years, each rival threw out his best story ideas and the other two shot them down. When Clay lost this "blood-on-the-walls" contest to Harold Hayes, he went on to the fabled *New York Herald Tribune.* Asked to create a Sunday supplement, he rejected pabulum and instead mirrored his primary-color vision of New York. It smacked readers with glaring cover images of their city and hooked them with irresistible food and cultural features. He drafted the paper's two best reporters, legends-in-the-making Tom Wolfe and Jimmy Breslin, and hounded them into producing must-read stories almost weekly for four years. Wolfe, the tidewater Virginia gentleman, had a fiendish eye for deflating the vanity of Manhattan swells. Breslin, the snarling Irish bad boy, had a thirst for Damon Runyonesque guys and dolls.

When the *Herald Tribune* folded in 1967, Clay raised a million dollars and combined it with his severance pay to give birth to his dream—the first magazine devoted entirely to one city: *New York.* It was 1968 and the country was coming apart at the seams with two shattering assassinations, of Dr. Martin Luther King Jr. and Senator Robert Kennedy. New York City was in an economic tailspin. Racial fury seethed in Harlem while Columbia's antiwar students were chanting "Revolution!" I was there in graduate school.

Out of the turmoil of 1968, Clay fathered a new generation of star journalists, among them Gloria Steinem, whom he first turned loose on politics and later showcased with her own magazine, *Ms.,* inside the pages of *New York.* Clay and his tribe invented an alternate New York, a circus of street culture as seen through the eyes of a new young generation of escapees from the suburbs. Most of his writers were rebels with a cause—free living and loving on the New Frontier, far from the confines of white flight, fascinated by every ingredient in the urban stew pot, the Big Apple.

It was within this turmoil that Clay and I began our relationship, challenging each other with ideas, chasing stories, wrestling through the feminist revolution to educate (or annihilate) each other, falling in love, and resisting the convention of marriage. After a whirlwind seventeen-year courtship, we finally married in our middle years, in 1984, and adopted a child.

Clay was a progressive, but he never had any fixed ideological point of view. There was no formula his writers had to fit. He often said people do their best work when they are valued for their personal vision and not just for their professional skills. This became the "Felker effect."

Clay's duplex apartment on Manhattan's Upper East Side defined him. It was the stage set upon which, starting in his thirties, he learned to play the role of the quintessential New York editor. Buttons on the phones were always alight. The door was always open. People streamed in and out, talking, asking, pitching. Emerging from the elevator, guests found themselves looking down from a balcony into a sunken living room. Framed by cathedral-sized windows behind him, Clay occupied a big club chair by the fireplace, devouring soft-boiled eggs and five daily newspapers.

"Look who's here!" was his welcoming bellow to breakfast guests, as if they were the most important people in the world. Clay's greatest gift was to be a natural mentor. He lent himself to be used as an opportunity for others' development, becoming a protean assemblage of all the talents he nurtured. If he thought you could do it, he made you believe you could.

Milton Glaser, the Bronx-bred artist and graphic designer who was Clay's partner in starting *New York* magazine, was amused by Clay's constant astonishment at the ways of the city. "He never developed the thick cynical veneer of so many other editors," he said. "Clay was always vulnerable to fresh ideas and possibilities."

Various aspiring novelists tried to fictionalize Clay, but none successfully captured the man behind the scenes. I believe my daughter Maura, the stepdaughter he adored, came closest.

"When I was around five or six, I began to form the impression that he was magic," she has written. "Whenever Clay thrust out a hand for a taxi, a Checker cab appeared, even though there were hardly any left in New York.

I'd look up Second Avenue at the tide of yellow, and there wouldn't be one in sight. The next thing I knew I was climbing in and opening up the jump seat, trying to remember when I'd looked away.

"When we went somewhere with him, he'd often just start off walking impossibly fast, down some dark street. I'd yank my mother to keep up in her heels. If I asked how much longer, he'd stab a pointed finger into the air and grunt, 'Just, just, just.' And then suddenly he'd stop and there would be a door, and we'd go in, and there would be great music, a splendid room, some unbelievable delight, people sounds, something happening. It was magic. So I learned, like everyone else, that even though you didn't know where you were going, if you were with Clay it was going to be fun, and probably fascinating, maybe even spectacular."

Inflated by ambition, Clay finally flew too high. He spent too much to buy *The Village Voice,* hired a chef for editorial lunches, and launched a West Coast version of *New York,* a poor cousin called *New West.* Perversely, the moguls who prospered by investing in his success—who loved dining out on the buzz about his magazines—were quick to betray him. In 1977, they sold him out to the Australian press baron he had introduced to New York, Rupert Murdoch.

Stunned by the hostile takeover, Clay's staff walked out en masse. From a tabletop in the nearest restaurant, ironically called Chicago, Clay addressed them. "Don't give up your jobs on my account. Get some money out of these bums!" He went on to buy, create, or edit many other publications and fostered the highest dreams of his protégés to write their own books, create their own magazines, start their own media companies. Their names are legion. Dozens of the artists who worked for Clay and Milton became renowned art directors, designers, and painters shown around the world. A tribe—and a bond—was formed by those seven years of journalistic utopia that we all enjoyed at the early *New York* magazine.

Clay would have appreciated the opening paragraph of his July 2, 2008, obituary in the *New York Times*: "Clay Felker, a visionary editor who was widely credited with inventing the formula for the modern magazine, giving it energetic expression in a glossy weekly named for and devoted to the boisterous city that fascinated him—New York—died on Tuesday at his home in Manhattan."

The *Times* went on to say: "The West Coast became his second home. And while he loved teaching, nothing ever quite equaled those high-living and hard-working days when New York City was his muse and *New York* magazine his darling."

From Clay's perspective, however, it was the last seventeen years of his life, despite intermittent illness, that he found the most rewarding. It was a golden opportunity to advance to the guru stage and teach while learning from yet another generation of the brightest young journalists.

Throughout the long undoing of his body and throttling of his ability to command a room with his booming voice, Clay's spirit expanded in intensity. He showed as much interest in the personal lives and aspirations of his home health aides as he had in his up-and-coming writers and editors. He fostered the dreams of their children. A quote from Albert Schweitzer sums up the magic he passed on.

In everyone's life, at some time, our inner fire goes out.
It is then burst into flame by an encounter
with another human being.

To his last breath, this was the Felker effect.

THE MAKING OF A
CAREGIVER

one
THE CALL

The call came to me in a beauty salon.

"It's not benign."

"Not benign?" I repeated dumbly.

"The cyst on Mr. Felker's neck, it's not benign."

The caller was my husband's surgeon. Blunter than ever.

"But two years ago after the biopsy, you told us—"

"The pathologist recut the old biopsy slides. It's cancer."

Two peaceful years before, the surgeon had scooped out a lump on my husband's neck, a cyst quickly verified as "benign." End of crisis.

But cancer is cruel, implacable, perverse. It tricks smart oncologists and defeats brilliant surgeons. The supposedly benign tumor had come back, bigger than ever. Weeks flew by as I tracked down doctors, compared hospitals, listened to stories from friends, and scavenged the Internet for alternatives. Dizzy from conflicting opinions, many delivered with more egotism than expertise, I didn't know whom to trust. It began to dawn on me that my life, too, had changed radically. I had a new role.

Family caregiver.

I didn't expect it. I wasn't prepared for it. Nobody briefs us on all the services we are expected to perform when we take on this role. If want ads for the job existed, they would look like this:

HELP WANTED: Untrained family member or friend to act as advocate, researcher, care manager, and emotional support for a parent or spouse, sibling or friend, who has been diagnosed with a serious illness or chronic disability. Duties: Make medical decisions, negotiate with insurance companies or Medicare; pay bills; legal work; personal care and entertainment in hospital and rehab. Aftercare at home: Substitute for skilled nurse if injections, IV, oxygen, wound care or tube feedings are required. Long-term care: Medication management, showering, toileting, lifting, transporting, etc. Hours: On demand. Salary and benefits: 0.

I never dreamed that I was about to spend many of the next seventeen years as a caregiver, fighting for the life of a man who refused to give up. And I had no idea that nearly fifty million other American adults were stumbling along the same unpredictable path—trying to take care of their parents or other relatives or supporting a partner through chronic illness. The prevalence of this mostly ignored passage is staggering: In almost one-third of American households somebody is serving as an unpaid family caregiver.

WHY I WROTE THIS BOOK

This book is aimed at helping you take charge—a gift you owe both your loved one and yourself. My intention is to illuminate the challenges and rewards inherent in the caregiving passage—to identify universal patterns in the chaos and give the journey a form that makes sense. This may well be the most important passage of your life. It will revive old issues in your family. It will pit your own dreams for your middle years against the needs of your elders. How you handle this crisis will shape how you feel about yourself and almost certainly change you in ways that follow you to the end of your days.

In 2009, I was honored to serve as AARP's Ambassador of Caregiving. I appealed to the most trusted organizations that assist caregivers to introduce me to families who represent common challenges and different cultures. With a producer and cameraman, I traveled the country for months interviewing hundreds of caregivers. The thirty families we chose to film bring to life the emotional journey. I posted their videos on the AARP.org website and wrote journals that point to resources. You can see these videos on my website: www.gailsheehy.com.

In this book I also offer my own raw experience of each phase of the caregiver's journey. Our story offers a possible catharsis for readers who are going through the crisis right now. Each of the stories within highlights creative ways to meet the challenges, practically as well as emotionally and spiritually. I invite you to learn from our mistakes: thinking we have no authority because we're "just family"; passively accepting first opinions; taking on the whole burden; not believing we deserve help; not researching where we can find help; often giving up our jobs, friends, and financial security; ignoring our own health; and forgetting what gives us joy. You don't have to make these same mistakes. This book offers you insights, tools, and wear-tested strategies that will enable you to proceed with confidence.

COLLISION OF LIFE STAGES

In my books and speeches since 1995, when I published *New Passages,* I keep predicting liberation ahead—the advent of a Second Adulthood, starting in one's midforties and fifties. At that proud age, having checked off most "shoulds," people generally feel a new sense of mastery. Haven't you done your best to please your parents, your mentor, your boss, and your mate, and now it's time for you? The children are making test flights on their way to piloting solo. Your parents have become giddy globe-trotters, piling up frequent-flier miles and e-mailing playful photos of themselves riding camels.

Free at last! (Or at least, freer.)

This is the time to revive dreams deferred years ago. A new passion—a skill, a cause, an enterprise—surely looms just ahead. Life takes on richer meaning, rekindles old talents, reveals new ways to give back. Now you can finally earn that degree, start your own business, run for office, master another language, invent something, or write that book you keep mulling. And isn't it time for that dream trip, the one sure to relight the fire between you and the snoring body on the other side of the bed?

Then you get The Call. The one that changes your life, diverting all your hope and energy to an entirely different priority.

It's a call about a fall. Or a stroke or a cardiac arrest. Or the call is about

Dad. He's run a red light and hit somebody, but he doesn't quite remember how it happened. Is it his eyes? Or his mind? You don't really want to know because you still won't win the argument about giving up the car keys.

The Call throws most of us into shock and denial and a frenzy of learning how to take charge. We don't know the medical lingo. We have no idea how to navigate our way through the patchwork of care alternatives, insurance regulations, Medicare rules, or the conflicting advice of traditional doctors versus holistic practitioners. And we have no concept of how long, how much it will cost, or how we will pay for it.

My experience is being shared all over the world by countless millions of unpaid Samaritans who take care of adults suddenly unable to take full care of themselves. Whether through love or necessity, family caregivers confront extremes of compassion, grief, and exhaustion that others may never encounter, much less imagine. And it's not all about old people taking care of really old people.

Today's average family caregiver in the United States is a forty-eight-year-old woman who holds down a paid job (more than half work full-time) and spends twenty hours a week providing unpaid care for an adult who used to be independent. One-third of family caregivers are actually on duty forty or more hours a week. One-third also still have children or grandchildren under the age of eighteen living with them and take care of two or more people, usually parents. Not surprisingly, one-half report a high level of burden and nearly one-half say their own health is fair or poor.

And this role lasts for an average of five years.

An overload of responsibilities? Yes, but more—it's also a collision between conflicting stages of life. As adult children, we are now in the passage of our middle years, long past expecting our parents' financial support and soon to be free of supporting our own children. Ripe for Second Adulthood, we envision a new life of novel ventures. But this expectation coincides with our parents' passage into Elderhood, the final great psychological stage. Suddenly we find ourselves the family's designated hitters—our aging parents' last-resort protectors.

But I'm not ready! you cry silently. *My children are still needy, my job is hanging by a thread, my mate is whining through a midlife crisis, and our dog is dying— give me a break!* When your life is squeezed between rising needs and falling hope, escape is tempting. But if we abandoned this work, who would take over? Even if some other good soul were ready and waiting, the chances are that delegating a loved one's care to others may be more upsetting than facing the job yourself. Convenience is no match for guilt.

We must work out a whole new way of relating to our parents, or to a life partner who is weakened and frightened by illness. But this interplay between two of life's greatest passages can become whatever you make it—a time for regretting or for rejoicing. Seen as the latter, it opens up the greatest possibilities for true intimacy and reconnection at the deepest level. The sharing of strengths and vulnerabilities, without shame, fosters love. And for some caregivers, this role offers a chance in Second Adulthood to compose a more tender sequel to the troubled family drama of our First Adulthood. We can become better than our younger selves.

The bottom line is that most of us believe we should take care of our parents as they get older. Fate or genetics will also command many of us to tend a husband or a wife whose health is compromised when they're still in early adulthood or midlife. Others will feel responsible for looking after a stricken sibling, life partner, or close friend. And some caregivers are already into advanced age when they nobly attempt to keep alive a failing spouse or elder.

Why, I wondered, did so many caregivers I interviewed adamantly refuse to recognize the vital, professional-level job they were performing? The most obvious reason is that women have been socialized to believe this is their responsibility once they pass menopause, or if they never married, or if they have no children of their own. And until recently, medical professionals showed scant respect for the family caregiver. The job was typically seen as custodial work best handled by low-paid domestics. Fortunately, that is slowly changing. Geriatricians and many nurses and social workers now bring in the family caregiver as part of the decision-making team.

More and more, the family caregiver is the backbone of our broken health-care system.

Every caregiving family is different. A diagnosis that comes out of the blue will thrust us overnight into the first phase—what I call Shock and Mobilization.

two

WHY DIDN'T WE TALK
ABOUT THIS BEFORE?

What was I thinking in that beauty salon just before Clay's surgeon called to announce, two years after the fact, that we had a new visitor in our lives—cancer? A profound issue: whether I could still fit into last year's theater suit. That night, we were joining friends for Zubin Mehta's farewell concert at the New York Philharmonic. As I hung up numbly, I remember thinking, We will never be carefree again.

I was premature. I didn't expect my husband's usual greeting when I returned that evening—a hearty headline shouted through our apartment—"Girl Reporter's Home!" I expected to find him slumped, eyes glazed, staring at the TV. Instead, he was in the bedroom, all dressed and looping his formal black tie.

"Handsome," I said.

He wrapped me in his arms. "Are you scared?" I asked.

"No," he said calmly. "We'll get through this. Together."

That was the first conversation. It set the tone for all the rest. Clay's way of handling the crisis was simply to carry on with life as planned, to approach treatment as work, just another job to be done.

I wasn't yet in my midfifties when I got The Call. My husband was in his sixties. Like most new caregivers, I thought the crisis would resolve itself in six months or a year and then we would go back to normal.

My husband and I had never had a conversation about the what-ifs. That was a mistake, given that we married late and already had children from previous lives.

When I first met—or heard—Clay Felker in 1965, he was bellowing into a phone, "What do you mean, you don't have our reservation!" His big shoulders and square-cornered head didn't fit his tiny office with its half-high partitions at the New York Herald Tribune. To me, a cub reporter frozen in the doorway, he looked like an overgrown character out of Alice in Wonderland. I was intimidated. But, of course, I was also attracted to this fierce life force.

After our courtship of seventeen years—we were both casualties of marriage to unfaithful mates—we were married in 1984 in his bachelor apartment in Manhattan with two grown daughters in attendance, my daughter Maura, from a previous marriage, and our adopted daughter, Mohm, whom we had found in a camp for Cambodian refugees. Looking on in amazement was our tribe of writers, editors, artists, publishers, photographers, and literary agents, who gave toasts teasing us for leading them on a merry Rolodex chase through our turbulent premarital relationship.

Seven years into our marriage, we were as attached in love as we had been in work. Clay would often remark, "With you, I'm never bored." And I still felt the tingle of excitement mixed with a frisson of intimidation when I came home and heard his voice rumbling through the door of our apartment. A magazine and newspaper editor with a voice loud enough to penetrate walls or travel several flights of stairs, he kept the door always open to a parade of writers, artists, academics, political insiders, Wall Street ears, fashionistas, newbie journalists, anybody with a fresh idea. We had a wonderful life.

Then, The Call.

Only in retrospect did I wonder why we hadn't talked about the inevitable: growing older. How might we face the assaults of body and mind? Who would take care of whom? How would we pay for it? Americans tend to wait until we are too old and too sick to have decent, affordable choices for care in our golden (or rusted-out) years. Planning ahead is preferable—if you can face it. If you can't, you risk plunging into confusion in full crisis mode.

That crisis had begun when the growth reappeared on Clay's neck. He saw the same surgeon and we waited for the results of another biopsy.

Our cheerful denial began vanishing as soon as the surgeon sat us down for a candid briefing on Clay's condition. I accompanied my husband, which I soon learned is essential. The patient is likely to tune out whatever news is too

*threatening to take in. The caregiver has to be the ears, the notetaker, the advo-
cate. But we, too, may listen selectively. Medical consults drive straight through to
the emotions.*

*"We recut the original slides, at your wife's request," the surgeon said.
He referred to the biopsy slides of nearly two years before. New slivers revealed
the tadpole of cancer missed earlier, now grown into a full-sized ugly toad. Obviously chagrined, the surgeon reviewed Clay's "case" in desensitized medical
lingo.*

The notes read:

*June '89: Felt node on right side of neck. Diagnosed as brachial cleft cyst.
August '89: Resected at St. Vincent's Hospital, NYC.
December '90: Mass reappeared on same side of neck.
March '91: Needle biopsy negative.
May '91: Another needle biopsy. Negative. But mass larger.*

*Mass resected. Seventeen lymph nodes removed. One node found to be positive
squamous cell carcinoma. Metastatic.*

*Not pausing to suggest any oversight on anybody's part, he summarized: "My
recommendation—radical neck surgery."*

*It felt like a rabbit punch to the back of our necks. It shook our usual confidence
in medical professionals. We had no interest in blaming anybody. Whenever we en-
countered bad news that couldn't be changed, our mutual reaction was to move forward, not look back.*

*But "radical neck surgery"? The shock was too great to absorb. We wanted to
stop the world and grab all possible frivolity before facing the guillotine.*

*"Let's put off treatment until after the Fourth of July," I coaxed. "You always
love going to David's party."*

*Clay was dubious but wavered under persuasion. David Frost, one of his best
friends, staged an annual lawn party in London that Clay prized. Meantime, I decided to put on my investigative reporter's hat and scour the worldwide Internet for
alternative treatments.*

*Searching under "Head and Neck Cancers," I found a doctor's website called
"CAN HELP." The man who answered in Port Ludlow, Washington, was not an*

M.D. but a Ph.D. physicist. *"The biggest mistake you can make is to do radiation alone. Head and neck tumors spill into the blood and lymph nodes, so when you have a recurrence—"*

"When? Not if?"

"Okay, if you have a recurrence, then all we can do is cut again. And mutilate."

I e-mailed an oncologist in Dusseldorf, a Wolfgang Schafe. *"I favor chemo, together with hypothermia,"* he wrote back. *"Not radiation. If you get a recurrence after radiation, you can't penetrate it with chemo. Mutilations become ever more gross and finally disastrous. You have no head and neck left."*

Working the Internet blindly can be terrifying. I decided not to take dire warnings seriously until I googled the professional association focused on Clay's disease and checked with more than one medical professional. An oncologist at the most famous cancer center in the United States, Memorial Sloan-Kettering, weighed in. *"Time is of the essence. I recommend preventive chemotherapy. Cytoxan. Adriamycin. 5FU."*

Maybe it was the eff-you part that raised my hackles. But I didn't like the sound of those poisons. After another Internet search, I called the oncologist back with some hard questions. Cytoxan damages the DNA. Adriamycin damages the heart wall. 5FU lowers the white cell count. *"How is this chemotherapy preventive?"*

He launched into a pitch for his drug menu as an experimental protocol. He was obviously eager to recruit subjects for his research. I said, *"Ten years ago, they used to give just about everybody 'introductory chemo.' Patients' platelet counts went so low, many died of infection."*

"We are more sophisticated now," the oncologist countered. To be fair, joining an experimental protocol can be a fine choice, if the patient believes in the doctor and checks out the results already posted for such treatment in other parts of the country or the world. Patients in clinical trials have the benefit of being monitored very closely.

I found out that chemotherapy had not proven beneficial for squamous cell cancer of head and neck (at least in 1991). So I put the question to Clay in a negative way. *"Do you want to be a guinea pig for somebody's protocol?"*

"Not a chance."

AFTER THREE WEEKS OF *staggering between the medical authoritarians and the wackos, we began looking for trusted friends who had been through the investigative process on a disease like Clay's. They made sense based on real experience and were glad to help.*

We listened to our dear friend Deborah Szekely. As proprietor of the oldest health ranch in North America, Rancho La Puerta, and a breast cancer survivor now in her eighties, Deborah is a fount of wisdom on how to nurture health from the emotional and spiritual angle. She gave us sound advice: "The key to this phase of the battle is to take control of the process to the degree you can."

Clay called a friend who was also battling cancer, the movie director Frank Perry. Clay admitted he was reluctant to reveal himself to anyone. "I know, I was the same way," Frank said. "Men don't like to show our wounds." But Frank gave us the same prescription Deborah had for dealing with the Shock and Mobilization phase: "Take charge, man, because what you find is, the only person who will battle for your life is you." And your caregiver.

Finding the Right Doctor

When I found the name of the most highly regarded head and neck surgeon in New York, I called the New York Academy of Medicine to check him out. Dr. John Conley (now deceased) had learned his trade as a battle surgeon in World War II—good training. He had pioneered nerve-sparing techniques for reconstructing the head and neck even during radical surgery. He had written the book on it and was revered by medical students as a teacher.

Tall, erect, snowy-haired, Dr. Conley stepped out of his office on Central Park West to greet us as if we were guests for tea. He had the gracious manner of an Oxford don. "No, not chemo!" he protested on hearing about the oncologist's pitch. "It will poison your liver, your kidneys, your intestines—that's overkill."

I told Dr. Conley we were overwhelmed by all the conflicting advice.

"You've had a curveball thrown at you by life," he said with great empathy. "You need to take a weekend off and be close and let your thoughts settle."

A wise man. We had to develop a game to meet the curveball.

Mulling over our consults with different doctors, we began to fret about Dr. Conley's age. He was on the brink of eighty. Could we count on an octogenarian to hold steady through a long and meticulous operation? "Have no shame," advised a psychologist friend who had guided some of his patients through cancer treatment. "Ask for a follow-up consult."

This time when we sat in Dr. Conley's waiting room, I noticed a bookcase with a dozen small volumes of poetry titled Vocal Painting. The author—John Conley. It turned out that this doctor was a Renaissance man: poet and surgeon, scientist and ethicist, flutist and painter. We had a gut feeling that he was to be trusted. We asked him, "How many of these three- or four-hour surgeries do you perform in a week?" This is a vitally important piece of information. Studies have shown that the more continuous experience, the greater the success rates.

The doctor held out both hands. "I recognize that Mr. Felker is a sensitive man," he said. "You want to know who you're partnering with."

Partner—that was the word we were looking for. Between doctor and patient and caregiver, treatment must be a collaborative process. It is essential that you as caregiver speak up, and right from the start assess whether or not this is a doctor willing to enter into a collaboration.

"I do three of these surgeries a week," Dr. Conley continued. "All three to five hours long. I am very steady." All the while the surgeon spoke, his hands remained suspended in midair, still as a tabletop.

"There are only two things I ask of you," he said. "I like to work with classical music in the OR. And I want you to tell me, the morning of surgery, 'We know you're going to do a splendid operation.'"

We heartily agreed to his conditions. I used this intimate moment to ask if Clay could have a Walkman with a healing meditation tape to use in the recovery room, definitely not protocol at the time. "I'll do better than that," said Dr. Conley, being an enthusiast of complementary mind-body medicine. "I'll give you a plastic bag and hang it on his chart so it can go with him into the OR."

Clay and I grinned at each other. We had asserted some control. The surgeon had also shown us both confidence and humility. Together, we had all three entered into a very human contract.

My prescription for entering the Shock and Mobilization stage is this: You never want to go into this game without a medical quarterback.

WHAT IS YOUR STORY?

But suppose Mom is just forgetting more than usual, or a spouse keeps mysteriously losing weight. That might be called a *creeping crisis*. Awareness seeps through only slowly, screened by fear and self-protective denial. Only later do we lash ourselves: *Why didn't I notice earlier?* We all wonder . . .

Why is this so hard?

Am I doing anything right??

I feel so alone . . .

That is why I had to write a book dedicated to understanding and bolstering the family caregiver. I am continually shocked by the gaping holes in the medical and nursing care available to middle-class Americans, particularly to those who fulfill the grand promises of our ever-increasing longevity. The presence of a family member who will act as a fearless advocate is not just essential—it is a matter of survival.

The secret of caregiving success took me years to discover. Quite simply, we cannot do it alone. No one can. We must create a support circle—a circle of care. We need to choose doctors and nurses and social workers who will be our advocates—voices of recognized authority who will speak up for the rights of patient and caregiver to determine the goals of treatment. We need to grow a network of family, friends, and veteran caregivers to help us understand what we're going through and pitch in wherever they can.

But first, we must come to believe that we are deserving to ask for their help. Only then can we anticipate caregiver burnout before it takes us down. We need concrete strategies to get through all the phases. We must also prepare a path for our own comeback. Before we lose our loved one and our sense of purpose as caregivers evaporates, we must reconnect with the lifelines that used to give us joy, and replenish our emotional attachments.

I couldn't write this book until I had walked the full circle of caregiving and come back to life myself. Until that point, I was frankly uncertain that I would survive to tell the tale. It is not uncommon for a caregiver to die earlier than the person into whom we pour our love, sweat, and tears. Yet I ultimately found new life—precious life. And I want you to find it, too.

three

THE INNER PILGRIMAGE

In my 1976 book *Passages,* I traced the journey of adult life as a series of stages of growth, each preceded by a crisis or transition that I called a passage. As we master the tasks of each stage—assuming we do—we grow in ways that prepare us for the next passage and stage of growth. And so life proceeds.

The caregiver's journey is different. It does not proceed from stage to stage in a neat fashion. It is definitely not linear. It feels like we are going around in circles, thinking we have resolved a crisis only to have it return or be superseded by a different, unexpected crisis.

The question is not *if* you will be called to act as a family caregiver—that call will come to most of us at some point—but how you will respond. This passage compels us to approach an uncertain future with a new philosophy. I caught a glimpse of what that might be while I was walking the spiral of growth.

AT A CHURCH IN Portland, Oregon, I gathered with other caregivers for a daylong retreat. There, I found myself walking a labyrinth. It led me in an ancient spiral pattern. This one was inlaid in a wooden floor. I came abruptly on sharp twists and turnings. Suddenly I had to switch directions. I thought, *This is just like caregiving.*

The ancient labyrinth pattern is not a maze. A maze is a riddle, meant to trick and trap you with many misleading paths and dead ends. A labyrinth has one well-defined path that eventually leads to the center and then back out again. A maze creates chaos. A labyrinth orders chaos. We cannot get lost. However, the path is not visible, nor is it predictable—and that reflects our journey as caregivers. If we proceed with patience and faith, walking a labyrinth becomes an exercise in practical spirituality.

As I walked the labyrinth, I began to feel a sense of flowing. Nothing was forced. I imagined some gentle gravity pulling me along. I noticed the other caregivers walking the circles in silence. It created a shared intimacy and reverence without distraction. As the spiral led me into the center, I felt a cleansing and quieting. The mind chatter had mostly stopped. I felt peaceful. Contemplative. I did not receive any cosmic answer to my immediate problems as a caregiver, but I don't expect any thunderbolts when I pray, either. I did feel my heart and mind open to two things: acceptance and hope for the future—as uncertain as it may be.

FOR ME, WALKING THE labyrinth became a powerful metaphor. Out of my seventeen years of experience as a caregiver, and hundreds of interviews, grows my understanding of the emotional, physical, spiritual, and practical demands on a family caregiver. It starts with The Call and can become a calling. For me, the calling is literally to speak to and for millions of silent caregivers.

Most of us will go through what I call "turnings"—significant changes in the condition of our loved one that demand new coping strategies. Each new turning requires a shift in attitude, different tools, and more help. We caregivers also have our own turnings, bombarded by conflicting emotions that force us to question our motives and reshape our attitudes. We have so much to learn, not only how to become fearless advocates for our loved one but also how to take care of ourselves at the same time.

Eight turning points appear to be universal as we travel the full journey of caregiving. The path is not linear. We often come back to the same turning we've been through before, but we know better how to navigate it. We start out as caregivers, but with time, we grow into care managers. This becomes a professional role.

Instead of stages, then, this book is divided by Eight Turnings of the Caregiving Labyrinth. The more clearly you understand these turnings, the better you will be able to address your loved one's needs—and your own. Each turning includes real stories about real caregivers solving real problems like those facing you, as well as carefully researched strategies.

A capsule of each turning follows below. The rest of the book will be laid out, turning by turning, each one offering a collection of strategies that can empower you to meet the challenges with confidence.

EIGHT TURNINGS AROUND THE LABYRINTH OF CAREGIVING

I. Shock and Mobilization

Your entrance to the labyrinth of caregiving starts with Shock and Mobilization. You get a call that your mom can't be found, or your dad has been rushed to a cardiac unit, or your spouse has a frightening diagnosis. Where to start? Who to call? You mobilize. You start sprinting—grabbing for answers—it's dizzying. Time speeds up and you are working off adrenaline day and night.

As you begin chasing facts and opinions and run into contradictions, you will feel disoriented, as if swooping up and down on a roller coaster. Your emotions run wild. You may wake to the first light of morning in a sweat, convinced you never slept.

To start the day more calmly, try breathing exercises. Give yourself ten minutes to sit in the dark. Breathe slowly, deeply, from down in the diaphragm, hold it, and slowly exhale. To override your racing thoughts or mind chatter—typically four hundred words a minute—focus on one word or phrase or mantra. Or try a statement of gratitude: *Thank you, God, for this day.*

I know, I know, your mother always told you the same thing. Just try it.

II. The New Normal

You realize, perhaps for the first time, that you have a new role—family caregiver. And this isn't a sprint. This is going to be a marathon. You are living with a new uncertainty, and you are not going back to the old normal.

This may also be a welcome reprieve. A disease process has been interrupted and now may be reversed. Waves of humble appreciation for life may sweep over you and your loved one. Go with those waves. Let them pull both of you away from your usual habits and routines. If it's a life partner, try crazy experiments—an exotic cuisine, a sport you both gave up, a new avocation. Volunteer in a soup kitchen. Go biking, fishing, or hiking together. Take up yoga or a new language. Give away your well-worn clothes and buy entirely different ones. Move to a houseboat. Live in another country for six months. The point is to collaborate with your partner on a bold change in your lives. These are great boosts to the immune system.

If it is a parent whose health status is threatened, pick up your traditional visits. Make surprise visits. Send zany presents. Get your parents online, on Facebook or Twitter, and set up their profile. Introduce them to a sport they can play in their living room, on a Wii. Take them on outings to unexpected places—a comedy club, a drumming class, an auto show, a political rally.

You and the person you're caring for will create entirely new pathways in your brain by participating in unfamiliar activities. Whipped into action, the body responds with natural mood elevators.

III. Boomerang

Everything has settled down into a new normal routine. It's been months, maybe a year or more. You're handling it, thinking *OK, I can do this*. And suddenly, BOOMERANG! A new crisis erupts. The original illness roars out of hibernation. Or aggressive treatment causes a backlash of complications. Or the family member who was still robust and had been caring for your unwell parent suddenly suffers a surprise setback. Now they both need help. You are the backup.

This is one of those turnings that you have made before. You are back at Shock and Mobilization, but you know better now not to be passive and accept the first doctor's opinion. This time, you need to designate one physician as your medical quarterback who will assemble a team and call the plays. You may want to consult a research guide. You will certainly want to explore complementary, nonmedical treatments that can boost the patient's immune system and foster a positive attitude.

It is essential to call a family meeting and get others involved, since it is now clear that this will be a chronic, or recurring, health condition. Now is the time to begin seriously caring for yourself. You need to learn how to shift out of crisis mode and into a healthier gear, since this may be a long journey.

IV. Playing God

By now you've become a seasoned caregiver. You're good at it. You are the only person your loved one trusts. You also believe you're the only one who truly understands what he or she needs. People say you are heroic, and you are beginning to believe it. You are Playing God.

But the truth is that we can't control disease or aging. And if we keep trying, we will be overcome by stress and fatigue. When all our efforts fail to protect our loved one from inevitable downturns, the failure will feel like our own. Eventually, we have to accept that some things are totally beyond our control. Clinging to unattainable hopes simply causes more suffering. But we can change one thing—our own attitude.

V. "I Can't Do This Anymore!"

You were convinced you could do it differently. You'd be fine. But one day, a year or two or three later, you break into tears, totally fatigued. Same thing the next day. You've given up so much. You're cracking. You absolutely must come up for air or you'll go down in despair.

Call for help! There are resources in the community that you are probably not aware of. With imagination, you can pull together a care team. You need to take breaks. Everyone needs a vacation at least once a year. But most important, you must start taking care of yourself on a daily basis. Carve out at least one hour every day to do something that will give you pleasure and refreshment. Take a walk. Have coffee with a friend. Go to the library and read a book. Work in the garage. Listen to music. Chop wood. Walk a labyrinth. And know this: Your loved one also needs some time with other people who offer stimulation of a different kind.

VI. Coming Back

This is the crucial turning. It now becomes clear that your loved one is not going to get well and will become more and more dependent and needy. You are approaching the center of the labyrinth. This is a place of sadness and reflection. You may touch the depths of despair. But it is here that caregivers who survive begin the effort of coming back to life.

People often say, "I can't wait to get my old life back." But that is not the way it happens. You are changed by this long passage. You can't go back to your old self. The middle of your journey is the time to begin thinking about coming back to find a new self.

I know it sounds selfish, but the reality is that you must continue on the path of life. Your loved one is on a different path. There is peril in remaining so attached to your declining loved one that you lose your "self" and go down with the person who cannot come back. Too many long-term caregivers retreat into isolation or addiction or depression, despairing that nothing will ever change. Caregivers sometimes set up their own illness or accident, unconsciously wishing to be taken care of themselves.

It is here, then, at the center of the labyrinth of caregiving, that we need to begin releasing our loved one. Letting go. It is a slow and painful process. Of course, most of us will rebound with any signs of hope that he or she is getting better. But relaxing our attachment allows us to begin receiving images of our new life. Releasing and receiving is what the caregiver needs and deserves. It makes it easier to begin anticipating the grief of loss.

This is the time to resist isolation and reach out to replenish your emotional attachments. Grandchildren? Old friends? A support group or a church group with people who will be eager to carry you across the abyss? Connect with other caregivers who will understand your situation and allow you to help one another.

What were your lifelines before caregiving? Remember your former transports to joy, whether in work or play. Pick them up again. Renew your efforts to find spiritual guidance. We all need some higher power to whom we can turn over our burdens and direct our prayers or meditations. Asking for reassurance that you will find the way out of the labyrinth is an active act of hope.

VII. The In-Between Stage

This is a momentous turning point for those who care for the chronically ill. Your loved one cannot be cured in an acute-care hospital, but he or she is not ready to die—and may live on for years.

Our health-care system has little to offer at this stage, except round-trips to the emergency room and readmissions to the hospital. According to a study published in *The New England Journal of Medicine,* one in five Medicare patients ends up back in the hospital within the first month. Why? Because insurers pay hospitals to treat disease rather than rewarding them for decent follow-up care that would reduce the number of re-hospitalizations. The estimated cost of return visits in 2004, the study states, was $17.4 billion.

I found a solution for the In-Between Stage in palliative care. In between hospital and hospice is home, where most people want to live out the long afternoon of their lives. Palliative care is a preventive care model. The goal is to prevent the crisis that would require readmission to the hospital.

You need to expand the circle of people who will assume some responsibility for aspects of care or just be present with your dependent loved one. Let members of your family and friends who have not been involved know that you have reached the end of your rope. Even long-distance, they can be helpful. And don't be shy about asking for assistance from neighbors, coworkers, your church, your community college, or social organizations. Find students from your local high school or college who need to do public service.

Surrounding your loved one with a circle of love is the best medicine of all. There is now scientific proof of this obvious human instinct.

VIII. The Long Good-bye

This is the last turning. No one can answer your most burning question. How long? Inevitably, there will be times when you see your loved one suffering that you will likely feel: *Why can't you die? It's enough.* Then, of course, you'll feel guilty for thinking such a thing. But it is entirely human and predictable.

It is important at this turning to have end-of-life conversations. Find ways to encourage your loved one to talk about his or her goals for this precious last stage of life. Suggest a life review. Talk about what has given his or her life meaning, and what will be passed on. Bring in a spiritual confidant, religious or pastoral, to talk about how to find peace in coming to the end of life.

What kind of medical interventions does he or she want—or want discontinued? This may have been spelled out in writing earlier, but if not, make sure a living will is up to date, very specific, and communicated to anyone involved in the care. Turn the decision making over to your loved one. This is his or her death, not yours. You are on a different journey.

WALKING THE PATH IN YOUR OWN WAY

I soon came to understand that without help, it is almost impossible to find one's way around the labyrinth of caregiving. The thread leading you out can be found through various spiritual practices. In Christian terms, the thread exemplifies God's grace, which is sought through prayer and contemplation and selfless action.

In Yoga, the thread is an inner serenity cultivated through breathing, meditation, and physical postures. In recent years, mindfulness meditation has become an adjunct to mainstream medicine based on clinical trials by Jon Kabat-Zinn, a molecular biologist who extracted it from Buddhism. It can be practiced with or without a religious orientation. Those with an intellectual rather than a religious orientation may seek the thread of "emotional intelligence," a path to self-responsibility. Others walk the path with faith in a personal destiny that will define their rightful journey.

In her gentle book *Walking a Sacred Path,* the Reverend Lauren Artress, canon of Grace Cathedral in San Francisco, writes that the simple act of walking the labyrinth "invites us back into the center of our being." She identifies the labyrinth as "the inner map of knowing in women." The use of labyrinths for healing and rebalancing began hundreds of years before Christ. With the building of the permanent outdoor labyrinth at Grace Cathedral in 1995, a replica of the labyrinth at Chartres Cathedral in France, the labyrinth movement was launched by Rev. Artress. Today labyrinths can be found in many secular as well as religious places, including hospitals, schools, community parks, and memorial spaces.

The central aim of this book is to take you on the emotional journey of this strange new passage. The world of caregiving is initially as foreign to most people as life on another planet. Yet caregiving is a predictable crisis, a likely event so scary that we prefer to consider it unlikely. Indeed, we spend years of robust life avoiding the very thought of any such scenario. Not for us. Oh, no.

Hence the utter shock when The Call comes. And the irrefutable need to prepare mentally and logistically before The Call. We must be ready, willing, and able. Not helpless. Not lamenting: *Omigod, my life is changed, how do I do this?*

I can tell you, from having completed the passage,

There is living through caregiving.

There is coming back after caregiving.

And there is life after caregiving.

If you accept this role, you won't be sorry, provided you read on. Learn how to walk the labyrinth of caregiving and save your own life. Come, take a walk with me.

four

TAG, YOU'RE IT!

At a health ranch in Mexico I overheard a conversation between two women confessing their delight—and guilt—at leaving behind their caregiving responsibilities to get away and repair themselves. Debbie Burger and Irene Garcia-Sabourin describe themselves as alpha females, accustomed to controlling their environment, their businesses, and their family dynamics. But overnight, at the peak of their forties, they were both tagged to play a role for which none of their education, training, or experience prepared them.

EVEN ALPHAS WEAR OUT

Debbie is a Japanese-American who runs her own roofing and construction company in Northern California. Irene is a Latina and vice president of a large insurance company with sixteen people reporting to her. Both were accustomed to working fifty to sixty hours a week, and, now that their children have been dispatched, they were enjoying hiking, biking, and romantic weekends with their husbands. All that had changed when Irene's still-striving husband was stricken with a life-threatening illness and Debbie's mother, already hospitalized, began to fail to the point of requiring a regular morphine drip.

They were the only ones available in their families to coordinate the care. Irene was the wife. Debbie was the only daughter.

Tag, you're it!

Suddenly, their expertly balanced worlds were turned upside down. As senior executives, wives, and mothers, they were confident they could remain in control. But serious illness and the sudden dependence of parents stunned them. For the first time in their adult lives, they had no idea what to do or how to do it. More baffling even than their clumsiness with doing medical research and making treatment decisions was the emotional roller coaster. A consult with one doctor would plunge them into unreasonable depths of despondency, but a day or two later a more hopeful prognosis would boost them to a false high. Every caregiver feels more or less the same. Most of us go on far too long pitching and tossing on the roller coaster, without asking for help or taking a break.

This is what attracted me to Irene and Debbie. They had done what I was finally doing; after five years of nonstop caregiving for my husband, I was taking my first real break. The two women didn't start out as friends; they were barely acquaintances through their husbands' work. But they recognized an unspoken bond between them: they were both in the caregiving life.

Behind them on the hiking trail, I overheard them talking about why they had both taken time off to care for themselves. They had cajoled and humored each other into "stealing" a week away at a health ranch—"for our own health, so it's not stealing," Debbie had corrected Irene. The intent was to sleep, hike, exercise, eat well, journal, sit and stare at a mountain in silence, walk a labyrinth, and share heart-to-heart talks about a way of life only caregivers can understand. But they continued to oscillate between delight and doubts about their decision.

Irene: *I wouldn't have come if you didn't drag me.*

Debbie: *You need this time for yourself.*

Irene: *It sounded totally selfish.*

Debbie: *I noticed that you threw up on the plane.*

Irene: *I haven't done anything for myself in the last four years. I just take Tom from chemo to chemo.*

Debbie: *I almost didn't come myself. The hospice people kept bugging me for the burial plans for my mother. I couldn't find them! They said, "We have to know—what if your mother dies while you're away?"*

Irene: *But you came anyway.*

I couldn't contain myself any longer. I caught up with Irene and Debbie on the hiking trail, introduced myself, and told them that I was collecting stories of family caregivers. They welcomed me into their conversation.

Debbie: *The night before I left, I went over to see my parents. My mom is sitting there, this little white-haired, hunched-over lady in her eighties. My dad was there, too, but he doesn't track well anymore. And there was also a private duty nurse I'd hired to look after them.*

Irene: *They're giving her morphine now?*

Debbie: *Uh-huh. "Mom!" I said. "You know I really love you and I want to be there for you." My mom's eyes were at half-mast. "But it's been a rough nine months. I need the next week—for me. I'm going to be in Mexico, so don't die!"*

Irene: *You said that to her!*

Debbie: *Her eyes came into focus. I couldn't believe it. "That's what I want," she said. "You should go."*

Irene: *Wow, great!*

Debbie: *I've really lost my mother in recent years. I've become the mother to her. But for that brief moment, she was back. She was my mother again. She was able to say, "I can see you need that."*

We hiked together over rolling hills for the next couple of miles, and we still had only just begun to share all that we'd experienced. Softly, Irene admitted, "You forget about yourself. You forget that you're a person. People think I'm this strong person, but I don't take care of myself. No matter how much I do for my husband and my parents, it's never good enough."

Debbie sighed. "The possibility of being weak even for a minute is frightening to contemplate, because there's so much hanging on our shoulders."

The responsibilities hanging on the shoulders of a caregiver differ in some important ways, depending on the illness of the loved one and the caregiver's own cultural background. Below, I have outlined five typical, but different, situations.

THE ACUTE CAREGIVER

The first distinction is between acute and chronic caregiving. Acute illness invades your life while you're making other plans. The caregiver who steps up to mobilize defenses for the patient has to become an instant expert on the disease, treatment options, insurance coverage, complementary medicine, hospital rules, and aftercare.

Hospitals today send people home quicker and sicker. The acute caregiver is expected, overnight, to take on the roles performed in the hospital by three shifts of skilled professionals, from the IV nurse to the dietician to the visiting specialists and resident doctors. You will have to learn fast how to talk to physicians and nurses and decode their clinical speak. It's like being dropped into a foreign country where you don't know the language.

But after the sprint of weeks or months of mobilizing to find and follow the treatment plan, the acute caregiver may be granted a welcome respite. It may even turn into a reprieve of years. There will always be a little startle when a call comes in late at night. But if and when another health crisis erupts, you will be better prepared to respond like a professional.

Irene Garcia-Sabourin, the Latina woman I just mentioned, was tagged to respond overnight to the sudden blow of a life-threatening illness.

My husband was diagnosed right off the bat with Stage IV colon cancer. We were cyclists. We rode a hundred miles a week. Very healthy. Never smoked. We had this incredible life and suddenly we were in the oncologist's office, after Tom's first surgery. The doctor put up the slides and said, "We're not dealing with anything easy here. It got into the liver. It's going to return." He rattled off different treatments and therapy options. It was a blur. He wound up saying, "It's important that you get yourself a lawyer and get your paperwork in order, because the chances that your husband will make it through the year are slim. Very slim."

I didn't even cry. I got sick to my stomach.

The emotional assault hits everyone hard. We shut down. The news doesn't sink in as believable. But Irene's story shows how, even with a grim prognosis, it is possible to find our way through the chaos and gather the confidence to jump-start the life that is left.

For the first few weeks, naturally, Irene just went through the motions. "I'm really vocal when it comes to what my parents need, but with Tom, if I can stick my head in the sand, maybe it's not happening, and he can take care of himself."

One of the biggest problems described to me by both caregivers and care receivers is the lack of honest communication. Feelings that we may consider unthinkable or unacceptable go unspoken. They fester and may later be expressed in angry outbursts, withdrawal or guilt-tripping, or the slow burn of resentment, creating a schism between people who otherwise love each other.

Every stage of caregiving calls for a necessary conversation. It's uncomfortable, but being honest in admitting fears and feelings is the way to open the channels of communication. In Irene and Tom's marriage, he was the more passive partner, accustomed to letting Irene take charge. Studies find that it's most common for men to assume their wives will take on the responsibility for shepherding them through illness.

The new realities of Stage IV cancer demanded action. Issues of financial peril were gnawing at Irene, but she didn't know how to voice them without making Tom feel like he was failing her. The fact was, Tom would have to stop working right away and probably wouldn't be able to work again. They had no disability insurance. Irene would be the sole breadwinner.

Irene describes herself, you may recall, as an alpha female, vice president of a large insurance company with sixteen people reporting to her. She reacted as many highly functioning people do in this first phase. When her mother offered to move close by to help her, Irene said, "No thank you." Her children kept calling from college to ask how they could help. But Irene was in full rescuer mode. "I told them all—no, I can handle this."

After a few more weeks, Irene and her husband did pull themselves together and have a series of honest conversations, which put them on a very different road from the dead end projected in their initial consult. "The first thing we have to do is be totally honest with the kids—they're adults now," she told her husband. He agreed, as long as they didn't tell anybody else.

Irene ignored the attitude of the first oncologist, who had summarily dismissed her husband with a death sentence in a year. She did research until she found a more holistic oncologist. This was, literally, a lifesaver.

"He turned out to be a guy who wanted to work with us toward living," she says. He suggested putting Tom on an experimental drug that had just been released. Irene listened as the oncologist talked about all the studies until she felt assured that he was knowledgeable. "I could finally let my guard down," she told me. She asked if he would be their medical quarterback; the doctor was more than willing. "The doctor said that since Tom had no family history of cancer, he was young, in good health, and a cyclist, he was a perfect candidate. Tom was willing to take the treatments every week."

Tom insisted that they put their home on the market. He could no longer take care of three acres, and what if something happened to him very soon? Irene would be left to sort through the oversized garage full of car parts and tools that served his hobby. He wanted to clear it all out. It was important for Tom to reclaim some of his independence by planning for the future. In the process, he was signaling his immune system that he was worth fighting for.

Irene and Tom gave up only what they absolutely had to, and the more they pursued their joys, the more unexpected energy they found. Irene maintained her big job. It kept her from obsessing about her husband's condition and helped practically with the financial ability to supplement his medical treatment with complementary therapies and short trips.

Tom fought on for four years beyond his diagnosis.

"Our lives changed completely," Irene told me. "We started marking off a list of things we'd always wanted to do. We traveled. We became even more avid cyclists. We kept one step ahead of the cancer with surgeries and chemotherapy. Tom went through a lot, but the average person wouldn't know it to look at him. He didn't have the look of cancer. And when I say we 'lived,' we really lived."

THE CHRONIC CAREGIVER

Mary Furlong was furtively checking the voice mails on her BlackBerry while in the middle of a business meeting when she heard the *rat-ta-tat-tat* message from an EMS medic: "Your mother's fallen and lost mobility in one leg." Mary is a sixty-year-old dynamo who is always traveling. That call stopped her in her tracks. "I had nine months to prepare for the birth of my first child. I had nine *hours* to prepare for the dependence of my mother."

Mary had to believe this crisis was temporary. "As soon as I find the right wheelchair for Mom," she told me gamely, "it'll be okay." She might have to cancel one trip to make time to take Mom around to doctors, then go back to her own life with a pledge to help out with paying her bills and submitting insurance claims. But if Mom didn't recover mobility, or if she fell again and insisted on remaining at home—which is the strong preference of over 80 percent of older Americans—Mary would be faced with the responsibilities of a chronic caregiver.

A chronic illness or condition presents as a *creeping crisis*. It comes on slowly, and you're not quite sure what "it" is. The hazy signs of early dementia, for example, are usually met with hiding by the elder and denial by family members who don't want to believe the worst. When your loved one develops several chronic conditions that recur and go into remission and recur again—for example, MS, Parkinson's, or diabetes—you never know how long your role is going to last.

So many questions . . .

Should I take a leave from my job? Or steal time from my employer to make those interminable phone calls to doctors? Or let my sister or brother take over and just write checks? Or move in with Mom until she gets better? What if she doesn't? Shall I move her in with us—how will that sit with my new live-in boyfriend? If Dad is still around, how long can he take care of her? Should I look into assisted living? These are the kinds of questions grappled with by the caregivers you will read about in this book, questions that suddenly become first priority and beg for inspiration from the lived experience of caregivers who have already found answers.

MEN ARE CAREGIVERS, TOO

Dr. Brent Ridge, a geriatrician at Mount Sinai Hospital in New York City, often gets panicky calls from men who are accustomed to running everything from companies to health-care programs. "My father just had a stroke and my mother isn't strong enough to care for him," he heard from the CEO of a major publishing corporation. "I have no idea where to go to find out how to help them."

"Nobody knows how to do this when it's thrust on them," Dr. Ridge acknowledges.

If you are a man doing hands-on care for your wife, or trying to look after your mom or dad long-distance, you may feel alone, embarrassed, angry. Many men are programmed to believe this is women's work. But others I have observed are right at the bedside, administering injections, changing IV bags, or working out a discreet dance for placing Mom on the commode. I came to appreciate men's ways of caregiving.

Today, men are estimated to assume one-third of the caregiving efforts. Studies usually emphasize that men do less of the tedious, hands-on, heartbreaking "shit work"; that is left to women. Men more commonly take on executive tasks like managing finances and legal and insurance issues. That role can be onerous, too, and it continues after the loved one's death, with estate issues, hospital bills, and possibly a business left by the deceased. But what impressed me in watching male caregivers was their action orientation. They often step back and figure out a better way for the whole family to manage the situation and reduce tensions.

I have an indelible image of male caregivers. One night, shortly before a well-loved politician died, the house was overflowing with extended family, and the toilets backed up. When the septic tank overflowed in the backyard, the youngest brother got on the phone to his buddies. Soon six men were silhouetted under a bright harvest moon, digging up the waste tank to make it possible for the dying politician to continue to be cared for at home. Those young men were happy doing shit work!

Other male caregivers whose journeys I followed were astonishingly loyal and stoic about sticking by a wife with a debilitating condition. Jon Strum, for instance, is a fifty-four-year-old real estate agent in Los Angeles who has been through most of the turnings. When he first experienced Shock and Mobilization, he and his wife were having coffee at their neighborhood Starbucks.

"Why is your little finger twitching like that?" Jon asked.

Jean looked at the hand that was holding her cup of coffee, "I don't know. I should get it checked out."

They went together to see an orthopedist. He gravely intoned, "You need to see a neurologist." It was clear from the MRI that she had multiple sclerosis.

"Ironically, the diagnosis was delivered on Jean's birthday," Jon recalls. "She was thirty-seven. Vigorous and beautiful, a screenwriter, and not the kind who is a waitress by day. She actually sold scripts and worked as a gun-for-hire doing rewrite work for studios."

Over the next four months, the little tremor in Jean's pinkie first consumed her hand and then that arm, then spread down the other arm and into the other hand. She was no longer able to write. At the moment of that first diagnosis, Jon told his wife, "You know what, it's just one more push on our way to realizing that our life must change," he says. Jon gave up his business and for the next three years acted as his wife's full-time caregiver at home while he tried to find another career. It had to be one that didn't require him to be in a corporate office from nine to five but would still offer an income sufficient to pay for all that insurance didn't cover. The only profession that seemed to fit the bill was one in which he had no interest, real estate.

"I learned to find things I enjoyed doing within real estate—building businesses and helping others to problem-solve," he reports. "Several of my agents understood real estate but didn't understand business. They paid me as their coach."

Caregivers find out who their true friends are. As Jon's wife became increasingly immobilized and, like many people with a degenerative illness, sank into depression, the couple became a lot less fun. Friends could only come to their house and sit around. Visits dwindled, then stopped. "Seven years into this," says Jon, "I realize that nobody makes it out of this situation alone. I went out of my way to develop a new network of friends—not the easiest thing to do at fifty. They visit Jean and remember her on her birthday and holidays. But they also work at getting me out of the house."

The one thing his new network of friends has in common is that they are all women. About two-thirds of those afflicted with MS are women, which means that the great majority of their caregivers are men. "And men are not good at reaching out to a social network," says Jon. He is grateful for learning a technique natural to women in crisis. In cases of progressive MS among couples, an overwhelming majority of husbands eventually abandon their wives. Jon fully empathizes. He says it's "because it is overwhelming for one person. And we tend to think that if we're going to own that responsibility, it's our obligation to always be there."

THE LONG-DISTANCE CAREGIVER

Given the reality that most baby boomers work and often have to travel or relocate to satisfy an employer, a new kind of service is springing up—senior concierge services. Buckley Anne Fricker is a lawyer and married mother of three who learned, while working in her mother's elder law practice, about the unmet needs of aging parents and their overworked boomer caregivers. Adult children of clients would often come in looking not for sophisticated estate planning but for life-enhancing services to revive their parents' joie de vivre.

"I wish I could hire someone just like me to visit my dad," adult daughters often say. What good is it for our parents to get to the end of life if they are unable to benefit from some of the experiences that always brought them joy, like arguing about world politics, or visiting the latest art exhibit, or just going out for an ice-cream cone? So Buckley looked for highly educated stay-at-home moms and retired professionals who would be interested in part-time work that would be socially meaningful. She launched a new kind of concierge service in 2005, Buckley's for Seniors.

"We visit middle-aged and older clients stricken with debilitating diseases whose spouses have to work and leave their mates alone for many hours," says Buckley. "Our more affluent clients use our services several times a week, to take them shopping or to museums or luncheons." Family members provide extensive notes on the physical and mental status of the clients, their doctors, and their likes and dislikes. Staffers then use special software to constantly update that information and keep family members apprised of the activities, concerns, and well-being of their loved ones. It all sounds dry and mechanical until you see Buckley in action, checking up on her clients and their assigned companions.

WHEN PHILLIP FERRARA TURNED ninety, his daughter, Antoinette, got antsy about having him and her mother thousands of miles away in Hawaii.

She insisted on moving them to a suburb of Washington, D.C., where she worked in the State Department. But shortly after she settled them into a condo in Arlington, Virginia, her husband was appointed mission director of the USAID office in Budapest, Hungary. Antoinette wrestled with herself for weeks over a conflict that seemed insoluble. How could she abandon her father and mother when they had just uprooted themselves from their home on a beautiful island? And how could she deny her husband the chance to take a major step up in his government career? Fortunately, her father made it easy by giving his blessing.

But The Call that posed the greatest challenge to Antoinette as a long-distance caregiver was the one about her mother. Phillip Ferrara invited me to talk to him about this momentous decision.

"Welcome to my cubicle," Phillip said with a wry smile. He stood up proudly, wearing a well-pressed dress shirt and taupe gabardine pants. Running a hand through a surprisingly full head of gray hair, he boasted, "It's an Italian thing." He apologized for his one-bedroom condo in an assisted-living apartment house run by Sunrise. After more than fifty years of marriage, he still has a wife but he lives as a single man. Phillip began giving me his side of the story of the losses of his last few years.

"My wife was diagnosed with Alzheimer's," he said tonelessly. "We lived in Hawaii, but my daughter thought it would be better if we moved up here to Washington. Then she moved to Budapest with her husband. That of course has been a problem for me. So I am anxious and depressed much of the time."

Phillip poked an index finger to each temple and rolled his eyes. "After all, I am ninety-three. Just saying that age is depressing."

But Phillip was in a rather jaunty mood because he was being visited by his vivacious companion Nikie Micheli. She is one of the dozen passionate staffers who work for Buckley Fricker's senior concierge service. Nikie visits Phillip three times a week. She helped to arrange an adoption for his beloved cocker spaniel when Phillip could no longer walk him. Buckley herself helped Phillip with one of his earlier painful transitions. His daughter was serving in Kosovo when he had to give up his big condo to find a safer situation for his wife with dementia. Buckley helped to pack him up and move him and hang his pictures in the new, smaller unit with assisted-living services.

"She did a lot of things my daughter would have done if she were here," Phillip told me. But Buckley and her staffers often function at a deeper level of psychological support for seniors whose children are not around. They become trusted confidants. When I asked Phillip what they provide that he treasures most, he said, "I find it hard to make major life decisions all by myself."

The most painful decision of all was whether or not to move his wife a few floors below into the Alzheimer's unit. He sank into his easy chair and stretched out his feet onto a fuzzy mat, remembering the long period of indecision. At that moment Antoinette phoned him from Budapest where it was 12:30 in the morning.

"Hi, Dad," she said sweetly over the speakerphone. For my benefit they relived a couple of clashing conversations they had over the decision about Phillip's wife. Antoinette, having been out of the country for months, had no idea how difficult it had become for her father to manage her mother as her disease accelerated. Antoinette was dead set against her mother being moved. That had only made her father feel even more guilty than he already did. The strain of indecision was taking a toll on Phillip.

It was Buckley, the concierge manager, who sat with Phillip and framed for him what he thought was an either/or decision.

"There is really only one choice," Buckley told him. "To make sure your wife is safe and doesn't raid the bathroom cabinet in the middle of the night and take a dangerous medicine, or go wandering out of the building while you're sleeping, you have to move her to the Alzheimer's unit. You can see her anytime, but there she'll be under constantly watchful eyes."

Phillip agreed to move his wife. Antoinette finally came around: "I knew Buckley had my father's best interest at heart and my mother's, too," she told me. "So when she weighed in, and my dad explained his thinking, I figured that I had to go with that."

Buckley's for Seniors serves only the wider Washington, D.C., area and parts of Baltimore. Companions can step in to fill the gaps between medical assistance by home-health-care aides and the absent family members. E-mail: Info@buckleys4seniors.com. You can also visit the website, www.buckleys 4seniors.com, or call 703-918-9330.

Senior services of this sort will be springing up around the country as parents live longer and their adult children work in a globalized economy.

STRATEGIES

Are Your Parents Safe and Sound?

Older people generally hide their vulnerabilities, fearing that helpers will curb their independence. In reality, the sooner they get help and make their homes safe, the longer they can retain their independence.

What to do: Stay in your parent's home for a few days. Get to know his or her social world. Who are the people who could look out for your parent? Does your dad have a buddy at the American Legion hall? Does your mom play bridge? Introduce yourself to their doctor, the mail carrier, the neighbors, the local police, the pharmacist who fills your parents' prescriptions, the regulars at the diner where Mom and Dad stop for coffee, and anybody else linked to their lives. Take down all these names and their contact information and pass around yours in return. Ask people to call you.

If anything seems amiss, entrust a friend or neighbor with keys to Dad's or Mom's home before you leave town. It might be wise to pay somebody a small fee to ring their doorbell and take a quick look every few days.

What Are They Eating?

Seniors lose taste buds and crave highly salted and seasoned foods. Adriane Berg found out her mother was living on pizza and Chinese food, both easily delivered. When her mom went to the supermarket, she didn't bother to read the labels and came home with packaged foods high in sodium and sugar.

Berg, as the founder and CEO of Generation Bold, has a savvy eye out for anything that can help busy boomers in their caregiving role. Golden Cuisine, she discovered, was a line of prepared meals for seniors that carry FDA nutritional labels and are low in sodium, sugar, and fat. But they were served only at assisted-living facilities and not available to the lay caregiver.

So she created Golden Cuisine Direct, forty different meals that are frozen and can be ordered online and shipped to one's family member. I tried out the Country Herb Chicken and the Cheese Manicotti and was pleasantly surprised at the flavor and texture. "What we try to avoid is some of the chemicals and ingredients that are inherently bad for seniors, that can contribute to dehydration and cardiac dysfunction," Berg says. A sodium substitute, Saltwise, is used, and flavor is punched up with herbs such as thyme, oregano, peppers, and curries.

To order, go to GoldenCuisine.com.

"Nana" Technology to Close the Distance

When I visited Andrew Carle's eHuman lab at George Mason University in Fairfax, Virginia, he couldn't wait to demonstrate his concept of "Nana technology." An expert in assisted living and senior housing, Professor Carle keeps abreast of electronic devices that allow caregivers to check up on their loved ones wherever they are.

"Let's say my mom is in Memphis, a thousand miles away from me," he says as he points to a plasma TV screen on the wall. "She has a video portal on her kitchen wall and I have a video portal on my kitchen wall. Whenever it is on, and we are in the same room, it is just like she is right there. We chat. When she wants privacy, it's like closing the door to her bedroom. She just turns it off. But we can leave it on all day, so when the kids come home from school, it's 'Hi, Grandma' and 'Hi, kids!'"

- **Video Portal Technology.** This technology is already available (Accenture, the company that developed it, calls it "a

window on the world"). But the price has to come down
before these devices become available on the consumer
market. They are a fancy version of Skype, the hugely
popular computer software.

- **Skype.** This software application has paved the way for adult
children to make free voice calls to faraway loved ones,
even in foreign countries, provided Mom or Dad also has the
service. Users receive calls on their computers over the
Internet. It's not the easiest way to make a long-distance
connection, but it is either free or no more expensive than
the same rate charged in other countries for calling a
landline. Computer-savvy families can put together a family
reunion, for example, by using the Skype audio conference
system.

Skype for Windows has been putting families face-to-
face through two-way visual contact since 2006. With a
computer video camera attached to your computer monitor,
Skype allows you to see the person you're calling, full
screen, even as they see you, in real time. This way you
know what's going on with your parents on a regular basis,
rather than waiting until the next holiday and shelling out an
expensive plane fare. The cameras can be purchased for as
little as under $20, and they are simple to plug into the
USB port of any contemporary computer.

When Professor Carle called his aunt in New Jersey, a
box popped up on her computer screen, alerting her that he
wanted to say hello in person. All she had to do was use her
mouse to click on the Skype icon and type in her password.
Voilà! Her nephew was suddenly in her kitchen smiling at
her. As they chatted, he could show her concept models of
future technologies, like the "GPS Shoe," a sneaker with a
built-in chip that can locate an elder who has wandered off.

For holdouts from the computer culture, the following are two much simpler devices that are popular.

- **The Jitterbug Wireless Phone.** The Jitterbug is a simple, oversized mobile phone designed to make it easy for older people to see the bright color screen and large numbers and get help to make calls. They can access all options by answering simple yes and no questions. The wireless service, provided by Verizon, allows the user to dial "O" to reach a live, twenty-four-hour operator who will greet the caller by name, provide directory assistance, and connect his or her calls. The operator can also add names and numbers to update the customer's phone contact list.

  The phones themselves cost around $150. Airtime cost for the Jitterbug, starting at $14.99 a month, is one of the most expensive prepaid plans on the market (in 2009), more than T-Mobile prepaid and more than PagePlus, a Verizon mobile virtual network operator. Information is available at Jitterbug's website: www.jitterbug.com.

- **MyCelery Service.** The name of this service is a play on the Latin word *celeritas,* which means "speed." Lots of older people like to handwrite letters, but they would like to speed up the sending of snail mail. MyCelery allows the user to send "mail" without a stamp or without having a computer or an Internet connection. Grandma can send and receive notes and photos using a simple fax machine and a single home phone line. MyCelery sells the service to turn the user's handwritten pages into e-mails. Grandma can also receive e-mails. They will be recognized and automatically printed out on her fax machine.

  The user's caregiver is designated as his or her "celery buddy," who fills out a form and sends in the addresses frequently used. MyCelery then manages the user's address book. Users can send individual messages or one message to their entire family at the same time, just writing "Dear Family."

The service costs $13.98 per month for color messages or $8.98 for black and white. Users can use their own fax machine, or buy a preprogrammed fax machine from MyCelery for $119.00 plus shipping. To inquire or make an order, call toll-free 1-866-692-3537. Or access the website: www.mycelery.com.

CULTURALLY SCRIPTED CAREGIVERS

The role of caregiver is often assigned, early in life, by family dynamics or cultural expectations. It usually falls to the daughter. In traditional families, it's the daughter who never married, or the eldest daughter, or the gay daughter, or just the daughter, period. Great numbers of dutiful adult care providers do not identify themselves as "caregivers." Whether African American, Asian, or Latina, they accept "this is just what we do, as daughters."

"Asian women are just expected to drop everything and take care of our parents when they get old or sick," says Gemma Kim, a Korean American social worker I met in Portland, Oregon. "We don't even have a Korean word for 'caregiver.'"

As the youngest of five children, whose father died before she was born, Gemma was preordained to become her mother's caregiver at an early age. She was barely out of her teens when her sixty-three-year-old mother fell ill. Suddenly she was in sole charge of a sick, jobless widow who could not speak English. Gemma's social life came to an abrupt end. She spent every spare hour translating for her mother and caring for her medical needs. Her siblings were either self-employed and working seven days a week, or they lived on the opposite coast. Naturally, they relied on her.

Tag, you're it!

Gemma is now in her forties and still caring for her mother. As she told me all this, Gemma suppressed a nervous laugh and said, "I feel I became a caregiver before I had fun."

She married at twenty-six and completed her graduate education. Although she loved her job as a social worker at the Asian Health and Service Center and had a thriving private practice of her own, she was lost in her labyrinth, still pulled in too many directions: "I have to take care of my own family and do right by my clients, and at the same time, I have to take care of my mom. Whenever her health is not good or she has to have surgery or she falls, I'm the one who has to run."

After almost twenty years of attending to all of her mother's medical needs, while working full-time and trying to please a husband who sees running the household as entirely women's work, Gemma burned out. She had no idea how to create emotional distance. "My mom is in my head twelve hours a day, even in my dreams. One time I dreamed my mom was confused and fell in the street. It was very troubling. Consciously and unconsciously I'm always thinking about her."

One day Gemma heard about a local source of possible relief—a six-week course called "Powerful Tools for Caregivers" (PTC), developed by Legacy Health System, a hospital chain in Portland. Gemma was intrigued. Like other leaders in Portland's Korean community, though, she was wary after reading that the course emphasizes "I" messages over "You" messages. They objected to "sharing" their feelings and to using the "I" word, as in "I need." "No, no, we wouldn't do that," Gemma insisted. She had rarely expressed her inner feelings—anger, anxiety, depression.

"I just stuffed all these feelings inside me," Gemma told me. "It's really hard for Koreans, or any Asians, to talk about family matters. We talk in more collective terms, so your own feelings are not important. And we don't really express our feelings in front of others."

Kathy Shannon and Leslie Congleton, pioneers who started the PTC course, had both struggled with family members in cognitive decline. They were determined to spread the program to other cultural groups. "We had outreach workers go into the Korean community and find people who had experience as caregivers and wanted to train as class leaders," says Shannon.

"But we didn't change the material," she emphasizes. "If you have a great program that addresses common issues, it crosses cultural lines."

Once Gemma and other caregiving Korean women attended a pilot session, they began to ease away from the taboos that initially held them back. "They wanted to speak for themselves," recalls Shannon. Soon the dam broke, flooded by rising emotions. Participants discovered that everybody else harbored similar feelings, which they now felt permitted to share openly.

Training has since been provided for more than a thousand class leaders to teach the PTC program in twenty-eight states. Israel and Ireland are both interested in adopting the program. For a complete description of the course and resource information, see the section "Powerful Tools for Caregivers" in Chapter 16, "When a Couple Is Divided by Dementia."

Gemma credits PTC with saving her life and her marriage. She learned how to communicate her feelings and even to ask for help from her sisters. Using "I" instead of "you," she was able to say: "I feel really tired and stressed out, can you do this for me?" Or "I can do this today, but can you do it tomorrow?"

Having empowered herself, Gemma began training to become a PTC leader. She had the teaching guide translated into Korean and Chinese and introduced both courses at the Asian Health Center. Now that she understands the need for a caregiver to take a break and get away, she is dreaming less of her mother. Her dreams now float her on hot-air balloons to the faraway places she reads about in travel magazines. She has promised herself a trip.

WHO CARES FOR THE CAREGIVER?

In 2007, I wrote an article for *Parade* magazine entitled "Isn't It Time to Care for Our Family Caregivers?" Back came heartbreaking letters from readers describing their worst nightmare—caregivers who gave up so much to do right by their ailing parents that they sacrificed any prospect of independence for their own later years.

The government's response to this crisis is the opposite of what's needed. Instead of subsidizing people who quit their jobs to take care of their loved ones, the government has slashed Medicare benefits and funding for home-health-care agencies. Nonprofit organizations, too, are shifting more care-related costs and services to family members.

Even in a flourishing economy, family caregivers often leave the job market temporarily and then never find their way back. But in the economic recession reverberating around the world in 2010, many more are drowning in debt and the weight of elder care for which nobody subsidizes them.

One in six family caregivers lost a job during the first half of the 2009 economic downturn in the U.S. More than 20 percent had to share housing with family members to save money, according to a national survey by the National Alliance for Caregiving and Evercare, a division of UnitedHealth Group.

A huge proportion of these people lost their own health care. Why? Because fate drafted them out of the paid workforce to do the selfless work of caring for ill spouses or parents. In their eyes, the government inflicted catastrophe on innocent citizens—not only themselves, but all taxpayers, since every jobless, doctorless caregiver necessarily becomes dependent on working taxpayers.

The most heartbreaking aspect of my research was to see heroic family members being ground down by the staggering costs of taking care of a loved one, long-term, at home. It comes as a shock to many boomers to learn that Medicare does not pay for long-term care. Medicaid, the government program of subsidized health care for elderly poor Americans, spent $97 billion in 2007 on long-term care. You think that's a lot?

The estimated economic value of unpaid contributions of family caregivers in 2007 (at the going rate of $10.10 an hour) was $375 billion—more than three times as much as the government outlay. This figure is cited in the 2008 study "Caregiving in the U.S.," by the National Alliance for Caregiving and AARP. And it doesn't count the later costs of caring for caregivers, who typically ignore their own health even as they give up their jobs and forfeit their own financial security.

This myopia is creating secondary health costs—declines in caregivers' own health. Many recent clinical studies show that long-term caregivers are at high risk for sleep deprivation, immune system deficiency, muscle and joint problems, depression, chronic anxiety, loss of concentration, and premature death. "The tragedy is the family member—usually the wife or daughter—gets so stressed out emotionally, her own health is compromised until she can no longer provide the care, so the only option left is to place the care recipient in a nursing home—the last choice of everybody and the most expensive for taxpayers," says Lynn Friss Feinberg. She is a pioneer who founded the Family Caregiver Alliance in San Francisco over thirty years ago as a grassroots program to improve the quality of life for caregivers of loved ones with cognitive impairments. It has grown to include the National Center on Caregiving.

THE UPSIDE

The chance to give back some of the love and compassion and tender care to the parents who were there for us, or the life partner with whom we exchanged solemn wedding vows, or the brother or sister whom we once rivaled and emulated, is a gift. Often, the caregiving commitment brings a loosely knit family closer together, as long as each member is made to feel valuable for his or her unique contribution. The joint effort can be a surprising emollient in dissolving what seemed like indelible antagonisms between sisters or brothers.

The worst solution is to dump the whole load of caregiving responsibilities on one family member. If one person sacrifices much of his or her life to perform the relentless role of caring for a person who is declining, sooner or later either the caregiver will become angry and frustrated and lash out at the patient, or the sick person will learn to manipulate the passive caregiver and may become the abusive one.

A major goal of this book is to redefine the role of caregiver from solitary sacrificial lamb, shouldering the whole burden alone, to compassionate coach who learns how to attract and assemble a circle of care. The pool of recruits can be surprisingly large—family members, friends, neighbors, coworkers, community resources, student volunteers, perhaps some paid aides. With direction and inspiration, they can keep the caregiver healthy and give the ailing family member the greatest elixir—warm human connections.

What makes a successful caregiver?

Studies on the impact of family caregiving focus exclusively on what goes wrong. Thus a common fear is that individuals who accept the job will get stressed out and become emotionally and physically exhausted, be forced to give up their job and lose their friends, and ultimately sacrifice their health and financial security. Tragically, this is the downhill spiral experienced by roughly one-third of America's caregivers, principally because our society does not reimburse family caregivers or support us in any meaningful way.

But no study or book that I know of has focused on the experiences of caregivers who are coping or thriving. From studies on caregivers over the last thirty years, the Rosalynn Carter Institute estimates that about a third of family caregivers decline in health and well-being and age prematurely. Another third adapt to the stresses with varying degrees of success. Many do learn new skills and become more empowered in all areas of their lives. And another third say their lives have been enriched by acting as family caregivers.

"The successful group is the one we never study—the people who say their lives have been made better," says the institute's director, Dr. Richard Birkel. "We don't understand what distinguishes each of these three groups, but it is definitely not just income."

You will meet people from all three groups in this book, but the emphasis is on those who have found the gifts of giving care, survived the grueling months or years, and come back to new life enriched in some way.

First Turning:
Shock and Mobilization

five

How We Mobilize

Anyone facing serious surgery needs help in dealing with the anxiety. Stress overload makes people stupid. Solid research has proven it. When we become overstressed and don't know how to pull out of it, a cascade of hormones is released that creates a nasty chemical soup in our brains. The longer we remain in that state, the harder it becomes to pull out of a negative downward spiral. And that spiral interferes with healing.

Doctors' usual way of dealing with anxiety is drugs. Caregivers can act as a drug-free antianxiety medicine. It just takes being present. When my husband faced radical neck surgery, we had to find a way to let go of the nightmarish visions of deformity that we had been warned could be the outcome. Clay and I did meditative breathing exercises together. I talked him through calming visualizations. Most important, we were introduced to the benefits of self-hypnosis before surgery.

Seeking Surgery Without Stress

Dr. Stanley Fisher, a clinical hypnotherapist and personal friend (now deceased) who worked with Dr. Mehmet Oz at Columbia College of Physicians and Surgeons, had tested the efficacy of self-hypnosis in minimizing the trauma of a serious operation. He explained that the body considers surgery an attack. When the knife goes in, the body reacts just as it would if an attacker stabbed you as you were

putting the key in your car door. Your body sends out a cascade of hundreds of
hormones that jack up your heart rate, breathing, and blood pressure and that
suppress your immune system. If you are really under attack, the stress response can
save your life. But it's detrimental during surgery. The more tense the tissues of the
body become, the more bleeding will occur and the longer healing will be prolonged.
"So you want to train your unconscious to know the difference," Stan explained.

But could the unconscious send messages to the muscles when a person is
under anesthesia? Yes, Stan told us. The more primitive parts of the brain become
acutely aware of any sensory information and can access preoperative hypnotic
suggestions.

Clay was not by nature a navel-gazing, om-chanting kind of guy. But in a
couple of sessions, Stan trained Clay how to close his eyes and with the simplest
steps, put himself into a trance state and then give his body instructions for how to
respond to the surgeon: The doctor and I are working together to get me
better. I invite the doctor to cut out the cancer and throw it away. I will stay
calm and relaxed. *Immediately after the surgery, in the postoperative hours, he*
would play the tape to give the body another message, focused on healing: There
will be very little bleeding. The wound will remain clean and dry and free
of infection. I will go back to doing things I like to do.

Stan told Clay the more often he practiced, the easier it would become to slip
into a hypnotic state. His anxiety would lessen. He wouldn't need as much
anesthesia or painkillers. He would lose less blood and recover more quickly. I had a
biofeedback session to pinpoint my own anxiety triggers and learn how to
counteract them. Through all these efforts, my husband and I became connected at
a much deeper level.

The evening before surgery my daughters and I created a pleasant space inside
the clinical cubicle of Clay's hospital room. The idea here is to minimize the sudden
breach between the patient's normal world and the abnormal hospital environment
by introducing familiar totems of happy times. Sprigs of fresh lavender from our
garden overwhelmed the solvent smell. On the windowsill we propped favorite
photographs—a romantic one of the two of us frolicking in the surf, Clay tan and
handsome and virile as a sea lion, and a Churchill bulldog portrait, under which
we hung the leader's famous motto: "Never, never, never, never give in."

My sister and our daughters served up a feast of crown roast of lamb on china
plates and sponge cake smothered in cream and berries. We played games. Clay

loved the zaniness of it and brightened still more when Dr. Conley stopped by. He didn't have to remind us to tell him he was going to do a splendid operation.

All seemed buoyant until the nurse came in to take Clay's blood pressure.

It was abnormally high—155 over 100. I was relieved when Dr. Fisher appeared to give Clay one last practice session of self-hypnosis. Five minutes into the effort, Clay broke out of the trance and said, "I don't know if I can do it, Stan. I haven't been practicing and my shoulder is so knotted up . . ." Suddenly, his head dipped to one side.

"It's the tension," Stan said. "It's all right."

Clay was so tense that he fainted, yet remained frozen in an upright position. After a minute or so, his body shuddered and in one great spasm he slumped over, arms dangling. His face turned mustardy. I tried to put my arms around him.

"He's in shock," Stan said calmly.

"Shall I call a nurse?"

"He'll come out of it."

I closed my eyes as I thought: Oh, Clay, what have we done to you with our hocus-pocus hypnosis? But his reaction is not uncommon among patients awaiting surgery. Anxiety may cause the body's circuit breakers to turn off the system for a brief rest. Just as a computer shuts down when overloaded with tasks, so an overstressed person may need a quick time-out followed by rebooting.

When I opened my eyes, Clay had come to. He yawned, casually mumbling about feeling nauseous and having eaten too much. "I think I'd like to lie down." He didn't know he'd fainted.

On his back, his belt loosened, unguarded, the real thoughts he'd been working so hard all day to push down below the surface of consciousness began scuttling up like moles.

"What if they take out my tongue and I can't talk?"

"That won't happen—you've prevented it legally and we have the word of your surgeon," Stan said.

"I'm not sure what I'll be when I come out of this surgery. Will I be deformed?"

"These are real questions. Genuine fear. Just let yourself have these thoughts," Stan counseled. "You've been pushing them away all day."

"I was thinking this morning as I swam laps," Clay mused. "I was feeling so good, and suddenly the thought came—is this the last time I'll be able to swim this way? Arm over my head?"

"Honey, in two weeks you'll be swimming laps again the same as always," I interjected.

"No, Gail, don't tell him that."

Startled, I looked at Stan.

"We can't know how he'll be in two weeks from now. His fears are real—let him go with them. Everyone who faces serious surgery has these questions. If you try to push them away, they'll rise up and overwhelm you."

From this episode I learned that it is easy to make the mistake of cheerleading too hard. When we rush to reassure a loved one that everything will be hunky-dory in no time, we burden him or her with unrealistic expectations on top of his or her own fears.

Stan's next words were the most important: "The real reason you're so afraid is that you want to live. You have a life worth fighting for and you're going to do everything to help the surgeon fight his battle for the best result."

Clay's color gradually returned. I could see the veins in his hands flatten out. I asked the nurse to take his blood pressure.

"120 over 70."

"Amazing," Clay said, "I haven't had blood pressure that low in years. I believe this stuff—my mantra really works!"

Reprieve

A smile flickered on his relaxed face as he was rolled into the room from recovery. The Walkman was in his ear. He had done his work. "Jazz," he said hoarsely.

"You're talking!" I flipped out the recovery tape and popped in "Sing, Sing, Sing." Clay loved the swing era and this raucous song, written by Louis Prima, was made a classic by the Benny Goodman band. Later that day Dr. Conley came bouncing into the room, wearing his natty plus fours after a round of golf.

"You did a great operation," we chimed almost in unison.

"We did it together," he said.

AT 10:00 A.M. ON a Sunday, our daughter Mohm and I stepped out of the elevator on the head and neck floor of St. Vincent's Hospital. Before we rounded the *first corner, Clay loomed in the hallway—smiling, striding toward us, big and broad-shouldered and costumed again as a whole man in his tattersall checked shirt and summer-sand suit.*

"Hey, catch this handsome dude!" I snuggled into his arms, planting a kiss.

"I feel human again." His big voice, his good humor, were back. Out rolled one of his long deep tromboney laughs. "I'm down to 189—a record—and I feel good. The human body is an amazing healing machine, isn't it?"

We moved out of the hospital like sojourners at the end of an unforgettable vacation. In a funny way the whole experience was a getaway from the workaday routine that keeps us all from delving into deeper realms of existence. We had been touched by the many expressions of love and concern from our friends. Clay's generation had conditioned him to hide fervent feelings of affection, especially for other men. This experience had opened him up. He pondered the change:

"When you're faced with extinction, you think, what am I hiding from?"

"Beautiful," the doctor pronounced a week later as he removed the bandage and surveyed his handiwork. "You haven't had one drop of blood after this whole big operation. You handled the surgery absolutely way above average. The body is healing very fast."

"Well, I had confidence in what you were doing," Clay said.

We had done what Deborah and Frank had told us was the key to this phase of the battle—take charge where we could. We had formed trusting partnerships with two brilliant professionals who helped us mobilize both medically and psychologically. And we had learned how to use mental imagery to train the mind to react calmly under extreme stress.

"It's your spirit that triumphed," I told Clay.

"No," he insisted, "we did it together."

———

STRATEGIES

Empower Yourself

Here's what I learned the hard way about responding to the Shock and Mobilization phase.

Start the Conversation Before the Crisis

Only a third of Americans say they have talked with a family member or friend about providing them with care in the future. Despite this head-in-the-sand behavior, most Americans still believe that a close family member will "be there" to care for them. My husband and I had not talked about the what-ifs, despite the fact we were both in midlife. The best strategy is to start having such conversations—with your spouse, your parents, your siblings, and your children—early and often. Don't wait until a crisis adds more tension or your loved one isn't well enough to participate fully.

Interview Doctors

Speak up! In your initial consult with any doctor, determine if he or she is willing to be a partner with your loved one and with you, as the caregiver. You have every right to interview the doctors who want to treat your family. Your primary task in the mobilization phase is to be a good reporter.

Doctors can be brilliant and compassionate. They are also human, fallible, and rushed. Notice whether the doctor takes a thorough history, not just rote facts about allergies and frequency of bowel movements. Does he or she ask what the patient lives for? How various treatments would affect the patient's quality of life? Some doctors see you as a guinea pig for testing a new drug; others seem focused on scheduling.

THREE QUESTIONS YOU MUST ASK:

- Will you be the one to coordinate the care? Or who will?
- Will you help us decide among different treatment options?
- Will you help address pain and other side effects of treatment?

Seek a Second Opinion

You can now consult a doctor or seek a second opinion, from home, using your computer and a web camera. Telemedicine is exploding and more options will become available.

The famous Cleveland Clinic offers an online medical service that can connect you to top specialists when you are faced with a serious diagnosis, or for a more routine medical or nutrition consult. The website is https://my.clevelandclinic.org/eclevelandclinic/myconsult/default.aspx.

MDLiveCare is another live health-care delivery system where you can consult certain kinds of doctors, on demand, 24/7, from anywhere. It offers a national network of board-certified U.S. physicians (pediatricians, dermatologists) and licensed therapists and nutritionists. These in-person consults can be done via real-time video, phone, or secure e-mail, regardless of your location. The website is www.mdlivecare.com/. The regular mailing address is 700 Banyan Trail, Suite 200, Boca Raton, FL 33431, or call 786-419-4661.

Consider Treatment Options

Draw out your family members' questions and concerns. If you are still confused or have unresolved questions, ask the doctor for a follow-up consult. Take a tape recorder into any important consult, or at least a notebook. Doctors rarely object. Get it all down. You will be surprised at how you and your patient hear what you want to hear or exaggerate the negative. It's normal. You are both under great tension. Weeks later, when you're making your final decisions, these notes will be pure gold.

If you are going into an important diagnostic consult with your wife or husband, take along a third pair of ears—an adult child, sibling, or friend. A neutral observer can later validate or challenge your own gut reactions.

Use Guided Imagery—Your Insurance May Pay for It!

At a recent West Point course in Enhanced Performance (ACEP), I learned that Clay and I and Doctors Conley and Fisher were almost twenty years ahead of our time. Utilizing guided imagery on a CD to train a patient beforehand to accept the assault of surgery with "detached interest" rather than tensed defenses is now a technique that has gone mainstream.

The mind cannot distinguish between a highly vivid image and the real thing. Our nervous system will process the imagined information very much the same way it would the actual experience. That insight can be used to fortify a patient before any fearful procedure.

Creating visual imagery is a *skill.* Here's how the army trains its soldiers to practice developing a mental imagery CD. Using every one of your senses, imagine the following about the experience:

What will it look like (in the OR)?

What will it smell like?

What will things taste like?

What will it feel like (when the surgeon operates while I am under anesthesia)?

How will you feel when it's over? (Happy the tumor is gone.)

Our hunch back then—that the less stress around any invasive procedure, the shorter time it would take to heal—is now demonstrable fact. Blue Cross/Blue Shield of California conducted a trial with remarkable results, showing that practice with guided imagery CDs resulted in shorter hospital stays and less medication. The company saved an average of $2,000 per surgical patient.

Blue Cross/Blue Shield now offers a significant discount to patients who choose the Guided Imagery Option. For information, call the company's Alternative Medicine Service Center, part of its Options Program, at 800-514-6502.

Ask About Quality of Life Under Treatment

Only when patients do this will the side effects and aftereffects of surgery and drugs become less ominous. Palliative care focuses on the relief of pain, stress, and other debilitating symptoms of serious illness. Palliative care can be delivered at the same time as treatment that is meant to cure you. Most large hospitals have a palliative-care team of doctors, nurses, and a social worker. Ask for a consult with the palliative-care team to help the patient match goals for quality of life with the treatment chosen.

Check Out Hospitals

Rankings and ratings on hospitals are made available by not-for-profit groups like the National Committee for Quality Assurance (NCQA), which issues an annual report card on hospitals after they pass a rigorous, comprehensive review. The Leapfrog Group, supported by companies who agree to buy health care that meets certain safety and quality standards, also rates hospitals' performance on patient safety, high-risk procedures, and intensive care. If your specialist has privileges at only one hospital, it still pays to check it out. If you are disappointed, you may want to look for another specialist. The Leapfrog Group's website is www.leap froggroup.org, or call 202-292-6713.

The Joint Commission on Accreditation of Healthcare Organizations is the nation's leading nonprofit accreditation group that encourages quality and safety standards among health-care facilities and gives a seal of approval to those that meet its standards. Quality Check is JCAHO's online search service of accredited hospitals, laboratories, and nursing homes. You can search facilities by accessing www.jointcommission.org/QualityCheck.

Google Without Freaking

As I mentioned earlier, working the Internet blindly is scary. In our case, it became almost comical. Don't take seriously the dire warnings of treatment side effects or survival statistics until you have talked with more than one medical professional and consulted the specific disease organization. The "median survival" rate refers to the person in the middle of the curve. That means that given any one hundred patients using the same medical treatment, 50 percent will live longer than the median. Survival statistics are based on the use of a particular drug or medical treatment. They exclude all patients who add any nonmedical supplement from nutrition to prayer.

Absorb the Shock and Process Together

Don't immediately leap into action. Pause to let the news sink in. You and the patient need time together. Advice from friends and family may be useful but also contradictory. After all the consults and a firm diagnosis, take a weekend off from everybody else and just sit with nature or music or take walks or bike rides—anything to rest your minds and remember what you both have to appreciate. In a calm and receptive state, you are more likely to receive an insight or inspiration and know which direction feels right.

What if you and your loved one can't agree? It's the patient's call. Ask him or her who should be told and who shouldn't at this early stage. Job security may be at stake and bad news travels fast. As a caregiver you must respect your loved one's wishes here.

Develop an Action Plan

List quality-of-life goals and the steps needed to achieve them. Focus on what's right with you and your loved one, not what's wrong. Discuss treatment outcomes—what does your loved one want and not want? Then talk about possibilities for a future beyond this crisis. What new dream might he or she now be willing to consider?

Don't cheerlead too hard and burden your loved one with unrealistic expectations on top of his or her own fears. Remember— you don't have control over everything. This is a brand-new experience. Be patient with yourselves as you both learn to adjust.

Create an e-mail tree or Twitter to update family and friends while you're spending time in the hospital without any idea of the outcome. It will save you the exhaustion of talking to each family member and being overloaded with their responses. Calm yourself with music or a book on CD to shut out the din of the hospital. Ignore criticism: Remember, you're doing the best you can. So is your loved one. Practice patience. When your sister or brother calls in from the other side of the country to insist that you're headed in the wrong direction, remember this:

The farther away they live, the quicker they assume you don't know what you're doing.

National disease organizations are excellent resources, able to answer your first questions about the diagnosis you or your loved one has just received. Find a complete listing of such organizations and contact information in Resources.

six

WHAT TO DO ABOUT
MOM AND DAD?

So often, the conversation starts with spats about driving the car. The adult child visits and takes a white-knuckled drive as a passenger with Mom or Dad. It's plain the parent just isn't safe behind the wheel. Sez who! demands the parent, outraged at any suggestion of incompetence in a skill performed for fifty years or more.

DEALING WITH PARENTAL REBELLION

Like most adult children in the sandwich generation, Ginny put off having The Conversation with her parents. Ginny is not yet quite fifty and unusually fit but stretched too thin over the past few years, both physically and emotionally, as the gathering crisis with both her mother and father gained momentum. She has a typically prickly teenage daughter who feels neglected and a husband who doesn't want to hear another word about her parents' health problems.

For the first couple of years, she stumbled through the fog of half-knowing that is familiar to anyone who sees the early signs of dementia in a parent. When Ginny finally uttered the words to a doctor, "Mom is not the same," her cry for help was met with the doctor's casual reassurance after a cursory exam: "Everything is fine."

In addition, she got nowhere trying to persuade her father that his heart was too unstable to risk driving on California freeways. He refused to see a cardiologist: "Too expensive." He continued to clean the pool and repaint the house, ignoring frequent chest pains. Ginny tried taking charge. She made the appointment with his cardiologist and drove to her father's house. "Get in," she said. "I'll drive." He exploded in rebellion.

"No, you're going in my car!"

"No, Dad, you're having chest pains, you can't drive."

Her father jumped into his own car and peeled off, leaving Ginny sputtering in his driveway. She tailed him to the doctor's office, but by then his symptoms didn't ring alarm bells and the doctor did nothing. Weeks later, he had a heart attack while driving to the hospital and was rushed into surgery for a triple bypass. From then on, whenever Ginny saw an unfamiliar number on her caller ID, she felt twinges of dread. Then she got The Call.

"Your father ran a red light and hit another car," reported the state trooper. "How could that have happened?" Ginny asked. There was a respectful pause. "Your father doesn't remember."

This was the shock that finally prompted Ginny to mobilize. She dialed the hotline of the Family Caregiver Alliance in San Francisco and told the preceding story. "It's the time bomb we've been waiting for," Ginny added.

Donna Schempp, the senior social worker, invited Ginny to come in right away for a free consultation. With their consent, I joined them in a friendly family room of the Family Caregiver Alliance with tulips and coffee cake on the table. Their dialogue is so instructive, I reproduce it here:

Ginny: *I'm dealing with this thing with my parents that's gotten totally out of hand.*

Donna: *You need to take your father for a driving test at a school that specializes in evaluating elderly people's driving skills.*

Ginny: *He'll never go.*

Donna: *This is a trick, but tricks can work. Tell him if he passes the test they might not revoke his license. That will motivate him to take the test. Of course, with luck, he'll fail it.*

Ginny: *Since my dad's emergency bypass, he's not making good judgments.*

Donna: *One of the first signs of Alzheimer's is loss of judgment.*

Ginny: *What are the causes of dementia?*

Donna: *There are twenty-five different causes. (See Chapter 16 for more information about Alzheimer's.) And a lot of behaviors look like dementia but could be from other causes. It could be medications, it could be dehydration, Parkinson's disease, ministrokes. Alzheimer's sometimes develops out of depression.*

Ginny: *Maybe that's my mom. She definitely shows the beginning signs of dementia. Dad calls me and says, "Your mother forgot to make dinner." I tell him, "Dad, you've been calling me for the last three years about that. Just take Mom out to dinner." But it's hard to see the way they live. There's tons of junk mail all over their house. Mom doesn't wash her hair anymore. My dad doesn't see it.*

Donna: *Who do you get emotional support from? Do you have any siblings?*

Ginny: *My sister and I are both on crisis patrol. She gets all emotional. We're not close. But I don't want to be my parents' nurse and housekeeper! Is that mean?*

Donna: *No, it's natural. You need some help.*

Ginny: *I hired a care aide. My mom threatened to fire her.*

Donna: *I often sneak nursing care into the house through the housekeeper. If they resist, saying it costs too much money, just pay from their bank account and tell them the nurse is a volunteer. We call it therapeutic lying.*

Ginny: *I'm making myself sick over this.*

Donna: *It sounds like you are dealing with two people with dementia. I want you to call the Alzheimer's Clinic at the University of California, San Francisco, and ask for a diagnostic test. It's offered free in most medical centers. We can offer you a class called "It Takes Two." It would give your dad some tricks to deal with your mother's dementia behavior. You and your dad could go to the class together. Dealing with dementia is counterintuitive.*

Ginny: *My mom won't do anything I tell her.*

Donna: *Your mom is no longer rational, logical, or reasonable. That's the most important thing for the caregiver to understand. You can't tell her to do something and expect her to connect the dots as to why it's good for her. One trick to get her to a diagnostic center is to take her out to lunch and then just "drop by" the center.*

Ginny: *Everything you're saying is great, and logical, but everything is a big fat no with my father. So what do you do in that situation?*

Donna: *If we can get Mom diagnosed, it's going to be easier to get Dad to give up driving. He may also suffer from some dementia, but if he thinks the main problem is her and not him, he will be more compliant in doing what's best for himself.*

Ginny: *How long will all this take?*

Donna: *It's not a quick fix. It's a process. One step at a time.*

Ginny: *All I do now is cry.*

Donna: *For the long term, you need to have a family meeting with your dad and your sister. Get everyone on the same page or as close as possible. If you have a neutral facilitator from the outside, it could really be helpful.*

Ginny: *I think he'd be too frightened.*

Donna: *Have a list of your questions. You can say, these are the things we have seen: Lapses in judgment. Is your dad safe driving? What does the doctor say? Express your concern about whether your mom is showing the beginning of dementia, or is it depression?*

When Ginny's father refused to be part of a family meeting, the social worker suggested she come in with her sister and Donna would be the facilitator. The sisters' relationship began to change. Ginny used to think she was right and her sister was wrong, period. She came to understand that her sister has a different way of coping than she does. Once they began to work on a mutual goal to create a safety net under the parents they love, they found themselves growing closer, and the care of their parents was better and easier.

STRATEGIES

Hotline Help for Caregivers

In most U.S. communities, online, and on my own website, www.gailsheehy.com, you can find numerous helpful hotlines. Reach out! Ask for help!

The Family Caregiver Alliance (FCA) is a great place to start. Based in San Francisco, FCA has pioneered in helping families provide long-term home care for the past thirty years. FCA's Donna Schempp heads a team of dedicated social workers who take calls on their national hotline Monday to Friday, nine to five Pacific time. "We usually deal with people in crisis," Schempp says. "They find us on the Web, or through a social worker at their doctor's office or another social service agency, or by word of mouth. The problem is that most caregivers wait until they're desperate because they've been trying to do it all alone for three or four years."

If you live in the Bay Area of Northern California, FCA will do a preliminary phone consultation. They may suggest an interview in their home office in San Francisco, or a home visit by one of their social workers to assess your family's caregiving needs and housing situation. Even if you don't live in the Bay Area, your call for help will be answered. These are not five-minute calls. FCA's interviewers want to know salient facts about you, the caregiver—your own age and health, your loved one's medical condition and outlook, your relationship, expectations, and finances. FCA workers are then able to search their database and recommend resources in your area. FCA also offers workshops, classes, conferences, and discussion groups. Visit the Family Caregiver Alliance online at www.caregiver .org, or call its hotline at 800-445-8106 or 415-434-3388. Office address: 180 Montgomery Street, San Francisco, CA 94194.

Brain Training for Dad—and You, Too!

I was introduced to the software CogniFit by Adriane Berg, the marketing expert previously mentioned. "The big problem is that people live longer, but they don't live better," she says. "So training your brain is one part of a healthy lifestyle. There is the nutrition aspect, physical aspect, stress aspect, and now you've got the brain aspect." Like a deteriorating domicile on *This Old House,* "Get your brain rehabbed!" Berg implores.

Ten years ago, this idea seemed far-fetched—even radical. But science has proven *brain plasticity* improves cognitive ability when you train the brain. CogniFit was created in 1999 by Professor Shlomo Breznitz, a celebrated psychologist who had more than thirty years of experience in brain research while president of Israel's University of Haifa, and he was the founding director of the university's Center for the Study of Psychological Stress in 1979.

The software begins with a baseline assessment of the user in fourteen key cognitive abilities, ranging from working memory to spatial perception. The assessment reveals an individualized profile of the cognitive skills that are working well for the person, and those needing the most rehabilitation. Throughout cognitive brain fitness training, the software adjusts to the individual's improvements or setbacks.

In the early stages of Alzheimer's, family caregivers can suggest that their aging loved one take the initial assessment as an objective determination of the senior's ability to drive independently and safely. Berg says that some elders have improved enough by using CogniFit "to the point that they can use a computer to be in communication with people around the world. This allows them to get stimulation whenever they want it and talk to their grandchildren."

For more information visit www.cognifit.com or call toll-free 866-669-6223.

Become a Reporter and an Advocate

On Memorial Day in 2009, my friend Anne called me to cancel our plans to go to a parade. "I have a problem with Mom," she said. Her mother, who was widowed and lived alone in a semirural beach community on Long Island, had fallen and hit her head with a blow severe enough to require hospitalization. Anne had to pick her up at the hospital and drive her to Anne's sister's home in Connecticut.

Anne's matter-of-fact recitation suggested a deeper concern. It surfaced as we spoke: "Mom isn't making a lot of sense. Maybe, I don't know, it could be, who knows, signs of dementia?"

These are the first sounds of a chronic caregiving crisis. Anne's mother was a feisty political woman and right-to-life crusader who had been married to a sheriff. After her husband's death, she insisted that she stay on in their beach house by herself—no help needed. She ignored her age, which was thought to be in the early eighties.

But it surfaced in my short talk with Anne that her mother had fallen eleven times in the last year. And after the recent fall where she hit her head, she had been very confused and forgetful. Anne suddenly feared her mother might be showing the first signs of Alzheimer's.

"I don't know what to do," Anne said. I suggested she call the local Area Agency on Aging. "What's that?" I gave her a quick answer and asked if she might consider a geriatric care manager. "What's that?" she repeated. "We need to talk," I said. She agreed, but she was working overtime and had some problems with her kids who were being tempted by drugs and dropping out of college. Her sister, who was going in for knee replacement surgery, wouldn't be able to keep her mother for long. And her brother lived in Pennsylvania. It's a typical story of members of the sandwich generation, pressed between the delayed adolescence of their children, the prolonged senescence of their parents, and the first signs of their own body maintenance problems.

I told Anne I'd write out a list of strategies to get her started. Following are the steps I suggested that any caregiver can take at the first indication of a problem with a loved one.

Call Your Local Area Agency on Aging

AAA stands for Area Agency on Aging, a free one-stop shop for care of older Americans that is funded by the federal government. The Triple As, as they are called, can be found in every state, county, and possibly even in the city or town where you or your loved one live. It's free information, no income requirement.

A phone volunteer or social worker will answer, listen to your situation, and send you to the community providers of service that meet your family member's needs. These services may include in-home aides, meals, the closest adult day-care program, and free transportation. Services vary from county to county depending on the county's budget, the time of year, and the population in your area. Social workers at the Triple As know how the game is played locally and can plead your case. They can help you find out if your income level qualifies you for any financial reimbursement. But don't hesitate to call because you think your parent won't qualify; regardless of income, or whether or not you can pay for services, everybody needs information. Some Triple As offer a care coordinator who can assess your loved one's needs and the safety of your home.

And good news: Most Triple As also offer support programs for family caregivers, sometimes counseling, and some offer respite care (breaks from caregiving). If you run into a wall, go back to your Triple A office and tell them, "That didn't work. What else can we do?"

To find your local Area Agency on Aging, go to the Eldercare Locator website (www.eldercare.gov) and type in your zip code; or call 800-677-1116. You will be connected to a caseworker. Give a brief description of your loved one's situation.

Consider a Geriatric Care Manager

If you and your family members are all working and living in different states, you may find it necessary to hire a care manager. Sometimes called geriatric care managers, these are professionals who often have extensive health-care experience. Some are social workers or nurses or they have worked in the fields of psychology or gerontology. Most are freelancers, but care managers can also be found through government agencies (see below for contact information).

Care managers have the background and skills to assess the needs and strengths of the patient and the rest of the family. They recommend appropriate services and solutions, and they can also negotiate for and coordinate services of which the family may be unaware. Care managers are the experts in this complex world of caregiving. They speak the language, know the shortcuts, and can easily maneuver on your behalf.

Private care managers can be expensive. Fees range from $80 to $250 an hour depending on where the patient lives and the care manager's level of expertise. Medicare doesn't cover care managers. Most long-term-care policies won't cover them either.

You may want to consider a onetime consultation or short-term engagement. In the first weeks of caregiving after a health-care crisis, even a few hours of a health-care Sherpa's guidance can save you from bureaucratic brush-offs, blind alleys, and your own fears.

Very likely you will meet resistance from your loved one when you introduce a care manager. Patients fear losing their independence. Break the ice by arranging a friendly, low-key meeting between care manager and patient. Identify their mutual interests and set up an outing or a game they can play in the next meeting. Early trust is vital. You don't want your mother blowing up and firing the care manager before they even know each other.

To find care managers in your area, go to the website of the National Association of Professional Geriatric Care Managers (NAPGCM), www.caremanager.org. Click on Find a Care Manager. Type in your loved one's zip code or location.

Find Out Why Mom Is Falling

On Anne's behalf, I consulted the director of research at Mount Sinai Alzheimer's Disease Research Center, Mary Sano, a neuropsychologist who has worked in this area her whole life. "The first question is why is the person falling, not does she have Alzheimer's," said the expert. "Trauma to the head can produce mental confusion. But since this woman has been falling repeatedly, it could be a movement disorder—early Parkinson's or a balance disorder (possibly the result of a tumor or infection). Or it could be a medication-induced situation where she's getting sudden drops in blood pressure—orthostasis—or a cardiac problem. A good internist could do the initial tests and get a hint of which direction to go in, and refer to the right specialist."

If Anne and her siblings report that for the past six months or more Mom has been losing things, not paying bills, forgetting what she's read, asking the same questions over and over, those clues are significant enough to take her to her primary-care doctor, or the health professional who knows her best, and start an investigation of possible cognitive impairment.

Investigate a Medical Alert System

Most of us who have an elderly mother or father living alone or far away, worry about the nightmarish possibility that they might fall and be left for hours or days, unconscious and undiscovered, with a bleed in the brain that could be fatal without emergency treatment. Even a neighbor may see lights and a TV screen and assume everything is normal.

With a medical alert system, the owner simply pushes a button on a battery-operated pendant or bracelet that he or she is wearing. It sends a signal to the response center. Within thirty seconds an associate pulls up a computer screen that lists everything about the person's medical condition. The associate will then phone local resources—a neighbor, family member, or emergency help—depending on the situation. The largest provider is Philips Lifeline, but many smaller companies offer this product, also known as personal response systems (PRS).

Create a Notebook

Before you start making the rounds of doctors, gather all the information about your parent's health history, doctors' names, hospitalizations, and medications. Get it all down in a notebook with lots of dividers.

Ask your parent to sign a written request to release his or her medical records to you. Fax the request to your parent's doctors. Don't be afraid to ask your parent's physicians for help in understanding the information. They may illuminate the findings. Now you have the clinical speak at your fingertips for all the calls you will make. The more knowledgeable you sound, the more likely you will be able to engage medical professionals and assure they will take you seriously.

Boil down the main points into a cheat sheet, print out multiple copies, and send to the appropriate family members so they can be empowered with the same information. Keep it updated!

To keep things straight, use a separate section for each agency, facility, or physician you contact. This will preserve hurried phone information and help you compare conflicting recommendations later—that saves you time and energy in making decisions.

Following are key list items:

1. Name and contacts (e-mail, phone, fax) for each agency, doctor, nurse, or social worker. Make sure to memorize the name and something personal about the head nurse; she is your best friend.
2. What services does the agency provide?

3. How do you apply for each service? Requirements?
4. Who can help you apply for services?
5. Will the patient be assigned a caseworker or care manager?
6. Is there a waiting list?
7. Which services are free?
8. Is free transportation available?
9. Are any services offered for the caregiver?

Have the Conversation with Your Siblings

Once you begin to understand the system, set up a meeting or a conference call with your siblings to talk about dividing up the tasks. You've already done the hard part: gathering information. Once you arm your other family members with a faxed copy of the patient's cheat sheet/medical history and contact info on the facility or physician they will be visiting, they will be more inclined to help and do the follow-up work.

Get a Diagnostic Workup

If a parent has had numerous falls and has also been having some memory lapses over the last six months or more, call the Alzheimer's Association 24-hour hotline (800-272-3900). Wherever you are in the United States, when you call this number between nine A.M. and five P.M. local time, your call will automatically be connected to the Alzheimer's Association office nearest you. A representative will talk to you and offer guidance even without a diagnosis of cognitive illness. If you are interested, you can be referred to the nearest diagnostic center for a full workup. After the diagnosis, call back and the hotline will recommend further assistance. The Alzheimer's Association recently created a "Caregiver Notebook" to help you keep track of medications.

Make an appointment with a neurologist. This was the advice

given to me, on behalf of my friend Anne, by Robin Fenley, director of the Alzheimer's and Caregiving Resource Center at the Area Agency on Aging in New York City. Whatever is going on in a parent's brain that may be causing him or her to have repeated falls may not be associated with dementia, and it may not be Alzheimer's. But an Alzheimer's workup would also include the neurologic component and be able to rule out other causes.

SECOND TURNING:
THE NEW NORMAL

seven

SEEKING A NEW DREAM

How long does it take to recognize yourself as a caregiver? This is the first barrier on the journey into the labyrinth of caregiving. You can sprint for a month or two, maybe even six, but when the Shock and Mobilization phase becomes a marathon, you can't keep passing the water stations. You have to stop, refresh yourself, and reach out for some help.

Eventually, you will find your way into establishing a New Normal. This is the second turning. If acute treatment of your loved one has been successfully completed, you may be jubilant. Reward yourself.

However, if you are now dealing with a person who has a chronic illness, or the multiple conditions so common among older people, your own life will change. The ways in which you think about your own future will change. You have a new role—family caregiver—and the sooner you recognize it and see yourself as providing a highly professional service, the better you will be able to perform, without putting your own health and well-being at risk.

You and the patient may be living with a new uncertainty. This is the time to break out of old habits and routines. Together you can use the first shock of dangerous illness to jump-start your lives, to fight rather than flee, to make positive changes that help alleviate the uncertainty you both may live with indefinitely. It's a now-or-never moment.

AFTER HIS FIRST SUCCESSFUL *cancer treatment, my husband slid into a chronic depression. Like many who go on living with cancer, once he was no longer mobilized to defeat the enemy, he became nearly immobilized. Many aspects of his former life as a magazine editor and publisher were unrecoverable. He didn't believe in the publication he was now working for; it was formulaic. With the blot of cancer on his record, he was no longer an attractive investment for backers or employers.*

He couldn't adjust to this New Normal. With no ready outlet for his unquenchable curiosity, his spirit was slowly being crushed. He kicked around at home, moping over his minor investments, reading papers and watching TV.

In hindsight, it seems possible that a major loss of self-worth may have weakened his body's defenses, triggering serious illness. Many mornings stretched close to noon before Clay got out of his sweatpants and dressed for the day. He drifted for more than a year. It was hard on our marriage. Depression is contagious. It can become a family disease.

It took another shock to catapult us into making a dramatic life change. It came less than two years after my husband's dramatic recovery from squamous cell cancer in the neck. Now it was something tender in his abdomen. We found ourselves in another doctor's office. Clay was diagnosed with lymphoma. But this time we knew: Don't take the first doctor's word. I asked my dear friend Dr. Pat Allen, a gynecologist who knew everyone at New York Hospital/Weill Medical Center, to suggest a specialist with long experience. She made an appointment for us with Dr. Morton Coleman, who was director of the Lymphoma Center, one of the foremost blood cancer centers in the country, and a physician known for his humanistic approach.

"This is a low-grade non-Hodgkin's lymphoma," he told us. "It's indolent. The median survival rate at your age is ten years. But since you have no symptoms, and early treatment with any drug won't improve your life span, I'm going to leave you alone." At first, that sounded like giving up, but it was quite the opposite. "My advice," he went on, "is this: Go out and live your life—the two of you—do something wonderful you wouldn't have dared before."

Stunned, we sat mute. This wasn't the usual dehumanizing ten-minute physician consult. This doctor was talking to my husband man-to-man, as a person of action and intelligence, who was depressed by losing his former life. And he was including me, the caregiver, as a full partner in our experiment in healthy living with cancer.

We walked out of that office on a cloud of reprieve. It did not sustain us for long; clouds never do. We had to act—tear up the life we had spent decades building in the densely connected world of New York publishing, strike out for a new place and a new way of life that would stimulate and mobilize us. It took a community to help us find the right path.

Former colleagues of Clay's wanted to help. These were the writers, editors, artists, photographers, and staffers whose careers he had started, shaped, or promoted over the years. Secretly, they created an informal working group to brainstorm about how to get Clay back into action again. This was a gift of caring.

The initial impulse came from political journalist Mike Kramer, who enlisted Milton Glaser, Clay's partner in starting New York *magazine; Steven Brill, founder of* The American Lawyer *and* Court TV; *Gloria Steinem; Tom Wolfe; journalist and later playwright Aaron Latham; and others. "What about a dinner to celebrate Clay for all he's done for journalists," Michael suggested. "We could raise money at the dinner, to perpetuate Clay's memory."*

Milton looked up with his ironic smile. "Wait a minute. The guy's still living—I think." Milton wanted to offer Clay a new lease on life, as a guru to another generation of journalists. He said, "Clay is a maker of magazines; that's what we have to perpetuate." His vision was to create a center where people could learn how to think up magazines, under Clay's direction. That mission could excite support to raise the funds to endow such a center at a university. The group agreed that Clay would never be satisfied just serving on the board of an inanimate chair in his name.

Simultaneous with the group's patient search for the right home for such a center, Clay himself spent much of the next year searching for his own new purpose. We took long walks in a nature preserve almost every weekend while he chewed over the same question: What was it about his work that he most loved, stripped of title or setting? What big idea would allow him to give back from a lifetime of experience? If he could only glimpse that idea, we could then work together building a foundation to support the new dream.

This kind of work, I believe, is essential in recovering from any acute illness. From it emerges the pursuit that can give life new meaning.

When the answer finally hit him on one of our Saturday walks, it was clear as skywriting: he loved identifying and shaping young talent. That opened up a whole new avenue—what about starting a graduate program to make new magazines with young journalists? At the same time, the search group heard from the Graduate School of Journalism at the University of California, Berkeley. Tom Goldstein, a New Yorker who was then dean of the journalism school, ran with the idea and invited Clay to meet his students. Clay came back enthralled. The Bay Area of Northern California was a long, long way from Manhattan. But for us, life restarted beyond the Great Divide. Westward ho!

We moved to Berkeley for a semester to try it out. We were assigned to a faculty apartment and went back to brick-and-board bookcases and fighting over a single bathroom. Living like graduate students, we found a running track with an inspiring view overlooking San Francisco Bay and a sidewalk café where we had our oatmeal and coffee while reading the New York Times outdoors on winter mornings. We were young and in love all over again. We made this our New Normal.

Sacrifices We Rush to Make

Not everything goes quickly and smoothly in designing a New Normal. For us, as with many others I have interviewed, the adjustment unfolded in fits and starts. For the next three years I raced back and forth between East and West Coasts, struggling to keep up my professional associations in New York as I wrote another book and many magazine articles, yearning always to get on the red-eye and rejoin my husband in Berkeley. We rented a house in the Berkeley hills where each morning we took delightful hikes under the perfumed eucalyptus trees. Then Clay would go off to school, his professor's briefcase stuffed with stories by his exciting graduate students, and I would wait for FedEx to bring me another box of research for work on my overdue book. We were still in the prehistory of the Web and it wasn't easy to transfer computer files from one location to another. No sooner would I be close to finishing a chapter than it would be time for me to fly back east for a meeting with one of my editors.

The time came when we had to give up our New York apartment. I was willing to take that plunge, but Clay also wanted me to give up my little office in the city and the collegial experiences that come with it. That struck a nerve. My career as a writer was based in New York, the hub of media and publishing. Huddling with my *editors over eleventh-hour rewrites on a magazine article or pulling all-nighters in the final stages of closing a book, or showing up before dawn for a TV interview on breaking news—all these were thrilling to me. This is the cross-fertilization that saves the sanity of a writer who operates mostly in isolation. Clay was asking me to give up the world in which I functioned as a professional—exactly what had brought on his depression.*

The "something wonderful" we had done to stimulate Clay and set him up with a new career and a new home base three thousand miles from our children and my working colleagues was taking a toll on our marriage and my health. He felt lonely. I felt permanently jet-lagged. I was always running for a plane, running to make a deadline, running for my life.

The New Normal has to work for both patient and caregiver. The sacrifices we rush to make in the Shock and Mobilization stage, when we're driven by fear, often turn out to be unsustainable for the long term. Since my career was in high gear, I was now trying to do twice as much in half the time, while maintaining two homes and an erratic travel schedule. I couldn't face pulling up stakes completely. Grandchildren were on the horizon. I didn't want to be far away when it came time to hold my first grandbaby. And in the back of my mind was a future probability that I didn't want to discuss with Clay. At some point, either age or recurring illness would catch up with him. He would retire and need to return to New York. I was more than a decade younger than he, and I had to keep working.

Time, once again, for a conversation.

A New New Normal

One hot summer evening back east, we were overdressed to drive to a presidential campaign fund-raiser at the end of Long Island. We got lost. An hour late, we arrived at the gate, only to find it closed and bolted. The candidate had canceled at the last minute.

Whoopee! We were liberated from a stiff stand-up affair. Clay came up with a wonderful fallback: "Let's have dinner at the Chequit Inn." We loved the broad old-fashioned porch hung on the only hill on Shelter Island, and getting there by ferry was half the fun.

The ferry ride in falling twilight was romantic. We watched the moon fill an apricot sky. The wake ruffled up behind us, and we felt deliciously detached from the mainland's Saturday-night fevers. We joined the diners at garden tables, their faces glowing under the light of lanterns. I had worked out my speech. "Are we ready to have our Big Move discussion now?"

"Yes, I think so."

I began by reassuring him. "You know I love nothing more than being with you, sharing a day like this one." He said he felt the same way. The very thought of living by himself in Berkeley made him feel panicky.

I pointed out that he had a life structure in Berkeley—a role, a title, a class schedule, students, colleagues—a professional network. It was now his home base. "But my home base remains in New York."

"Why can't you move your office out to California?" he asked.

"Because my other world is in New York. It's where my children, my friends, my colleagues, my doctors, my support network exist. Even my hairstylist—hey, that's important!" He laughed. "As crucial as my relationship with you is," I said, "I'm afraid of moving away from everything else that matters to me."

For the first time he could empathize with me. He'd moved so often in his life that he was much less threatened by it than I. "You're well now," I said. "I want to go back to being your wife, the writer."

He said he wanted that, too.

I was proud that I had rehearsed the conversation and waited for the right moment to have it. We sat out on the old-fashioned porch under the amber lights, slowly sipping a vodka and tonic, and it was as if time stood still. The tender midsummer night caressed our bare arms. We gazed at each other like lovers on a third date. What a relief, I didn't feel like a caregiver anymore.

———————

eight

THE EDUCATION OF A FEARLESS CAREGIVING FAMILY

Nobody sails easily through the labyrinth of caregiving. But never fear: you will succeed. For proof, let's go beyond my words to one family's journey to success.

I give you the Colberts, an African American family in suburban Philadelphia, seven courageous sisters and brothers and their ailing mother whose turnings I followed for several years. I recorded how the Colberts adapted to each turning; how they groped, stumbled, learned, and progressed. And how, at last, they created a beautiful circle of care around their mother, reviving her health and spirits and bringing the whole family closer.

During the first two years, six of Helen Colbert's seven children hardly noticed the creeping crisis of her cognitive decline. The seventh, Harriet, saved them from paying attention. She took on all the responsibilities. The oldest daughter in a traditional churchgoing black family, Harriet never married and had no children. She was living with her mother and father in a two-family house in their staid Philadelphia neighborhood when her dad began failing. "Harriet took over as the primary caregiver for Dad and cared for him until he died," says her brother Louis Colbert, a veteran social worker in the field of aging. Soon after she was widowed, Helen Colbert's Parkinson's disease progressed and her diabetes accelerated. She was no longer the fireball of the family. She was eighty-four.

"Our other brothers and sisters assumed that since Harriet took care of Dad, she'd do it for Mom," admits Louis, embarrassed in retrospect that he and the others didn't offer to help. "It was the female sibling thing—old roles came up."

Harriet had been a promising artist, schooled at Philadelphia College of Arts and Pratt Institute in New York. Painting for her was once as natural and necessary as breathing; she couldn't imagine sustaining life without it. That was when she was young and aspirational. She had illustrated a children's book and was excited about doing a sequel now that she was in her midfifties and had more time. This was the dream of her Second Adulthood. Then her parents began to falter and lean on her. The transition from her passion as a painter into full-time family caregiver for her mother happened so gradually that scarcely anyone in the family took notice.

Harriet never thought of herself as playing an important role with a name: *caregiver*. She slipped into it, like so many daughters. From driving her mother to her doctor's appointments and preparing her medications, it escalated into bill-paying and balancing her mother's checkbook. The less her mother did for herself, the more she did for her mother.

"This is just what we do, as daughters," Harriet told me. She never considered asking for help from her four brothers. Why not? Her answer: "We were brought up to think you always give the best meat to the men and let them rest, because they work harder."

Work harder? Along with caregiving, Harriet herself worked fifty to sixty hours a week as a medical claims adjuster. When I questioned her retro attitude, she smiled ruefully and looked away. Her body answered. After a year of handling two jobs, she was running on half a night's sleep and feeling like a punch-drunk fighter. At that point her mother took to her bed and began refusing to eat much more than a spoonful at a meal. In time, she could barely walk. She became forgetful. Harriet suspected her mom had fallen into deep depression.

"She had lost her driver's license because her vision was poor," Harriet told me. "I had to drive her everywhere." But even when they went to church, her mother often felt too weak to get out of the car, so Harriet would quietly turn around and drive them back home. "Maybe she was just depressed about my father's death," Harriet mused. "After all, they were married for fifty-seven years. She had decided she didn't want to live anymore."

But the doctors never mentioned depression, and neither did Harriet. As an older black woman with memories of segregation, she accepted that her mother was just going through another of life's many struggles. And in her mother's generation, depression was not thought of as a disease requiring treatment; it was considered a personal failing. Not knowing what to do, the family decided that hospitalization would be best. It would assure Helen a complete medical checkup and allow for Medicare to kick in and begin paying for home care to help with Helen's activities of daily living.

They weren't expecting the devastating diagnosis.

"Failure to thrive," the doctor pronounced. He said Helen would have to be force-fed with a tube. It was another way of saying that Harriet's mother had lost not only her appetite for food but her appetite for life.

Failure to thrive. Louis Colbert was disgusted when he heard that diagnosis, especially when Harriet told him the hospital doctor had spent all of five minutes with his mother. After thirty years as a social worker, Louis recognized the doctor's dismissive attitude. It was all too common when the patient is elderly.

"That doctor told us our mother would be dead within six months," Harriet says. "He said she needed hospice."

STRATEGIES

Don't Miss Geriatric Depression

Depression is very common in elderly people with illness. Loved ones may be depressed because of losses in autonomy, such as difficulty in walking, hearing, and seeing; or just because they are alone and lonely and wish their children were more involved.

"Geriatric depression can be part of Parkinson's disease, it can be a secondary consequence of a stroke, even a minor stroke, and it can be part of cognitive decline," says Dr. Saeed Humayun, medical director of the Motion Picture & Television Fund, a giant health-services provider for members of the entertainment industry.

"Unfortunately, geriatric depression is vastly underdiagnosed. People just think the changes in behavior common in depression are part of aging: 'Mom is just getting old.'"

Often, as we see with the Colberts, the family is not receptive to hearing a diagnosis of depression. "How can you say Mommy's depressed? We're doing everything we can to make her happy." It makes the family look bad.

Ask for a Geriatric Depression Screen

If your loved one is staying in bed, refusing to eat normally, losing or gaining an abnormal amount of weight, and finding little pleasure in formerly enjoyable activities, these are classic symptoms of depression.

Frequently, children who do make an effort to visit their parent and suggest an outing will get a negative response. Then the children gradually withdraw, not realizing that there is a medical and psychiatric issue behind their loved one's behavior. "That leads to a vicious cycle of depression," says Dr. Humayun, who treats many such patients and their families. "Less stimulation, less activity, less conversation, and less pleasure in life lead to more and more depression, until the person has a declining ability to have any pleasure in any activity."

Get the Whole Family Involved

To be effective, a geriatric psychiatrist needs to determine any medical basis for the depression. Helen Colbert's decline was caused by a combination of her Parkinson's disease, the loss of her husband, and the loss of autonomy. Treatment involved not just medication but alerting the whole family to Helen's need for increased socialization and stimulation.

The best medicine for geriatric depression is to create a circle of care around the loved one.

THE COLBERTS' NEW NORMAL

If you start out by setting up a New Normal for a loved one with chronic illness, and you are the *sole* family caregiver, sooner or later, almost inevitably, you will begin to feel trapped.

Harriet Colbert did the compassionate thing by bringing her mother home from the hospital. The vast majority of older people express in surveys their desire to live in as natural an environment as possible in spite of their infirmities. Under the instruction of hospice, Harriet set up a hospital bed in the dining room and taught herself basic nursing skills by trial and error.

Within a week of coming home, her mother changed her mind dramatically. Helen began eating. First it was sugar cookies, then fried chicken, then ice cream, then hot dogs, and then more and more cookies. Harriet was baking all the time. The hospice nurse soon agreed with Harriet that her mother was not going to die on their deadline of six months, and hospice was terminated.

But after another three months of single-handedly caring for her octogenarian mother at home—cooking, washing, feeding, dressing, driving, medicating—Harriet was so tense and tired that often she could not even sleep. She knew her mother would be up and down all night. This reaction, called *sundowner's syndrome,* is common among inactive older people whose days lack a schedule. They sleep much of the day; when night falls, they become wakeful, often agitated, and want to play games, watch TV, or wander around the house getting into trouble.

Harriet worried that she wouldn't wake up in time to get to work by 7:30 for her sixty-hour-a-week job. "I have to make a living," she told her sisters and brothers. "*And* take care of my little mommy."

Her younger brother Brian offered to come over and sleep on the couch a couple of nights a week. A boyishly handsome man, normally laid-back, he was shocked at how his mother had deteriorated. She had always taken care of him, keeping him on track in school and nursing his sports injuries. Suddenly his world had changed. He had to follow her around at night.

"One night I heard a thump and a crash," Brian recalls. "I couldn't find her anywhere. Then I saw a foot sticking out of the tiny space between the washer and dryer. Somehow, my mother had crawled in between. She wasn't clothed. I didn't know what to do." It was very late but he woke up his older sister to retrieve his mother. Harriet was annoyed. "It's just a body. Deal with it. Don't destroy my sleep."

That night Brian wrapped his mother in a blanket, lifted her and draped her over his shoulder. To his surprise, she liked it. She called him "my elevator."

Harriet's sister Lisa began feeling guilty. "The rest of us just weren't as observant as we should have been," she admitted. "Harriet is so giving and kind, we let her do it all. One night I watched her try to walk up the stairs and just drop down on the steps. I knew she needed help badly, but she would never ask for it."

The company Lisa worked for, IBM, was relatively enlightened about balancing work and life, so she asked if she could work online from her mother's home, at least temporarily. Her boss approved.

"It was horrible!" Lisa recalls. She and Harriet laugh as they describe Lisa trying to hold a business conference call while her mother shouted nonstop in the background, "Sugar cookie! Sugar cookie! Sugar cookie!" Lisa's boss eventually got impatient about her prolonged absence, and she sensed a real danger of losing her job. Divorced and single, Lisa worried about leaving her two children home alone, one of them a combustible teenager. Lisa ate too much, slept too little, and battled toxic emotions—resentment, frustration, guilt: *This isn't working out; it must be my fault.*

Harriet considered retiring early—it would be four years before she qualified for Social Security. But that fantasy quickly evaporated in 2007 as recession began to bite a huge hole in the American economy. Actually, the two sisters had set up the best New Normal possible for their mother, without seeking any further help. But that was the problem. To keep their jobs and their own health and well-being, they desperately needed more assistance with caregiving, their second job.

STRATEGIES

Don't Be the Lonely Hero

After groping your way through Shock and Mobilization, it's a relief to create a New Normal that gives you and your loved one a renewed sense of structure. This can be tricky. You are entering the *heroic stage,* a term coined by Maggie Strong, founder of the Well Spouse Association. At this point, you may feel a surge of optimism leading to *over*confidence. You can handle it all. Conversely, you may feel guilty about neglecting your sick mother, or a need to make amends to a father from whom you've been estranged.

You may be in danger of giving up too much too soon.

I have known family caregivers to retire from their mundane day jobs for the seemingly more purposeful role of keeping a parent alive. Others drop everything to move in with Mom or Dad, expecting the treatment vigil to be temporary, after which they can return to life as it was. Be cautious. Heroic caregivers tend to see what they want to see. Some make hasty decisions that later fill them with regret.

It's one thing to take on primary responsibility for someone with an acute illness. It's a sprint, and most of us can do a sprint for some months. You put almost everything else on hold to deal with the crisis, pour energy into mobilizing to get on top of it, and at the end of treatment, you and the patient settle into a somewhat rearranged New Normal. A stroke or heart disease victim may return to more or less independent living with new preventive regimens. A cancer may be surgically removed or go into long remission, as happened in my husband's case. You hope your loved one will fully recover.

But with chronic illness, such as diabetes, any of the dementias, MS, or Parkinson's disease, changes creep up more slowly. The ebb and flow of the patient's symptoms develop unevenly and everyone hopes for the best. There is no one *aha!*

moment when you recognize that you are now a full-time caregiver, exit strategy and date unknown.

The fact is that a chronically ill person's future is inherently unpredictable. You may choose utter devotion to a loved one's journey and accompany him or her to the very end. But at some earlier point you must begin weaning yourself. The reality of family caregiving is that you must pay attention to two lives—your own as well as your loved one's.

Care for Yourself

You can only care for another person as well as you care for yourself. Imagine yourself as a parent on a pitching plane. When the oxygen masks drop, you put yours on first, then your child's. The same instruction goes for a caregiver. You cannot afford to get sick. To be a good care manager, you need to get your sleep and delegate some responsibilities to others. Pilots have copilots. You need one, too.

Make a to-do list for yourself—things *you* like to do, not caregiving duties. To save your health and sanity, you must commit to doing one pleasure-giving activity every day.

- Have coffee with a friend.
- Go to the library where you can read for an hour without being disturbed.
- Go shopping if it relaxes or energizes you. Better to do it out of the house rather than online.
- My favorite for rainy days was to lie on my back and prop my legs up on the wall and meditate to music.
- Exercise is your best friend, especially in a class where you have some social contact. Otherwise, you can get great exercise by walking, dancing, biking, or swimming for a minimum of twenty minutes at least three times a week. Consider learning a stress-management exercise, such as yoga or tai chi, which teaches how to find inner balance and relaxation.

BOOMERANG

When Helen Colbert went into diabetic shock one day, the two sisters rushed her to the hospital and found themselves back at the first turning again: Shock and Mobilization. But now they looked at it differently. This is the turning I call Boomerang. When the illness suddenly worsens or the wobbly care structure falls apart, the caregiver feels a new rabbit punch at the back of the neck.

The ultimate shock came from a hospital doctor who talked to Harriet and her sister Lisa about his success in easing another old woman out of life. "I can help your mother with a single injection." The sisters looked at each other in horror.

"Did that doctor just offer to kill our mother?"

It was so preposterous that one sister giggled, then the other, and soon they doubled over, laughing uncontrollably and weeping at the same time. Have you had similar conflicted feelings when the caregiving "crisis" mushrooms into one damn thing after another, for months or years? Running thoughts described to me by caregivers go something like this . . .

I'm "on" all the time—waiting for the next emergency call. I can't concentrate on work, I have no time for my kids. I eat so much, I must be doubling in size every day. And I can't sleep. How long will this go on? The rest of my life? I'm such a failure. If I were a really good daughter (or son, sister, brother, wife, husband, mom), I would behave with grace and patience, compassion and love. How can I feel angry and resentful? Nobody asks to get sick. They can't help it. The layers of guilt are piling up like dirty dishes. What kind of selfish brat am I? But I still want my life back.

Guilt-driven caregivers and those culturally scripted to dedicate their lives to sick parents inevitably sacrifice too much. They risk serious depression. This was beginning to happen to both Harriet and Lisa.

"You may want to check out our African-American caregivers' support group at church," Louis urged. His oldest sister Harriet's response was simple: "We don't do that," she insisted. "We take care of our parents. This is what we do."

But even Harriet knew they couldn't go on this way. Lisa dared to suggest that Mom might have to go to a nursing home. Harriet was appalled; that could never happen.

Secretly, Harriet's thoughts began bordering on suicide. "Sometimes I wonder what's the point," she whispered in my presence. "I don't have any children, nobody to take care of me in the same way. I'll just, you know, take some pills when I'm sixty-five."

PLAYING GOD

Louis Colbert thought he knew all there was to know about caregiving. He heads the Area Agency on Aging in a suburban county of Philadelphia. For the first year of his mother's decline, Louis had watched his sisters juggle all the hands-on caregiving at home along with their careers. He tried to "social work" them, he recalls, laughing at himself. "But they refused to identify themselves as caregivers." Louis recognized some avoidance. "Alzheimer's is more prevalent in the African-American community, but it's underreported and diagnosed later," Louis says, "so families struggle too long on their own without help or support."

It took another crisis before Louis evolved from passive cheerleader of his sisters' caregiving efforts to frontline advocate for his mother. He attended a Fearless Caregiver conference in his city, Philadelphia, and listened to the activist-author Gary Barg. For ten years, Barg has taken his conferences around the country to help boost caregivers' self-confidence. They are just as important to patients as their doctors, he tells them. "Your title is Fearless Caregiver Advocate," he says. "You want to gain the skills to become CEO of your family's Caregiving, Inc."

Barg says caregivers often isolate themselves and even resist help from others. "I try to motivate them to get their family members and trusted friends and neighbors to help. But there may be a deeper resistance, stemming from fear or shame: if I don't invite you to see what's happening to Mom or Dad, maybe it's not really happening." Barg writes a free weekly newsletter on his website (www.caregiver.com/fearlessconference/index .htm).

"I didn't click with how to be a fearless caregiver until I saw my mother being neglected," Louis told me. During one crisis, Helen Colbert had been moved from the hospital to a nursing home near midnight. The family wasn't notified.

Louis tracked her down by the next afternoon and found her traumatized from the midnight transport by strangers. Her glazed eyes seemed to swallow her face. Breakfast and lunch trays sat untouched on the windowsill. There was no evidence that Helen Colbert had been seen or treated in any way. Harriet and her sister Jenny had arrived by this time. Louis presented himself at the nurses' desk and demanded of a woman with an RN on her name badge, "Why hasn't my mother been given her medications?"

"We can't give her any medication because we don't know who to bill it to," the woman said. Harriet found out that his mother's insurance administrators did not want to be billed for another night's stay in the hospital, so she had been dispatched in the middle of the night to a nursing home that had only a provisional license.

That mobilized Louis. After consulting with his siblings, he called the medical director and insisted upon taking his mother home. The medical director flatly forbade it: "It would be an unsafe discharge." Louis found himself hollering at the doctor. "In our society, some physicians think of themselves as God, but you haven't even seen my mother!" Louis stood his ground. His family knew they could provide better care for their mother at home. And because he made his point intelligently, and repeatedly, the doctor finally backed down.

Now Louis was in complete charge. Driving his mother back to her home, he suddenly froze: *I don't know how to do this!* Despite years of experience in the field of aging, he couldn't imagine himself physically ministering to his frail mother. Tears leaked from his eyes. He turned so his mother wouldn't see them. He was terrified. It was one thing to challenge a remote medical authority who wanted to dictate the rules for his mother's care. It was another matter to become fearless himself.

He describes the awkward dance he did with his mom the first time he took her to the bathroom. "When I lifted her nightgown to sit her on the commode, she shrieked, 'I'm a married woman!'" Louis learned how to share the dance with his mother so she wouldn't be exposed and would maintain her dignity. She is still his mother.

Louis realized that he was making the same mistake as physicians who sometimes think of themselves as God. Instead, Louis asked God for help. Only then did he have the presence of mind to check out local resources.

STRATEGIES

The PACE Program

Louis found the national program called PACE (Program of All-Inclusive Care for the Elderly) at its website, www.npaonline.org. This is a Medicaid waiver program that helps seniors prolong independent living and stay out of hospitals and nursing homes as long as possible. The PACE idea is to give ailing elders a defense network—timely medical attention for early symptoms, adult day care, and training for family caregivers.

PACE uses an interdisciplinary team approach. The family sits down with the doctor, nurse, social worker, and director of the care site, and together they make a care plan. This saves care costs and often restores a patient's health via one-stop medical care, social support, and physical therapy. It reduces traumatic transitions between emergency rooms, hospitalizations, and nursing homes.

"They sent an aide to the house to wash and dress my mother and take her in a van to the facility two mornings a week, for a stimulating social experience, and for her medical care," Louis Colbert says. "All six of her specialists saw her right there, along with her case manager, her social worker, a nurse, a nutritionist, and the physical therapist. Most people enter PACE overloaded with eight or nine prescriptions from different specialists. PACE got ours down to three," says Louis.

Data show that PACE programs cost less than conventional care. Reasons include sharp decreases in costly services—fewer nurse visits, hospital admissions, nursing home stays. The program also gets high marks for medical care and improvements in

everything from physical functioning to quality of life, all this with
sick people at an average age of eighty.

Helen Colbert was bed-bound when she began going to PACE.
After two months, she could stroll with a walker and do some
gardening. Helen began to smile and laugh again.

"I CAN'T DO IT ANYMORE"

Two years passed. As the Colberts journeyed through the labyrinth of
caregiving, they kept adapting better. But the PACE program took care of
Helen for only two days a week, leaving Louis's sisters on duty around the
clock for the other five days.

Harriet and Lisa were still stressed. They finally saw the fallacy in the
old notion that only women can be caregivers. They sent an SOS e-mail to
the rest of the family, warning that they were getting ready to send Mom to
a nursing home.

This shocked Louis Colbert into action again. "I don't live with my
mother, so it was easier for me to avoid responsibility." He admits he was
content to keep a low profile as long as his sisters enabled him. But those two
words, *nursing home,* got everybody's attention. "One mother can raise seven
children," Louis decided. "But it takes seven of us to take care of Mom."

Louis called a family meeting. That is the crucial first step in creating a
circle of care.

THE FAMILY MEETING

On a bright Sunday in November, I joined the Colbert children in the
solid brick house in which they were all raised. Fall leaves fluttered onto the
porch from their Japanese maples. After sharing pizza in the backyard, we
cozied up in the living room on suede-covered sofas. Mama Helen was smiling and animated, a sunny presence now surrounded by all her children.

The seven siblings were asked what skills each one could offer and when
they could be available. Jenny, an accountant, said, "I can do Saturdays."

Brian, because of the kind of job he has, offered to sleep on the sofa several nights a week, in case Mom awoke in her dining room hospital bed. He had already become his mother's designated "elevator," carrying her in and out of the house. Louis appointed himself the care coordinator and took three afternoons and one Sunday a month. Lisa offered to take two weekday mornings and one Sunday a month. I asked Helen what Laurence does. "Very, very little," she said, smiling indulgently. "But he's my first child . . ." Everyone laughed.

That still left a few gaps. The family decided that they could each contribute $20 a week to hire a neighbor, Bernard, to care for Helen in between times. The Colberts now get together once a month, on Sundays, to review their mother's care and celebrate the victory of keeping Mom out of a nursing home and in her own home. They all have lunch or dinner together, which they never did before except on holidays.

What does this family tell you about caregiving? You'll never do anything harder. And you will come through it. But not alone. You need a circle of care. Once this family coalesced around their mother and collaborated on a schedule of shared care, they all felt rewarded. Helen Colbert had bounced back. Revived by being at home and being seen every day by one of her children and often her grandchildren, she showed far greater mental clarity.

Each sibling wanted to tell me what he or she was gaining from this experience.

Lisa: "Now I feel like we're really closer as a family." She winked impishly. "I have two daughters who understand now that their job is to take care of me!"

Brian: "I understand my brothers and sisters better." He looks lovingly at his mom. "Even now, she's still trying to be a mom."

Louis: "It is an affirmation of our spirituality and a testimony that our circle will not be broken."

Harriet was virtually reborn. Before the family rallied around to share the caregiving, she had envisioned sliding into depression and a "failure to thrive," just like her mother. She was resigned to ending her own life at sixty-five. Now she appeared relaxed for the first time in months. "I'm sleeping, a lot!" she said. I asked if she had a passion that she could return to. Her siblings pointed out her oil paintings on the living room walls. I gasped.

They were beautiful, soulful portraits. One was a self-portrait of Harriet in an earlier life: a fierce-eyed woman.

"Where did that feisty woman go?" I prodded her. "And what have you done with this extraordinary natural talent—you're an artist!"

"Oh, I put that aside a long time ago. I just never seem to have time."

I asked her if she had painted as a child. "All the time," she said. "It was like breathing for me."

"Caregiver, take care of thyself!" I declared. "When making art is like breathing, that's passion."

"One of these days," Harriet stammered, "when I find the time."

Helen Colbert's voice pierced through the mumbles. She wouldn't sit still for her daughter's procrastination. With a mother's authority, she said: "Sometimes you can make the time, you know."

"Do you think you will revive your painting?" I asked once more.

"Yes," said Harriet, now firmly. "I think I will."

Her mother encouraged her, as if returning some of the care she had been given. After all, mothers live to spur their children to do whatever gives them joy.

There *is* life after caregiving.

STRATEGIES

Balancing Work and Care

Ask if your company offers elder-care benefits. In one study, three-quarters of full-time employees doubling as part-time caregivers were beset with health problems, including stress, panic attacks, depression, insomnia, fatigue, pain, and weight loss. American business itself pays a stiff penalty when caregiving employees are distracted by their "second shift." They suffer attention deficit and can't focus fully on their jobs. They cause tens of billions in productivity losses and health insurance costs.

Some companies are taking note. As of 2007, one-third of

large American companies offered basic elder-care benefits. They range from unpaid leaves of absence, flexible spending accounts for care of a dependent, counseling, to backup elder care.

The more progressive companies also offer subsidized in-home emergency care, a geriatric care specialist on staff, and workplace support groups. Even if there are no benefits tied to elder care, your company may allow flexible work arrangements, job sharing, telecommuting, or a compressed workweek that allows you to share the care days with other family members or paid home health aides.

If your company turns a blind eye to this commonplace family obligation, speak up. Let the Human Resources people know it's smart business to help employees do the right thing for their families. Anecdotal evidence is that caregivers who are given flexibility in their work usually repay far more than their required hours, putting in extra time in the middle of the night or weekends.

How Can a Family Caregiver Be Paid?

This question is Topic A among the questions I get on my website (www.gailsheehy.com). So far, family caregivers are not paid or reimbursed under any federal program or by any insurance company, as far as I know.

California has a paid state family leave program. Public or private sector workers are entitled to six weeks per year to care for a seriously ill parent, spouse, child or registered domestic partner. Most employees receive up to 55 percent of their weekly wages. Fewer than ten percent of workers have done so.

A major federal law, the 1993 Family and Medical Leave Act (FMLA), provides up to twelve weeks of unpaid leave per year to care for a sick family member (spouse, child, parent), or a newborn, without losing your job or your health insurance. It works well, but it's not available to everybody. The law applies only to companies with fifty or more employees and you must have worked fifty-two days full-time or 1,250 hours during the previous year.

Many employed caregivers don't benefit because they work for a business with fewer than fifty employees.

A MetLife study found that caregivers spend an average of $5,500 a year of their own money, and long-distance caregivers spend an average of nearly $10,000 for those in their care. It's important to protect your long-term employment prospects, maintain your Social Security benefits, and preserve your sense of self-worth. Arguably, one big benefit of holding on to your job is the social stimulation—watercooler therapy—the gossip and jokes and teamwork that ease the isolation of caregiving.

There are glimmers of light.

In some states, a Medicaid program called Cash and Counseling pays seniors directly to cover their in-home care. It is available only to certain low-income individuals and families who qualify for government health care under Medicaid. The rules are determined by each state. The amount a family can receive depends on the Medicaid assessment of need and the prevailing pay rate for in-home-care aides in that state. It ranges from $6 to $10 an hour and doesn't include health insurance. It would represent a heavy pay loss for most working people, but it's better than nothing.

Seniors can then use the money to pay anyone of their choosing—including a family member—to provide care. They can also use some of the money to buy helpful home items such as kitchen tools, a new vacuum cleaner, safety equipment, or the like. Permissible services include cleaning, meal delivery, or transportation.

Cash and Counseling programs are currently in effect in Alabama, Arkansas, Florida, Illinois, Iowa, Kentucky, Michigan, Minnesota, New Jersey, New Mexico, Pennsylvania, Rhode Island, Vermont, Washington, and West Virginia.

Service Employees International Union (www.seiu.org) represents home health workers. It negotiates with individual states, because states set Medicaid rates. In parts of California, New York, Oregon, and Washington state, some family caregivers do get health insurance and sick days. Call your local Area Agency on Aging to find out about your area. The Triple A can walk you through the eligibility requirements. You can also go online for information about home services provided by Medicaid or community organizations. A great website for locating home aides and other direct-care workers is www.directcareclearinghouse.org.

Remember, the only way to juggle outside work and inside caregiving, without losing your mind, is to knit together a circle of care.

Recommended Reading

Share the Care by Cappy Capossela and Sheila Warnock (Simon & Schuster, 1995, 2004) is much more than a book. It's a philosophy developed by two caregivers who took care of a terminally ill friend with cancer for three years. Since 1995 this step-by-step model has empowered friends, neighbors, acquaintances, and coworkers to create *and* maintain a "caregiving family" over time. It explains how to hold a meeting to organize your group and discover the hidden talents within it. There are personal stories, resources, and twenty-four helpful Share the Care forms that save you the time and effort of making schedules and charts. Visit the website www.sharethecare.org.

nine
SIBLING WARS

We like to think that siblings are born allies and automatically support each other when parents falter. Not so, according to a major 1996 study by Cornell University sociologist Karl Pillemer and J. Jill Suitor of Louisiana State University. They concluded that siblings are not just inherent rivals—they're the biggest source of stress between human beings.

Anyone facing a crisis welcomes support. The warmest and most useful help comes from other people who have had a similar experience, the study verified. That's why caregivers get the best support from other caregivers.

Strong bonds tie sisters and brothers together all their lives. But those bonds were tempered in childhood by myriad rivalries involving differences in age, intelligence, strength, personality, ambition, parental favoritism, and so forth. When the emergencies of family caregiving interrupt the siblings' busy adult lives, primal rivalries and resentments are likely to be stirred up.

PLAYING FROM OLD SCRIPTS

As sisters are faced with the demands of caring for their aging parents, positions in the family drama that were played out decades before may resurface with a vengeance. Old wounds are reopened. Which sister was always the dutiful daughter? Which was the prodigal daughter? Which feels like the favored child, and which still nurses resentment that she got second best? Who is the family success and who is the "loser"?

The older child typically wields more power. The sibling living closest to parents often makes the important decisions. The unmarried sister may resent her wedded sister's assumption that she's the one to give up her life and be the primary caregiver. The sibling who controls the money can trump the others.

Sisters may start out quite tolerantly in the early months of Shock and Mobilization. But as the job of managing responses to an unpredictable disease becomes more overwhelming, primitive emotions rise to the surface. You may find yourselves back in your living room, acting like seven-year-olds fighting over which TV program to see.

————————————

GROWING UP, JANE AND Rebecca Loeb* were deeply connected and yet profoundly different. Jane, the first child born to David and Harriet Loeb, was the dutiful daughter. She was the high achiever who always knew how to fix things when they were broken. Rebecca was the complete opposite. As the baby in the family she was rebellious and unconventional, more artistic than responsible. The two girls locked horns over everything. If Jane wanted to paint their shared bedroom pastel pink, Rebecca would insist on bubble-gum pink. The Loeb girls did have a deep connection to each other, though, and they shared a sense of humor, which often kept them from going for each other's throat. At the first opportunity, Rebecca took flight to seek adventure and touched down thousands of miles away from her family.

Years later, when their parents became increasingly frail, Jane and Rebecca faced questions and issues that revived their childhood dynamics in their middle years. Jane, the oldest, was single and childless and lived in Boston near their parents. She held a lucrative senior position as a human resources executive and had the knowledge and contacts to know how to handle medical crises. Again, she assumed the position of being the one "in charge." But over time, she felt increasingly alone and burdened. Yes, she recognized that Rebecca lived and worked across the country, and was divorced and raising a young child, but resentment crept into her feelings about her sister. It became a rancid brew of the anger and envy she had expe-

————————————

* Pseudonym.

rienced years before: *She leaves home and never looks back. Why do I always have to be the responsible one? How come she always gets away with it?*

Jane called her aging parents several times a day. She visited often and orchestrated all their needs. In the final years, as her mother, Harriet, valiantly fought a rare kind of stomach cancer, it was Jane who accompanied her to countless medical consults, sat in waiting rooms while her mom underwent tests, and held her hand when doctors repeatedly imparted the grim prognosis. Jane was by Harriet's side in the final months as she lay in a coma and ultimately succumbed.

Rebecca harbored her own sense of isolation. Living so far away from her declining parents was a source of heartbreak and guilt mixed with secret relief. Her job was tied to her company's San Diego office. Money was tight, and she was perpetually exhausted from raising her daughter more or less on her own. Six or seven times a year, she flew back to Boston, but her participation was minimal compared with Jane's heroic level of caregiving. When their mother died, Rebecca arrived only in time to pay a late-night visit to the funeral home before her mother's burial the next morning. She wept as she lay over the still body, wishing she had been there to hold her mother's hand in her final days.

After their mother's death, Jane again forged ahead as the primary caregiver for their father. A vibrant man who managed to read voraciously into his eighties, he was determined to live out his days in his own apartment, despite being crippled by spinal arthritis. Jane had his apartment rigged with handicap accessories and fought with Medicare and Medicaid over insurance reimbursements, while paying thousands of dollars a month out of her own pocket for private aides.

Although the sisters rarely vented their feelings, the unspoken tension between them reached a crescendo. Rebecca, the distant sister, felt powerless. She offered to talk to aides and argue with insurance companies, and even suggested that their father move out to the West Coast and live with her. It was no surprise that he refused. Everybody knew that Jane was the one who handled things best.

All of Jane's pent-up resentments exploded the weekend she allowed herself a rare three-day vacation with office friends at a health spa on the Cape. When she phoned her father on her first day away, there was no answer.

Frantic calls to relatives got nowhere. Emergency medical workers finally broke into David Loeb's apartment. He was lying on the floor, dehydrated and semiconscious. He had fallen and could not get up. What followed was a whirl of hospitals and the decision that he needed twenty-four-hour in-home care. Jane managed the emergency, found a live-in aide, and paid most of the salary for the next four years.

After their father was buried in 2005, the sisters barely spoke. Jane's anger only swelled in retrospect, as she thought about the years she had spent as the sacrificial daughter. She fumed about the money she had spent caring for their parents. She exploded on discovering that Rebecca's retirement fund, accrued over decades of working for the same company, was larger than hers. The rivalry that shaped Jane's childhood view of her younger sister had persisted into middle age like some toxic chemical.

Ultimately, however, Jane, now guilt-free and excited about marrying her live-in boyfriend, wound up far more successful than her younger sister. Rebecca, who managed to keep her distance during family emergencies and free from the burden of caregiving, was left with less job security and a heavy load of guilt. The fact that they are both now in their fifties, middle-aged women with sophisticated lives, has not completely healed the old wounds.

But there is still time for peacemaking. Although the final crises of their parents' lives reignited all their childhood hostilities, the two women have never entirely cut off communication. They see each other more often now. Despite powerful feelings of resentment, they may well end up caring for each other. Sisterhood is powerful.

Jane and Rebecca's acrimony is not unusual, but there is nothing typical about sibling behavior when parents need caregiving. There may be as many variations as there are siblings, each shaped by a specific childhood history. What they usually do have in common is some money issue, says Beth MacLeod, a San Francisco social worker who helps families handle the strains of caregiving. Focusing on money can objectify the situation and sideline emotions. In her practice, MacLeod helps siblings clarify their priorities and deal with immediately relevant issues. As a neutral third party, she can nudge everyone out of their emotional trenches and invite each to contribute his or her special strengths to an aged parent's welfare.

"Anecdotally I've seen as many siblings work together beautifully as fight," she says. "I continue to be really impressed with how people in our culture take care of their parents. We always hear stories of neglect, abuse, and abandonment. But for every one of those stories, there are thousands of people who are never written about. They're the default class, those who give money for years as caregivers for parents who are slowly spiraling into Alzheimer's—the quiet heroes who take on far more than they should, emotionally as well as financially, but who do it anyway."

BROTHERLY LOVE

Brothers have traditionally let the burden of parental caregiving fall on their sisters. Men generally like to keep their participation at arm's length—writing checks and doing the parent's bills, maybe offering financial and legal advice. But today, Westernized men cannot count on being exempted from caregiving for their parents, any more than they can expect a working wife to be the only one who gets up to walk the floor with a howling infant.

In Portland, Oregon, I interviewed a graduate of the "Powerful Tools for Caregivers" (PTC) course, a brainiac who works for Intel, named Dick Casali. "I do figure analysis at the motherboard level," he said by way of introducing himself. But when it came to dealing with his own feisty mother, Dick was first to admit that all his logic and research skills were of little help.

As often happens, his mother's health and psychological well-being went precipitously downhill during the last six months of his father's life. A diabetic, she lapsed in administering her insulin and ballooned in her weight. That created strokelike symptoms. Dick was making frequent 911 calls.

"We went into crisis mode," Dick says. "My sister would come over and take care of her after work. Then we'd line up the next sibling who would fly in and spend a few weeks at Mom's house. You can only do that so long, because alarms start going off in other parts of your life that are directly related to the medical condition of the person receiving the care."

Dick confided to me, "All five of us got to the point of hating our mother. We were being pitted against each other, by Mother, and my brothers and sisters basically said, 'I want nothing to do with this.'"

In the PTC class Dick took, he learned how important a family meeting is and organized one for his siblings. His goal was to get his siblings to stop blaming one another for the situation. He tried out ways to communicate better—to get rid of the hidden "you's," as in "If only *you* had done that, Mom wouldn't have had a setback." Dick realized, "We had to start attacking the issue and not the people administering the care."

Dick was also very worried about money. He and his brothers had widely disparate incomes. He sent out an e-mail suggesting that each sibling make a do-what-I-can-best offer. In a follow-up family meeting, the siblings worked out that the ones who weren't able to help out as much financially could take greater responsibility for visiting and hands-on care. Dick also hired an elder-care attorney who saved the group from making potentially disastrous mistakes in transferring their mother's assets. He claimed it was the best money he ever spent.

In handling his role as the primary family caregiver, Dick learned leadership skills. He found a better way to communicate with his siblings, and he became valued as the one who organized family meetings. As Dick expanded his people skills beyond using logic and logarithms, he came to feel closer to his brothers and sisters and more resourceful in dealing with any life crisis.

SISTERS FOREVER

Caring for parents can also strengthen the frayed bonds between siblings. In my own family, I held the favored position as the only child for my first nine years. My only sister grew up in a very different household, one in which the happy-faced suburban family was crumbling as our father took to philandering and our mother took to her bed with "sinus attacks," otherwise known as the Irish cure, the drink. I became my sister's surrogate parent.

Decades later, when our mother began her premature decline from lung cancer and emphysema, my sister, Trish, and I seized the opportunity to help each other care for her. That commitment became as strong as the obeisance to the mother we both dearly loved. Together, we would shepherd her through her final years and make certain she felt herself cherished. We agreed that neither of us wanted to be left with a hangover of guilt.

Mom was remarried and lived in Florida. My sister and I both lived and worked in New York. We sat together and very practically sized up the strengths and limitations we each brought to the table. At the time my sister had more flexibility in her schedule and more patience with providing hands-on help. I had a more demanding job but more money. I paid for my sister's plane fares to Florida, and she would stay a little longer with Mom than I could. It reconnected the two of us, as grown-ups.

On a deeper level, which we recognized only in retrospect, we wanted to protect each other. We were both children of a recovering alcoholic, although shame and denial had kept us from acknowledging that reality. Both of us feared being drawn back into an unhealthy situation. As our mother's health worsened, and she had to give up swimming and sit inside, Trish and I began to go to Florida together. We could then alternate giving Mom baths, doing her hair, painting her toenails, reading and talking with her, and after we put her to bed, we could howl over private jokes and shared reminiscences. It allowed us to create a lighthearted mood around our mother. She loved having "the girls" home again.

My sister and I had an epiphany during this period. Our parents would die before us; our older husbands were likely to die before us. The longest relationship we would have in our lives would probably be as sisters. That primed us to put much more effort into it. We identified each of our weaknesses and hot buttons and agreed on BEWARE signs. We decided to duck behind e-mail when our conversations overheated. And we stopped being too proud or foolish to say "I'm sorry."

As a result of successfully tag-teaming to shepherd our mother to the end of her life, our own relationship became more equalized. I found that I could depend on my sister as fully as she could depend on me. I may be the older one, but she is just as often now the stronger one. As we became invested in a purpose larger than ourselves, our relationship changed and matured in ways that we both appreciate will pay dividends for the rest of our lives.

THIRD TURNING:
BOOMERANG

ten

WHEN IT COMES BACK

Everything has settled down into a new normal routine. Months or years may have passed since the original shock of life-threatening illness. For the lucky families, it never comes back. You are handling the changes to your loved one and thinking, "Okay, I can live with this," or you're counting on Dad to look after Mom or Mom to take care of Dad. For the unlucky ones, there is a sudden BOOMERANG! A new crisis comes out of the blue, swings around, and knocks you off your feet.

MY HUSBAND AND I *had enjoyed a long reprieve. We had passed the five-year mark since Clay's first cancer surgery and a full course of radiation in 1991. I believed we were out of the labyrinth. We must have beaten the Big C.*

The nearly six-year reprieve in California had been a peak of our renewed life. Clay fully embraced his new role as a teacher and guru to another generation of talented journalists. He was eager every morning to dress in his casual Lands' End professor's clothes plus a driving cap and gloves and purr in his secondhand Jaguar over to the Berkeley Graduate School of Journalism to be the silent partner behind the next magazine his students would be dreaming up. The new dean, Orville Schell, had captured a sizable grant to turn Clay's student magazines into impressive artifacts that would give the journalism school an edge. Clay felt useful again, appreciated, part of a dynamic mission in journalism.

That spring we had finally begun rooting in Berkeley. The Bay Area is a green and flowered paradise nine months out of the year. We had a modest rented house in the Berkeley hills where I wrote in a small attic room and looked down with envy on the neighbors' terraced garden. One weekend, as Clay and I drove by the neighbors' house, we saw a For Sale sign. We introduced ourselves to our neighbors, went over for wine and cheese, and by Monday morning we were ecstatically arranging a mortgage. We had the proceeds from the sale of Clay's apartment in New York.

The new house was a light box, surrounded on three sides by flowering pear trees or giant eucalyptus or the view from our deck of the magical garden. It was a Bonnard oil painting, no, wilder than that: a spontaneous explosion of calla lilies and climbing roses, sweet Meyer lemon trees and orange blossoms, and giant spears of flax plants pointing down the stone steps to a tiny pond alive with goldfish darting beneath water lilies. I was a stranger in paradise there, unfamiliar with this tropical flora. Our new Tibetan spaniel loved perching on the stone wall as guardian of the temple. Every morning I plunged into the garden and sniffed and clipped and gathered a few blooms for the house.

Then I could write all day without any sense of time passing. Writing and gardening were my transports to joy.

We had begun to build a solid friendship network with people we genuinely liked and who liked us for the right reasons. Entertaining was much more communal than it was back east. Everyone would bring a dish or a bottle of wine and sit out on the deck where pink dogwood and coral trumpet vine crept over the railings. Talk was the real entertainment, an impromptu concert of words, where some of the themes were familiar but broken up by new chords and intriguing dissonances. It was like listening to new world music and learning to love it. Busy making our new life happen, we were blindsided in 1997 by the cruelest word in the English language.

Recurrence.

The Call this time came from my soul sister, Pat Allen, who also happens to be my obstetrician-gynecologist. When Dr. Allen summoned me to her office in New York in late July of 1997, I thought it was my own inner works that had gone haywire.

"It's Clay," she said. "Recurrence. How much do you want to know?"

"Everything."

"A tumor at the base of his tongue," she pronounced with professional dispatch. "It's big. It may not be operable."

"Omigod," I choked, "I should have been kinder to him." (First response: It must be my fault.)

"I'm sorry, sweetie."

"How do you know?" (Second line of defense: Refute the messenger.)

"Dr. Coleman is out of town, but the results of Clay's CT scan came back," she said. "I called his office to find out." Pat was a colleague of Clay's doctors at New York Hospital. He had given her permission to confer with his doctors when he was absent. I was grateful that she was the one to give me the news.

"What would happen if they don't operate?"

"His swallowing would be compromised. Eventually they'd have to feed him through a tube."

"Could he survive that way?"

"Yes. But eventually his airways would be blocked by the tumor."

"Oh, God, he'd strangle to death? How long?"

"Maybe six months."

NOW THE MONSTER WAS back. I could only imagine what it would do to Clay—how to tell him? It turned out, he knew but he didn't want to know. The backstory came out later.

"My throat was always sore, starting last winter," he told me. "I thought it was an early symptom of bronchitis. But I didn't get bronchitis. It hung on into spring. I'd have examinations periodically—doctors would put a wire with a light at the end of it down my throat—but they found nothing. I'd had the cancer taken out six years before, so, sure, I thought I'd beaten it.

"One day I was shaving and I felt a twinge in my throat. The thought passed through my mind—oh, the cancer is back—but it was like remembering today is your first wife's birthday—there's nothing to do about it, so you let it go."

"You didn't say anything to your doctors?" I marveled.

"No. But I went back to Memorial periodically for checkups. Earlier this summer an ENT doctor gave me some antibiotics. That didn't help. I went to Dr. Coleman's backup. They took some CT scans. Then I didn't hear."

"But why didn't you tell me?"

"I didn't want to be old for you." A shrug went down his face. "I was afraid I couldn't keep up with you. And you would leave me."

I felt a stab of guilt. He was more than ten years older than I. The disease and toxic treatments had expanded that differential. He had slowed down a great deal. I was always pushing him to stay active, exercise, take weekend trips; I thought I was doing the right thing. But I also sometimes made cruel comments: "You're acting like an old man," thinking that would motivate him to move faster. I couldn't accept that he was indeed becoming older, easily fatigued, sometimes unsteady on his feet. And unbeknownst to both of us, he not only had a recurrence of cancer, his heart was blocked in its most important vessels.

Now I could begin to understand why, for the nine months before this news, Clay had often been irritable, withdrawn, accusatory. All that time he suspected the cancer was coming back. That gnawing fear had come up again and again, disguised in flare-ups with me. Whenever I had to travel to make speeches or meet with my editors, he would mutter that I was abandoning him.

We had lost ground in our journey around the labyrinth. In retrospect, I appreciated how we had approached his first cancer crisis. We had come close to being a single sensory mechanism, intuiting each other's every flinch of emotion, dropping our respective guards, and releasing ferocious creative energy. I had tried to encourage him to dare again to open himself up, to look at life with the eyes of his heart. Then he could see and feel the love. But it took this second life-threatening event to re-create the deep attachment that we felt between us during the first crisis.

This time, Clay's cancer did not fit neatly into the standard treatment options at Memorial Sloan-Kettering. His medical oncologist, Dr. H, was leaving Memorial. He reluctantly agreed to see us for a final consult. It was his last day and Clay was his last patient. He looked at Clay as a case management problem.

Perched on a rolling stool, Dr. H motioned for Clay and me to sit down and left our daughters, Maura and Mohm, to stand behind him. Then he held forth with a thirty-minute uninterrupted sales pitch for "the standard curative option for you in this setting—surgery."

He was brutally casual about the side effects. "The voice box frequently has to be removed as part of the process—even if it isn't involved with the cancer. The de-

tails of the operation would need to be discussed with the surgeon. You have to focus on surgery as your only option."

We were all struck speechless. There is preservation of life, and then there is the preservation of this man's life. Clay Felker without a voice? Unthinkable. There is never only one option. I tried to stutter out a question based on research that Pat and I had done.

The oncologist rolled back on his chair, squashing one daughter against a counter. He told Mohm she'd have to move and then launched into a tirade not unlike a defense attorney making the closing argument to a hostile jury: "I don't want to, in the same breath, talk about chemotherapy or implant. If you refuse the operation, we will come up with something for you. But that something would be an avant-garde creative option that even I could give no guarantees for."

The girls and I attempted to ask questions. Again, he ignored us. He rolled closer to Clay to render his final word. "You have to make a bottom-line decision—am I going for broke with my life?"

We dragged through the doors of that hospital at five o'clock on a Friday afternoon in August. The heat sucked out of us what little energy we had left. Expectant weekenders rushed past us wheeling designer bags toward cars and buses. We were not going anywhere.

Clay later told me, "The only thing I remember is that we were all together."

"What did that mean to you?" I asked him.

"Everything."

"Why?"

"I wasn't alone in this. People cared for me. People I loved. If I'd been alone, just lying in bed all weekend by myself, then I would have been . . . hopeless."

Pulling Together

We didn't even have our old New York home to go to; Clay had closed on the sale of his apartment in July. And I had given up my New York office as a peace offering. Moving is one of the top three stressors in life, right up there with divorce and the death of a loved one.

Serendipitously, only a month before, Dr. Pat and I had cooked up the idea of sharing a pied-à-terre in Manhattan.

It turned out to be the best decision I ever made. That apartment was the comfort zone that Clay and I and the girls crawled back to after the blow from Dr. H.

We were back at the Shock and Mobilization turning. And again, we were numbed by the shock. But this time we knew better than to allow our fears to run away with us. We needed the weekend to process the new assault. "I have to wait until I get all the facts before I let myself feel one way or another," Clay said. He also had an insight into the way he had handled a devastating blow in the past.

"None of this has been quite as much a shock to my system as losing New York magazine," he admitted. "I remember waking up in the middle of the night. I felt I was plunging into a pit—a black pit. I would be totally lost. It was the most frightening thing that ever happened to me. What was my future going to be? What was I going to do . . . with my life? It was my identity. The only ambition I ever had. I just remember making up my mind, 'Well, I'm not going to think about this.' So I repressed it. And that was not good for me. I never really let it happen to me."

Did that burn of inconsolable loss trapped in his throat, where the scream of pain was never allowed an exit, transmute into the toad of cancer?

On Saturday we took a silent walk through Central Park, all the way up to the Shakespeare Garden at 110th Street. We were wrung out afterward. As we lay back in an air-conditioned cab, Clay said quietly, "When you get to the end of your rope, you tie a knot and hang on."

I told him I would hold the other end of the rope and never let go.

By Sunday night Clay had made up his mind. "If they're going to cut out my voice, there wouldn't be any point in living."

I hardly dared to ask, "What's the alternative?"

"Just dying from cancer. Otherwise, it would be a living death."

Never Give Up

I knew by now not to accept one doctor's opinion as final. And certainly not a doctor who didn't respect Clay's terms for treatment. As frightening as it was to be left hanging at such a moment, we had to step back and seek another path.

Dr. Pat slept in our shared apartment for the next week to help us search for medical alternatives. She and I had tea on the sofa every morning at 6:30 A.M. Clay called her "My delivering angel." When all looked the darkest, she had a brainstorm. "Call Mary Greenbaum—she's a cancer survivor and the ultimate networker." Mary was in Nantucket but resourceful as always. She suggested I call Dr. Bruce Chabner, a brilliant scientist at Dana Farber Cancer Institute. He was on vacation. I left a capsule voice mail describing Clay's situation.

Within two hours of leaving the message, I had a callback from his daughter, Elizabeth Chabner, a twenty-eight-year-old medical oncologist. She had intercepted my message and already talked to the chief of radiation oncology at Massachusetts General Hospital, Dr. C. C. Wang, about Clay's case.

"Dr. Wang is phenomenal," the young Dr. Chabner told me. "He wrote the textbook on radiotherapy for head and neck cancer. He can be more aggressive. He has Clay's name, and he would be more than happy to see him."

I was astonished, again and again, at how often deliverance came from total strangers, like Elizabeth. I came to believe that these strangers were godsends. Instruments of a higher power. If we keep our hearts and minds open, start the day with a gratitude prayer, and reach out, eventually we get the information and inspiration we need.

So after a month in free fall without any satisfactory answers, we found ourselves on a rainy day in late August in the office of Dr. C. C. Wang, a Harvard professor known as the Gauguin of radiation therapy. He is a slight, graying Chinese man with a strong but clear accent, and his first words to Clay cut right through the fog.

"So, I hear you're big shot in New York. But there they want to cut out your voice box—so you come to me."

"You know how they are in New York—cutthroat," I teased back.

Dr. Wang chuckled. He examined Clay's throat, keeping up a casual banter while his wheels were obviously turning at the speed of a computer. Then he said the magic words.

"Your condition still has chance to be cured—our odds very good!"

Over the previous seventeen years, Dr. Wang had been a pioneer in developing a technique called hyperfractionated radiation *for treating people who'd had previous radiation. He explained that it would mean two brief* radiation treatments a day, five days a week, for about a month. "We have to be very creative," he said enthusiastically. Finally, a doctor who was not only willing, but confident about customizing treatment for Clay, not shoving him into a standardized slot.

This time I knew to ask the most important question: Would Dr. Wang be willing to coordinate all aspects of Clay's care—be the quarterback on our team? He said of course. The next day, Dr. Wang introduced us to the surgeon who would be following Clay's case, Dr. William Montgomery. "Call me Dr. Monty" is how this slow deliberate Vermonter introduced himself. He was still in his scrubs and green froggy slippers, having just stepped out of surgery. A Korean War veteran in his seventies, who had sewn up GIs' necks and heads on the battlefield, he had a down-to-earth manner that we liked immediately. He told us that Dr. Wang's treatment was extremely effective with squamous cell cancer. He and Dr. Wang were confident that the tumor could be shrunk to the point where surgery would be possible without invading other organs, and the voice box could be preserved, as Clay insisted. Dr. Wang assured us that he would be available to monitor Clay's comfort and pain level on a daily basis. We were so glad that we hadn't settled.

Dr. Wang left us with a Chinese proverb: "When chase a tiger, must run very fast."

————————

STRATEGIES

Designate a Medical Quarterback

In our fractured health system, it's hard to get a top doctor to coordinate your care team. Even so, you need somebody able to see the big picture, a doctor willing to help you and the patient compose disparate opinions into one coherent care plan. The job may fall to you by default, but try to avoid that.

You will probably see several specialists while seeking a diagnosis. Ask one of them to take charge and oversee your loved one's care. The concept of a physician acting as "medical quarterback" is an old one. What you are really asking is that the physician respects you as an informed caregiver and is willing to partner with you and the patient. The right kind of physician will welcome your participation. It worked for us, and when it didn't, we found another doctor.

In the case of cancer, the medical oncologist might refer you to a nurse or a social worker or a care manager, but somebody has to coordinate all three of those people. And if the physician is not on top of that, nothing will happen. The physician you want is the one who says, "Of course, I have already called the surgeon." Or "I'll confer with your cardiologist about whether or not you are a candidate for general anesthesia."

"Medical oncologists are focused on treating cancer and are seldom trained or have the time to address pain, symptoms, and side effects that have a profound impact on the patient's quality of life," says Rebecca Kirch, associate director of policy of the American Cancer Society. Some oncologists are now bringing in the primary-care physician to help with symptom management, particularly after treatment is over. Ask for post-op care. Oncologists often drop a patient abruptly as soon as treatment is completed. The ACS is trying to create a shift in medical culture, enabling patients to insist on quality-of-life solutions as part of medical care.

Consider Hiring a Research Guide

Deborah Szekely, whom I mentioned earlier, was another link in our expanding circle of care. She steered us to her medical researcher, Henry Dreher. He is a walking encyclopedia of alternative treatments and complementary medicine to fight cancer.

By scouring the latest studies on the disorder in question, a professional guide can cull and tailor the research to match the patient's age, sex, medical history, and particular biology. This will not only save you time and stress but also suggest complementary therapies or clinical trials, as well as guidance on insurance coverage and social support.

Guides and researchers go by various names: patient navigator, patient advocate, health-care advocate, medical researcher, cancer guide. The best of these guides will research treatments, put you in touch with leading doctors and medical centers, and help you through the maze of insurance coverage. To find one, you can contact HealthCare Advocates, Inc. (www.healthcareadvocates.com), which helps people with any medical condition to access the best doctors and treatments. If cancer is your concern, contact the Center for Mind-Body Medicine (www.cmbm.org) in Washington, D.C., and ask for their listing of cancer guides.

As mentioned, I consulted Henry Dreher, a cancer research guide and the author of *Mind-Body Unity* and *The Immune Power Personality: 7 Traits You Can Develop to Stay Healthy.* Trained by Dr. James S. Gordon of Georgetown University's Center for Mind-Body Medicine, Dreher consults with patients and caregivers in need of experienced help in researching cancer treatments and new protocols. He first asks the caregiver questions to find out which diseases the doctors have ruled out. He also suggests complementary, nonmedical avenues that can be beneficial and that may alter the survival rate: natural herbs and supplements, nutritional support, methods for relaxation and coping, exercise regimens, and psychological support. Then he plumbs the depths of the database that doctors use known as MEDLINE, the most comprehensive primary source for research in medicine. You can e-mail Dreher (hendreh2@aol.com) and find many helpful links to resources on his website (www.henrydreher.com).

You can use MEDLINE yourself (www.pubmed.com). It's made available free and online by the National Library of Medicine. But for those of us who are not trained academic researchers, searching the database is more than challenging. It's a brain cruncher.

Explore Complementary Treatments

A good nutritionist can suggest ways to bolster the patient's immune system and head off secondary reactions to medicine or surgery. Acupuncture and massage can relieve tension for both anxious patients and confused caregivers. Mind-body practices such as yoga, meditation, and tai chi are increasingly popular to reduce stress and help one think more clearly when making decisions.

eleven

CHASING THE TIGER

Suddenly, Clay and I had to move again. This would be the fourth time in the previous three years—now to Boston. Another gift—our daughter Mohm and her husband, Sean, lived in Boston. In no time, with their help, we found a perfect short-term apartment five minutes away from Mass General hospital. The owner recommended a concierge service that helped people set up a temporary living space while being treated at the hospital. They installed a computer, TV, VCR, and fax machine and gave us a list of restaurants they often called to arrange meal service. Sean brought over his college stereo and CD player. In half a day we had patched together the semblance of a pocket office and a very comfortable home.

I had a book to finish and two months to do it.

Maura and her husband, Tim, rallied around us, intuitively showing their love and understanding of what Clay needed. Maura put me onto Herbert Benson's Benson-Henry Institute for Mind Body Medicine, where we applied to join a cancer support group and take sessions on meditation, visualization, cognitive restructuring, yoga, nutrition—the whole works. Clay was open to the mind-body philosophy. The institute recommended that Clay walk an hour a day to stimulate his immune system. It was not a chore, since our apartment was a few blocks away from Beacon Hill with its quaint cobbled streets and antique shops and flying footbridges that took us to the Charles River and its harbor walks.

I sent an e-mail from Boston to thank the friends and supporters and health professionals who had helped us in the past, and to alert our newer friends about how to reach us in Boston. It was the beginning of a continuous conversation that created an emotional safety net beneath both Clay and me. It staved off the sense of isolation that too often closes down around both patient and caregiver when the monster comes back.

Our circle of care kept expanding. This is the most important role for the caregiver during this phase—reaching out and letting friends and family members know how to reach you and what you need.

Our dear former indefatigable housekeeper, Ella Council, arrived by train with enough supplies to keep the Ritz spotless. She insisted on staying weekdays with us, leaving her husband in New York to dog-sit with our Tibetan spaniel. Our close friend Lesley Stahl put us together with her generous sister-in-law in Boston, Paula Stahl, whose husband had survived a laryngectomy and went on to start up his own business.

Paula, as an experienced caregiver, knew exactly how to ease our transition. She welcomed us to town with a basket of video- and audiotapes and took Clay off to get a massage. Paula also knew the ropes in dealing with the radical treatment Clay was facing. "Just smile and tell each doctor you believe in him utterly," she counseled Clay. "But you, Gail, must not leave any doctor's office without a complete copy of your husband's records for the next consult. Don't let up until you get them."

Every caregiver needs a Paula in the early phases of this life crisis. I later read a study that supported my experience. The best support for a caregiver, both emotional and practical, is another caregiver, especially one who has been lashed to a loved one with a similar condition. They know what you need before you do. They can speak to your deepest fears without exaggerating them. A national survey of the social networks for caregivers of loved ones with Alzheimer's disease, by sociologists from Cornell University and Louisiana State University, found that caregivers boosted the mental health of other caregivers and also offered the most concrete practical help.

Don't Just Do Something, Sit There!

A fat smug September sun sat on the sills of our new home-away-from-home-away-from-home as I padded out at 6:30 A.M. to test our first morning from this *unfamiliar perch. Surroundings are so important when the world shrinks to a focus on getting well. I had placed bright ruby cyclamen plants all along the windowsills. We were high enough to see treetops and pockets of green between the sprawling complex of hospital buildings. We appreciated still being part of the natural world.*

Clay had his first zap at 9:00 A.M. A mask was fitted over his face and he was strapped down to hold his throat absolutely still to receive the hyperfractionated rads we knew would shrink the tumor. He returned to the apartment in high spirits—action had begun. Ella and I met with Paula Stahl's therapeutic cook, Martha, to learn how to puree veggies and make nonspicy soups and soften protein to pass with the least pain down Clay's burning throat.

I confided in one of Clay's best friends and favorite disciples of the New Journalism, Aaron Latham. Knowing that the two men went out to lunch together and "had a good talk," according to Clay, I assumed he had told Aaron about the cancer coming back. No. Not a word.

"Even when men talk, we don't talk," said Aaron.

On the third morning of our Boston sojourn, Clay rose intentionally at 6:30 to present himself in a living room chair as a ready candidate for meditation practice. Ella and I could hardly believe it. "You see Mr. Clay sitting like a statue, so still," she whispered. "He wants to do anything he can to get well." He had resisted the "touchy-feely stuff" for so long, but the Benson-Henry Institute had reached him with scientific evidence. And as Samuel Johnson famously said, "Nothing focuses the mind like the prospect of hanging."

When I read to him from a popular book on meditation, Jon Kabat-Zinn's Wherever You Go, There You Are, *he asked what the key passage meant, where it urges the practitioner not to do but to be attentive to the heart.*

I said, "Clay, as a man, you feel most manly when you are in action, affecting, making things happen externally. That is not the way to be powerful now. Now your power must be built up internally—the power to help heal yourself. You don't have to use your energy to affect things externally—you've delegated those major responsibilities to very capable surrogates and you'll go back and reclaim those roles—but right now you need to be in receiver mode. Take in all the positive energy being directed your way. Let yourself open up and be given to."

Clay nodded. He was back in his life with both feet. And I took on the advocate role full tilt. This is where I'm at my best. Give me a tough task of saving or

defending someone I love, and I will inflate like a colossus and fight fiercely,
whatever it takes. What I'm not so good at is listening. Watching. Intuiting. Not
doing. Just being present for Clay in ways that no one else could match.

———————

AFTER TWENTY-SIX RADIATION TREATMENTS *in fifteen days, Clay phoned*
me from the hospital to hightail it over. I was there in a shot, so excited and
apprehensive that I took the wrong elevator. "Where is he?" The nurse in the
makeshift basement radiation oncology suite went from one curtained treatment
room to another listening for the great Dr. Wang's voice.

"Here she is! My missing piece!" Clay announced like a headline. He was smiling
all over. Dr. Wang teased him: "Why you smile so big?" Clay told the doctor, as Paula
had taught him to say, "You're the man. You give me confidence."

"The tumor has shrunk by a third," Dr. Wang said.

"Whoopee!" I rushed into Clay's arms and hooted, "Okay, we're going to beat
this!"

Dr. Wang introduced a note of caution. "In China we have a saying. If wind
does not push boat forward, it is still making progress."

We knew he was right; we had a long way yet to travel, and speed was of the
essence.

Clay told me, "I prayed this morning—for help." That was a first for him.

I called Paula Stahl to share the news. "Your TLC is working. The tumor is
retreating behind it."

"I'm so glad, Gail," Paula said. "You are on your way to full healing—I
know it."

"I don't know how to reward you . . ." I stammered.

"You don't get it. My reward is seeing Clay's face after I took him for the first
massage and knowing he had had a good time. This is what we give each other as
caregivers."

———————

A WEEK BEFORE SURGERY *and we were on the roller coaster again, another slow*
crawl to the top, before the descent into hospital hell. But this time, we knew how to
mobilize ourselves. The whole week before the surgery was for filling up; we went
out every night. Clay sought out music. We went to Carnegie Hall for a concert by

*the Royal Philharmonic and sat holding hands through Schubert's Symphony no. 8
("Unfinished"). We felt the throb of pain and bursts of joy together. He said, "It's a
new way I can feel close to you—without words."*

The Conversation: What Will He Have Left?

"Tell me what you need to know." The speech pathologist, Tessa Goldsmith,
addressed Clay.

"Will I be able to talk after the surgery?" Clay asked.

Tessa formed her own words with total precision, softened by the music of a
South African accent. *"That depends on how much Dr. Montgomery has to take.
Your tumor is submucosal. Some healthy tissue has to be taken around the tumor,
to catch any floating cells that may have spread. So he's going to take out a fair
chunk of the base of your tongue."*

My head swam. Clay began negotiating. *"The thing is, I don't do anything but
talk in my work. I teach seminars and give lectures and even when I do consulting,
all I do is talk."*

"So you're very concerned how you're going to sound."

Clay nodded; to him, pain, disfigurement, none of it was as important as his
ability to talk.

"You must not use any of your voice for a week to ten days," Tessa said.
*"That's temporary, because you'll be breathing through a tracheostomy tube.
Afterward, you will need to work with somebody like me to restore intelligibility.
The base of your tongue is important for speech."* She paused. *"Also for pushing
down food in swallowing. You will need a feeding tube."*

Another unexpected blow. Tessa hastened to add, *"Temporarily—to allow you
to receive nutrition. What else do you need to know?"*

"Timing," Clay said. *"My second semester starts the third week of January."*

"Your surgery is scheduled, when, December 27th?" she verified. *"Realistically,
that's not enough time to heal."*

Clay slumped. *"That's a big disappointment. Getting back to teaching was the
biggest thing I had to look forward to."*

I came on like his defense attorney. *"Don't take that away from him now.
Maybe he'll heal quickly. Maybe friends will help . . ."*

Tessa Goldsmith wrapped up the consult with a promise to see Clay two weeks after the surgery and start him on speaking exercises.

JAKI JACKSON, MY YOGA *teacher, came to the apartment and asked me what I needed. "I feel locked up. All the giving and caretaking feels right and good, but there's not much coming back. Clay is in constant low-level pain. His nerve endings are too sensitive for me to kiss or even caress his face."*

She said she is constantly being stopped by women who are taking care of sick husbands—often not-so-nice husbands—"and they can't get mad because their husband is sick." Jaki suggested that I concentrate on standing poses. "They make you know your own strength. You can stand on one leg to consolidate all your will and strength, while the other side is being used elsewhere, so you don't feel depleted by caring for someone else all the time." It sounded logical. "Do you sleep with him?" she asked.

"Of course."

She nodded in her knowing way. "Mmmmm, then you are picking up all his feelings subconsciously."

I confessed that I was having panic attacks. Whenever I thought about a surgeon cutting out part of Clay's tongue, the perversity of attacking that place, the instrument he uses to connect with others, to praise or plant ideas, to fire off bursts of original thinking, the Socratic instrument by which he holds his students spellbound, the source of lovesounds . . . I couldn't keep my heart from leaping around like a frog shut in a jar.

Jaki explained that the throat area is the fifth chakra—the center of communication—but also of healing. It was hugely significant that this was where disease struck Clay, right where his life force was centered. "Tell him to breathe through his throat," she advised. "Then relax and receive healing from the support and love of his family and his friends."

STRATEGIES

Relieve Caregiver Stress

Stress is real.

Stress is measurable.

Stress can be reduced without medication.

Hit with a Boomerang, we can easily switch into high anxiety and get stuck in that gear. Soon life begins spinning out of control. Can you shift to a healthier gear? One good way is to hang on to routines that define normalcy in your life.

If you normally get up and stretch and shower before sipping coffee as you dress and watch CNN, don't stop. Even though you're not hungry, and you're much more anxious about catching the doctor than catching up with the latest world crisis, stick with what is most familiar. It will calm you and your family, especially if you have children living at home. The first memories we save as babies are the simplest routines of eating, dressing, bathing. They are also the last memories to fade for people in cognitive decline. Humans thrive on repeatable routines.

- **Breathe!** The single most helpful tool for caregivers is something we all know how to do from the instant we're born. Breathe! Breath is our first gift. Where did life begin? The Bible teaches that God reached down and breathed life into us. If anything teaches that we're powerless to play God, it is caregiving. We are just vehicles for God's breath—the breath of hope and life.

    Whenever we're afraid or anxious, our breathing becomes shallow and our lungs never quite inflate. So there isn't enough force to carry oxygen around to all the cells hungry for regeneration. The brain is thus deprived of the antistress hormones it needs to function calmly and clearly.

"I'm an educated person, I have a master's degree, but I didn't know how to breathe!" confessed Mae Boldin, a retired African American teacher. When she joined a Powerful Tools for Caregivers course, she was taking care of a beloved husband who had developed dementia. In a very short time, he had changed from her sweet-natured helpmate to an angry, volatile stranger. Once she learned that these were common symptoms of dementia and not her fault, not God punishing her, she was ready to learn the first tool caregivers need.

"I wake up now and take deep breaths from my diaphragm, hold the breath, and exhale slowly."

Just ten minutes of slow, deep, meditative breathing, I promise, will slow your heart rate, reduce the chaotic signals to your brain, calm your emotional state, and make it easier to think clearly and tune in to your intuitions. You will make better decisions with less energy.

Whenever you feel overwhelmed by caregiving responsibilities, take time out to sit still and breathe calmly and deeply for at least ten minutes. Let your mind flow freely with whatever ideas and images swim to the surface. Don't analyze or judge a thing. Just relax and observe the passing show. You'll arise surprisingly refreshed.

Google "breathing techniques." Dr. Andrew Weil offers three easy and excellent exercises to reduce anxiety or increase alertness.

- **Get Serious About Self-Care.** Once the immediate crisis passes, your adrenaline level will drop back down. You will begin to find another new normal. This is the ideal time to begin developing some health practices that will protect you before the next crisis. Be aware that when we "let down" at the end of a crisis, our bodies do, too, and we may experience a temporary depression. The patient often does as well.

Being a caregiver provides many excuses for skipping your necessary checkups, but don't do it. Make sure you get your annual checkup and find a doctor who knows something about the stresses of caregiving. Best idea: Ask to have your necessary tests performed at the same medical center where you take your loved one, and try to schedule them on the same day. Acupuncture and Chinese herbal medicine can be surprisingly helpful for mysterious aches and pains that develop under constant stress. Naturopaths and nutritionists can also help you to stay healthy, without drugs.

- **Find an Enjoyable Physical Pursuit.** I know, I know—you've had it drummed into your head that exercise is the best strategy for a long and healthy life. But surely you can find a form of exercise you'll actually enjoy. Walking in nature is restorative for the mind as well as aerobic for the body. Dancing is fabulous aerobic exercise. Biking is less aerobic but fine for clearing the head. Riding on an elliptical machine is superb aerobic activity, doesn't jolt the hip joints or punish the knees and can be done with hand pumps as well.

  Pounding on the treadmill is the best protection against osteoporosis, because it stimulates rebuilding of bone; and today, you can read a paper or watch TV or plan a trip on most treadmills.

  Swimming is wonderful for opening up the lungs and stretching the body. I've even borrowed a ten-year-old's scooter and pumped through the park—lots of fun! Any one of these activities should be done for a minimum of twenty minutes at least three times a week. Studies keep rolling out

that show consistent exercise is the best protector from just
about anything—falls, heart disease, even Alzheimer's.

- **Try Meditating.** All forms of meditation—yoga, tai chi,
  seated meditation, and walking a labyrinth—call for
  concentration on slow, regular breathing. Numerous studies
  confirm that during such activities, a person's heart rate can
  be slowed from a chaotic pattern to a calm and healthy
  pattern. Stress hormones can be reversed. This is the basis
  of Dr. Herbert Benson's famous relaxation response. Once
  relaxed, our bodies regain balance, our brains become more
  efficient, we make better decisions, and creativity returns.

- **Take a Break.** Make arrangements for any necessary fill-in
  help (family, friends, volunteers, or professional caregivers).
  Take a single day or weekend, at least once a month. Take a
  week's vacation within six months. Make sure you line up your
  support system so you can be confident that your loved one is
  safe and has companionship. And when you're away, *stay
  away.* Talk about different things, read that book you haven't
  been able to get to, and let your loved one know you will not
  be calling every night, but you can be reached if needed.

- **Eat Well.** Eat plenty of fresh fruits, vegetables, proteins,
  including nuts and beans, and whole grains. Caffeine, fast
  food, and sugar are quick pick-me-ups that also produce
  quick letdowns.

- **Reward Yourself.** Treat yourself to a massage, a manicure,
  a nice dinner with a friend, a funny flick, or a soothing
  concert. Take a break from anxiety and reward yourself for
  the superb care you give your loved one. Don't feel guilty
  about wanting to feel good.

- **Explore or Affirm Spirituality**. Whether religious or secular, families confronting a life-threatening diagnosis inevitably seek comfort, courage, and more—a sense of meaning or purpose. Believers of all faiths can find solace in their own creeds and rituals. But even nonbelievers, faced with existential issues, may find that talking with a trained spiritual counselor—priest, rabbi, minister, or other— awakens feelings of compassion and communion with all humans facing the same issues.

Hold On to Your Job

You need a focus for your mind beyond the cascade of "What ifs?" I remember being on a deadline to write a story about Saddam Hussein for *Vanity Fair* when my husband's first cancer diagnosis hit us. My editor was matter-of-fact about keeping our attention fully focused on our work. She deliberately refrained from asking me for medical updates. At first I was hurt. Later I thanked her.

Pull Close to Friends

These are people who knew you before your loved one's health crisis. They can empathize, without being in the pit of fear with you. They also remind you of who you are—your ambitions, fascinations, tastes, distastes, what makes you laugh loudest. Their friendship promises you a future beyond your current nightmare.

Seek Distractions

During the days or weeks of uncertainty between a tentative diagnosis and the final word, send out an e-mail to a few close friends and family members asking them to pass on anything amusing—a card, a movie, a book, a TV show. The laughter cure is real.

Seek Out Other Caregivers or Join a Support Group

Many caregivers I interviewed told me they were cool to this idea at first. "People like that will just depress me," they say, or "I don't do groups." But those who do join, later on, usually tell me they find they can laugh and cry and speak their true minds better among people who share a similar situation. And they gain a lot of know-how from the most resourceful members of the group. Caregivers who join groups held by the Alzheimer's Association almost universally praise them as remarkable.

The Conversation: The Night Before Surgery

Walking up the hill to our Boston digs on the afternoon before surgery, Clay doubled over with cramps. It was coming from the short procedure to implant a feeding tube in his abdominal wall. He was loathe to admit feeling pain.

Maura was waiting for us, having flown up from Brooklyn. She nuzzled next to her stepfather on the bed to read to him a story she was working on. His mind was diverted from the focus on his body and he reveled in being consulted as the editor. Maura and I played Schubert's "Unfinished" Symphony for him. "That's you," I murmured. "An unfinished man." He still had students to inspire, a memoir to write, grandchildren to see come into the world.

I asked if he would like a foot massage, and he whispered a hoarse, "Yes, that would be very nice." This was the one surefire stress-reducing technique I had found. Rubbing and stretching his feet, and finding the pressure points under and between his toes, would calm him and put him to sleep. I had asked a reflexologist to teach me what to do. But it wasn't my bootleg professionalism that worked every time. It was the loving human touch to the lowliest part of the body. It calmed me, too.

When he awoke in the evening, he was fighting the near certainty that he wouldn't be ready to resume teaching the next semester. Just then his friend the writer Aaron Latham called from New York. He'd had a brilliant idea. He could come out and team-teach with Clay for the spring semester. Clay was deeply touched. But he couldn't possibly allow Aaron to take on such a burden alone. Aaron and I protested. We would both help. His other colleagues might offer to come out to teach a class or two. And Clay would be in the classroom monitoring everything that went on.

"Clay," said Aaron, the gentle surrogate son, "I'll be your voice."

————————

THE MORNING OF SURGERY, before we walked to the hospital, Clay pinned me awkwardly in the privacy of our bathroom. "I don't know how to say this, to be politically correct, but, sweetheart, you are the center of my life. You are what creates beautiful homes wherever we are—it all comes from you—and I want you to know I think about it all the time."

At the hospital, looking quite serene, Clay went off toward the OR with his fingers trailing mine.

Later, a tap on the shoulder. I must have been asleep. I looked up at Dr. Monty, still in his froggy slippers and blue scrubs. He pulled off his face mask and gave me a smile. "The cancer is gone. He has great margins."

"Can I kiss you?"

"Please."

It was another godsend. We've been given great margins. My job from now on would be to widen the margins of our life.

————————

twelve
SANDWICHED!

Bonnie and David Heath are typical members of the sandwich generation—boomer parents who are pinched between raising their still-dependent children and carrying their parents over the threshold into late age.

The Heaths always looked forward to their nightly walk together.

It was their habit to step outside each evening to smell the flowers in their suburban neighborhood and unshackle themselves from the rigid schedules of work, commuting, and chauffeuring their teenage children across the infinite sprawl of Los Angeles. They talked, they laughed, they even walked briskly enough to keep their weight within an acceptable spread for a couple in their late forties.

The Call that first interrupted their lives was about David's mother, Raylene. "The EMS people are taking her to the hospital. She fell and shattered her femur," reported one of David's five siblings.

Even after Raylene finished a short stay in a hospital for acute rehab, she remained immobilized, with a plate in one leg and the other riddled with arthritis. Medicare rules decreed that she had "plateaued" and no longer qualified for "rehabilitation." She was now considered a "custodial care" case.

The Heaths had run up against the cruelest obstacle on the labyrinth of caregiving. Like many of us, they were stunned to learn that Medicare does not pay for long-term care at home. Since both Bonnie and David worked, Raylene's son David reached for a quick and temporary solution. He placed his mom in a nursing home. The drive was too long for her husband to visit her. Raylene complained bitterly: "They have Alzheimer's patients sitting in the hall in their wheelchairs, they give them dolls, they talk to themselves. I don't have my family anymore. Why am I here in a place where people are dying?"

Riddled with guilt, David brought his mother back home. Fortunately, David's father, Larry, had retired at sixty-four from his career as a successful film editor. To everyone's surprise, he was more than willing to accept the crown of family caregiver from his wife, who had raised their family of six children. He relished bringing his sweetheart breakfast on a silver tray. As the driver to get groceries and drop off dry cleaning, he felt necessary again, and he came to be proud of his cooking. The couple also hired an aide whom they paid privately out of savings.

This was a New Normal that seemed to work for everyone, as long as Larry remained healthy himself.

WHEN DAD BECOMES CAREGIVER

Many families describe their astonishment when the dad who was mostly absent during his career-striving decades makes a total shift, after retirement, from being competitive to becoming emotionally connected to family, friends, and home. As men's power orientation subsides, beyond fifty, the happiest men become more nurturing as they age, often for the first time. If they are able to show and satisfy a heightened need for human closeness, a need normally suppressed in their warrior days, they are found in studies to gain a corresponding rise in psychological health. These are the fathers, like Larry Heath, who take an interest in cooking or gardening, home improvement, and pets and grandchildren. They find new delight in opening their hearts and using their hands, rather than staying up in their heads or planning how to vanquish their rivals. Such men often become superb caregivers.

For two full years, David's dad was able to be the primary caregiver. And then—BOOMERANG! As so often happens, suddenly the strong parent can no longer compensate for the ailing one, and the responsibility shifts to

the adult children, who are usually unprepared. Larry Heath had been sliding into depression, unwilling to admit that he couldn't continue to perform
all the caregiving tasks. His balance deteriorated. Then one night he took a
bad fall on the way to the bathroom and suffered a head injury.

"The night we got the call from the paramedics about Larry, everything
stopped," says daughter-in-law Bonnie. "He couldn't cook. He couldn't drive
safely. He could no longer be the caregiver."

Larry was in the hospital for a week. "After he came home, he was different," says his son David, heaving a sigh. "We could see some dementia had
set in. We had to fight with him to take the car keys away, and we weren't
winning."

"I CAN'T DO IT ALONE!"

Suddenly, Bonnie and David Heath were turned into full-fledged members of the sandwich generation, a term they had never even heard. David
protested—he had no time on weekdays. He left the house at 7:30 for a demanding job at Universal Studios in film editing. He didn't get home until
twelve hours later. On weekends he was happy to take a half day to pay his
parents' bills and do financial planning. All the rest—getting Raylene dressed
and driven to the doctors and physical therapy, plus calming the tensions
between her and her husband, now that Larry felt robbed of his role as her
caregiver—fell to Bonnie, the daughter-in-law. It turned her days into a series of hundred-yard dashes.

"Being a substitute teacher, I'm up by six o'clock," she said as she rattles
off her schedule. "I have to make lunches for my kids. One son goes to school
at seven o'clock, I drive him. I come back. The next son has to be there by
eight o'clock, I drop him off, I get to my school. I'm off by three o'clock. I
have to go back to the high school, pick up my other son. I have just enough
time to change out of my work clothes, put on my mom gear, and run out to
pick up my mother-in-law, transition her into the car, take her to physical
therapy for an hour and a half, or take Larry to one of his six doctors, and
come home and say, 'Eh, what's for dinner?' "

Bonnie had no time to walk with or even talk to her husband. By 9:30 P.M.

they were both exhausted. She looked down at the bulge around her waist. "We've gotten fat. Sometimes now we even go to bed before our children." The children felt neglected and were worried about their mom and dad.

David attempted to joke about it: "If we didn't have errands to do on weekends, we'd never be together."

After nine months of doing all the driving and heavy lifting for David's parents, virtually by herself, Bonnie came to the end of her rope. "I kinda put my foot down and told David, 'I can't do it all. I love your parents, but it's not fair to me—something has to give.'"

David couldn't hear his wife. He needed to be the perfect Jewish son to a father he had worked with and worshipped. He kept telling Bonnie, "We're not going to let anybody fall through the cracks, so you just have to step up to the plate. That's what families are supposed to do for each other."

Bonnie knew they needed help. David's father refused to stop driving. The danger of an accident was one more blow she didn't think their family could absorb.

Fortunately, David belonged to the Motion Picture & Television Fund (MPTF), a venerated health-care organization in Los Angeles that operates like a supra union, offering a broad continuum of care for families of the film and TV industry. David and Bonnie were welcomed to bring in their parents to talk to a geriatrician, Dr. Saeed Humayun, the medical director of MPTF's Age Well program. An Indian-American geriatrician with silvered hair and a silky voice, this man exudes both compassion and authority. Dr. Humayun brought a progressive idea to MPTF in 1997: treat the family, not just the patient.

In his first contact with the Heaths, Dr. Humayun spent ninety minutes to gather a comprehensive picture, not only of their parents' physical history but also of their career and family and social worlds, their goals and capacities and passions. With all families, he also interviews the caregiver, knowing that the extra time spent forming a partnership with caregivers pays off down the line.

Together, the family agreed on a "life management plan" to keep the parents at home, remaining independent.

ONE FAMILY'S MEETING

Bonnie coaxed her husband to call the whole family together for a meeting. She reminded him that he had five siblings—five!—all living within an hour and a half of their parents. Why weren't they part of the circle of care?

David was reluctant to stir up old rivalries among his siblings. All five of his brothers and sisters were bosses of some kind—executives, film editors, a school principal, an insurance manager, a district manager, and an attorney. Dr. Humayun heartily backed Bonnie's instincts explaining, "I cannot close the loop of care for the patient without having family members become part of the team." David admitted that he couldn't lead a family meeting and keep his cool. Ultimately, he was relieved to have a professional offer to be the neutral voice.

All five of David's sisters and brothers were invited and four showed up, some with spouses. The absent sibling was patched in on a conference call. Larry and Raylene, both in wheelchairs, were brought in.

I was invited to observe. Raylene, who knew my books, had endorsed it. We gathered around a big table in a sunny room.

Dr. Humayun started it off by summarizing the medical findings of his assessment: "Mr. Heath has moderate to severe cognitive impairment." This pronouncement, had it come from one of the siblings, would surely have fomented considerable dispute from family members and from Larry Heath himself. When the neutral facilitator delivers the news, each family member—including the patient—has the same information and, the facilitator hopes, a similar understanding. Otherwise, family members' reactions are likely to be distorted by their own beliefs and fears about the illness.

Dr. Humayun, as a communicator and educator of both patient and the family, understood that his role was to talk to them in their own language and show empathy. He explained that Larry had a stroke that affected the portion of the brain that controls driving ability. Now Larry Heath spoke up forcefully, for himself.

"Dr. H. is the first person who told me how they establish whether you should drive or not. He was much more help than my own doctor, who just ordered, 'Don't drive.' It's a big thing to accept—never to drive again, but I made the decision," he said proudly. "I'm going to protect others and myself by not driving."

This was the first breakthrough. Bonnie smiled. The doctor was then able to move on to helpful recommendations for medication, exercises to improve brain function, and activities that he knew would give pleasure to Larry.

Jessica Caughey, the social worker, then raised the most critical issue for the mother. "Raylene has not been out of the house in eight months. We need to discuss how to get her up and out of her wheelchair."

Raylene, who had dressed handsomely and applied full makeup for the occasion, lobbied for the status quo. "My problem is, I need someone like Bonnie who knows how to get me in and out of the car. I feel very secure with Bonnie. Everybody else is working."

A visible expression of relief showed on some of the siblings' faces; yes, let Bonnie do it, Raylene trusts her. Bonnie had the chance to set things straight: "I've been driving them to five doctor appointments a week—and by the way, I *do* work. As a substitute teacher, if I don't show up, I don't get paid."

David pointed out that Bonnie was also the caregiver for her own parents in their eighties. What if there was an emergency and she couldn't show up for Raylene? He then made a brilliant suggestion that would be useful for any family sharing the care of someone who is wheelchair-bound.

"I'd like to see my siblings come over to Mom's house with their cars or SUVs and practice pulling up to the curb and getting Mom in and out." The choreography changes depending on the type of vehicle. It takes practice.

Larry Jr., the oldest son, gave his mother an out. "Mom, you're under a lot of pressure here; would you feel comfortable getting in and out of our cars?"

Predictably, Raylene shook her head. "No."

Two other siblings showed a willingness and coaxed their mother to let them help. Brother Bud stated the obvious: "We have to get Raylene to allow this to happen." The social worker then proposed a "training day." "Raylene, if your children all came over for a training day, would you let some of them drive you?"

Raylene loosened up. "I'd have to get used to it."

A second breakthrough.

STRATEGIES

Transfers Without Fear of Falling

Transferring anyone who is fearful of falling and unsteady on his or her feet is a major obstacle to defeating isolation and depression. Learning how to do it properly, however, offers an opportunity for physical intimacy and even a boost to your loved one's sense of mastery.

It's like learning new dance steps. You hug your partner, turn him or her—there's a rhythm to it—you can count it out and perfect your style. You're a dance team! Everyone will feel safe and effective and more independent, and your loved one will want to go out.

Most important is that someone shows the caregiver the right body mechanics, which involve using your legs instead of your back as you turn to move the person you are caring for from wheelchair to car. While the individual is still in the hospital, don't be afraid to ask a nurse or an aide to show you the procedure. If your loved one is already home, contact your local visiting-nurse service, home-health agency, or rehabilitation center, and ask someone there to put you in touch with a person who can train you to transfer the individual safely. When you're being trained, it's important that you use the vehicle you'll be using to transport the patient.

Moving someone from A to Z is much easier with a "sliding board" or "transfer board," a device that bridges the gap between two points, as in entering a car. The upper side of the board is slick, enabling the patient to slide easily. You put one end of the board under one hip and the other side on the seat of the car, then slide the patient over to avoid having to lift most of the body weight. A sliding board works fine with most cars, but not with SUVs, which are too tall.

GETTING MOM OUT OF THE HOUSE

The siblings turned to Bonnie to ask how she was able to get their mother to agree to go outside the home for more vigorous physical therapy. "I just don't buy into the guilt trip your mother tries to give me," Bonnie told them bluntly. "Raylene knows it doesn't work with me. I just tell her, not going is not an option."

Some of the siblings made excuses. "Raylene refuses to go out." "Dad is really getting better." The social workers were able to emphasize realities that are hard for any family to face. Dad was not getting better.

Jessica the social worker told them, "Larry is a prime example of a man who has lost a lot of control in various aspects of his life. Financial control has been taken away. He can't drive any longer. He's secluded at home unless someone takes him out. So he focuses obsessively on when he would be able to get into an assisted-living cottage on our campus. There's a long waiting list. Our job—all of us—is to help decrease that anxiety and improve his social and recreational opportunities so that he feels better about himself."

Then she offered a reality check on Raylene. "Your mother has not been out of the house for eight months—how would you feel if you hadn't been outside for the better part of a year?" Jessica said. "It's not good for anyone's mental health."

This spurred the husband of the eldest sibling to dig more deeply. "So, what we have to come to grips with is *why* Raylene won't allow us to take her out."

Mary, the oldest daughter, was then able to release the elephant hidden in the room. "I don't think my mother's psychological health has been tended to. She's been showing all the signs of depression."

That statement sucked the air out of the room. The staff was accustomed to resistance by adult children to such a diagnosis. "They think it makes them look bad," I had been warned by the geriatrician. A common response is "But we're doing everything to make her happy!" Dr. Humayun is aware of how often depression goes undiagnosed in the elderly. "It can be part of cognitive decline, or Parkinson's disease, or associated with even a minor stroke. The reason it's being underdiagnosed is that people, doctors included, attribute the changes in behavior—like not eating or sleeping well or refusing to go out—not to depression, but to the assumption 'Mom is just getting old.'"

It's Dr. Humayun's job to explain that treatment of depression is not just a matter of medication or going to a psychiatrist. It involves the children as well. It is necessary to look at all the dynamics in a person's life. Is the depression part of another disease, or a reaction to a medical condition like declining vision or being trapped in a wheelchair? Or is it because a parent is alone and lonely and wants his or her kids to be more involved? He noted a familiar dynamic in the Heath family:

"If the children make an effort and get a negative response, they withdraw, not realizing that there is a medical and psychological issue here that needs attention. That leads to less stimulation, less activity, less pleasure in life, which leads to greater depression and the declining ability to feel pleasure in any activity. It's a vicious circle."

Raylene spoke up for herself. She was frustrated with wanting to help her husband but unable while confined to her wheelchair. She complained, "He just sees me as a nag."

The social worker said cheerfully, "We're a democratic society. Let's have a vote. How many people think Mom could use a psychological counselor to talk to?"

Every hand went up, except Raylene's husband's. The social worker later observed that Larry might have been afraid to express a judgment.

Bonnie said she would like to see the family more actively involved with their parents' social activities. "Telephoning isn't enough. We need you to go over and take them out to a movie or lunch." Joe, the absent sibling, an attorney, piped up from an open speakerphone. "May I suggest setting up an e-mail tree? If I could see that they need coverage on October 17, I could schedule my appointments in half a day and drive down for the rest of the day and do as much as I can."

They all showed a willingness to do the same. Mary, about to retire, offered to tag-team with Bonnie, and Bonnie agreed to create a website with a calendar that could be shared. Larry Jr. was thinking long term. "What if we create a system and it breaks down? Can't we get together as a family every six weeks and look ahead?"

Buoyed by the evidence of so much love and support from all her children and their mates, Raylene asserted her own mental health assessment: "I'm willing to go for psychological counseling, but I also agree with Mary—Dad also needs somebody to talk to."

Mary agreed and moved on to future plans. "I'm going to have a birthday party for Dad. His eighty-third. Two subjects are off the table. Politics and religion."

Larry Jr. jumped in. "That just leaves sex."

Everyone laughed and left in a good mood.

UNEXPECTED BENEFITS

Four months later, on a Monday at 9:00 A.M., David Heath strides into his busy office at Universal Studios and scrolls through a blur of e-mails; it's going to be a blockbuster week of work. Before settling in, he picks up the phone to call his mother. They chat pleasantly.

"Her spirits are up," he reports. "You can hear it in her voice and feel it when you walk into their house now."

Was her depression treated? I ask.

"She wouldn't go to a therapist. But something better happened. I e-mailed my mother's own sister, Dorothy, and let her know that Mom was not getting out. She came to visit Raylene and saw her need for someone to talk to."

Raylene had just turned eighty. Dorothy was sixty-three, divorced and alone, and had just retired. She offered to drive down three hours every weekend and stay with Raylene and Larry. "She seems happy to reconnect with her sister and eager to spend time with her while she still has her," David told me. "It's taken the pressure off Bonnie, because Dorothy now drives my father to his medical appointments and does errands for him, all the while keeping up a lively conversation. His health is getting better!"

The benefits of this expanded circle of care were already enormous for both David and Bonnie. Dorothy was becoming Raylene's soul sister, a confidante she could talk to, and that had relieved Raylene's depression. Larry also had a reliable source of social and mental stimulation in Dorothy. This allowed Bonnie to go back to teaching and to spend more time with her own children.

Did David's siblings come around? I asked.

The Heaths credit the family meeting with opening up the minds of

David's brothers and sisters. His brother John, despite a serious illness of his own and two adolescent children, could be summoned for any fix-it job. Another brother was sending money on a regular basis for home health aides, and another made regular monthly visits to see his father.

Bonnie later told me, "David and I realized that you can ask for help, but when some siblings still don't help, we agreed that fussing about it is not worth ruining our marriage or our health. So we've eased off." This was perhaps the greatest breakthrough. It prompted Bonnie to look at what she needed to do to repair herself. "I noticed in pictures, oooh, I'm not looking well, and I don't feel well. So I dragged out my stationary bike and pedal thirty minutes a day while I read a book! I feel so much better. I am bound and determined to lose thirty pounds. And I'm hoping to resume our nightly walks."

Bonnie and David's children called a family meeting of their own, with their parents. They insisted that Mom and Dad have a lunch date every Saturday, just the two of them. These tête-à-têtes remind the couple to refresh their marriage. That is the tightest circle of love, one that will sustain them when parents pass on and children leave rips in the heart as they pull away to fly solo.

STRATEGIES

Expand Your Care Circle

By now you know you're a seasoned caregiver, ready for most crises. You also know you can't cope alone. You keep researching new expertise and tech tools for caregiving. But you need something even more important for yourself—a confidant, a friend or relative you can talk to honestly without being judged.

Research has warned us not to expect great support from siblings in a family caregiving crisis. According to a Cornell University study, siblings inject the greatest interpersonal stress. But anecdotal evidence, including the Colbert's family story in

Chapter 8, suggests that sisters may well rise far above sibling rivalry. In the preceding Heath family story, the medicine that pulled Raylene out of depression was not prescribed by a psychiatrist. It was an estranged sister who reconnected with Raylene, who cherishes her, and who offers the emotional tenderness, listening, companionship, and the nonjudgmental affection of a loving friend.

Sisters are sisters until the day they both die. And even then, as one brother once told me, he keeps the ashes of his two sisters in urns side by side in his solarium; they look out at the yard where they once played and fought over the one swing. He swears he can still hear them arguing over who can swing the highest.

Intimate friendships can be better for our health than a psychiatrist, who must, after all, keep a certain distance. Expanding the care circle around your loved one could mean calling on a rabbi or priest or minister, or a pastoral counselor, or a friend who has faced similar obstacles, or a care manager who may become almost as close as family. Other caregivers are also fine emotional cushions because they understand.

We know from scientific studies that older men who have four or more friends of either sex—the key being friends they trust enough to reveal their feelings to—live longer than men who depend only on their wives or on a few sports buddies. A ten-year Australian study, reported in 2009, found that very old people with a large circle of friends had a much better survival rate over a ten-year period than those with fewer friends.

Cultivate Your Social Network

Other recent studies and books trace lifelong friendships among childhood chums that extended their life span. In many studies of single people and friendships, friends are found to have an even greater effect on health than a spouse or family member.

Overall, as observed in the literature by Rebecca Adams, a sociology professor at the University of North Carolina, "Friendship has a bigger impact on our psychological well-being than family relationships."

This goes for both the caregiver and the patient.

How one deals with the stress of disease has an impact on cognitive function. People who worry a lot, or who have been through prolonged periods of depression, have twice the risk of cognitive decline. Once again, the best antidote to preserve the brain is an extensive social network. Dr. David Bennett, director of the Rush Alzheimer's Disease Center at Rush University Medical Center in Chicago, says it's not only how many people one knows but how many people one knows intimately and feels comfortable confiding in. It could be, Bennett says, that "the larger the network, the less likely they are to experience clinical Alzheimer's disease."

Empower a Parent to Decide Not to Drive

The senior Mr. Heath initially refused to accept that he had early signs of dementia. Some of his adult children had a hard time accepting that, too. Fortunately, Larry was still mentally present enough to engage in a discussion with Dr. Humayun and understand his diagnosis.

"It's a question of independence," explained Dr. Humayun. "Also a question of dignity and pride. Which of those three elements is most important to an individual depends on one's personality. In Mr. Heath, all these factors were at play. My job was to allow him to understand what his disease is, what his prognosis is, how it would change him, and that he was not the best judge of what he could do safely." The doctor showed Larry images of his brain and where the memory centers had been affected. "When I brought up the question of safety for himself and others, he was able to grasp that he could drive, but it could be dangerous. I didn't have to tell him, 'You shouldn't drive,' and that's the key. He was empowered to make the decision himself."

If empowerment doesn't work, there are other proven strategies. At the Family Caregiver Alliance in San Francisco, I had a conversation with senior social worker Donna Schempp about how to make the car disappear. "Sometimes it's good to put the blame on the doctor. In California, if you have a dementia diagnosis, the doctor is required to report it to the DMV. If he doesn't do it, you can report him yourself. He then gets a letter from the DMV saying he can't drive anymore." Donna smiles with the ruefulness of experience. "That doesn't mean Dad is going to listen."

One caregiver called her husband's insurance company and said her husband had dementia and shouldn't be driving. The company took him off the policy and sent a letter. Certain that her husband would not drive without insurance, the caregiver kept that letter up on the refrigerator.

Other tricks: Hide the keys. Park the car at one of the kids' houses or in a long-term lot. Take the car to the shop and say the shop has the parts on order, but it's going to be a long, long time. If you're dealing with someone with dementia, they won't remember.

Get Everyone at the Table for the Family Meeting

Should the first family meeting about caregiving include the patient? Preferably not, unless it's unavoidable. The initial meeting is for discussing an overall plan, an action team, and declaring a truce in old family feuds, all in the interest of a larger purpose. The patient should be included (if mentally fit) at a later point when all concerned review a professional assessment of his or her medical and psychological condition. All participants need to hear the full story together and ask their questions. This is imperative to counteract the patient's natural tendency to manipulate or play off

one family member against another. Include everyone taking part in
the care of your loved one—aides, friends, neighbors, and certainly
a care manager if you have one. Absent family members can stay
in the loop via a conference call or videotape.

- **Set the Agenda.** Most agencies recommend a predetermined
  agenda, to avoid a free-for-all. But when MPTF, for example,
  schedules a family meeting, the social workers urge all family
  members to attend, bringing a list of their own concerns,
  issues, and medical questions. The initial agenda is open,
  allowing participants to suggest items in whatever order they
  wish. After a free flow of the family's input, Dr. Humayun
  structures the agenda. He might say, "Of all the issues listed,
  we will take on the first five and put off the next five for a
  follow-up meeting."

- **Suggested Topics for an Agenda.**
  - Latest report from the patient's physician
  - Sharing of feelings about the illness
  - Daily and weekly caregiving needs
  - Financial concerns
  - Roles each person would like to assume
  - Needs of the primary caregiver
  - Problem-solving solutions
  - Summary

Find a Neutral Facilitator

The moderator at a family meeting should not be a family
member. Call the hospital where the patient was treated and ask
the social worker if she or he will gather the necessary medical
data and run the family meeting. Better yet, ask the social worker
before the patient is discharged. Social workers can also be found

in local caregiver organizations, home-health agencies, hospice, or private practice.

If your loved one is in a rehab facility, it is customary to have a regular care team meeting with the supervising physician, nurses, and social worker. A pastor, priest, or rabbi can be helpful, along with the doctor or nurse closest to the patient's case. (They will be paid only if the patient is present.) Psychotherapists are often trained in family counseling. If you are using the services of a geriatric care manager, he or she would have a global perspective and be an ideal moderator.

- Let everyone have a chance to speak and express their feelings. Important feelings, such as fear, anxiety, anger, may come out.
- Listen attentively and don't interrupt. Let the facilitator remind the group that speakers are limited to so many minutes, giving everybody equal time.
- Stay focused on the issues at hand. Family members bring a lot to the table—old scripts. You can't fix the family. That's not the goal of this meeting.
- Don't try to solve all issues right away. Record the thorniest problems and go back to them in the next meeting.
- Use "I" messages ("I can only imagine how hard this must be for you") rather than "you" messages (as in "If only *you* had done that, Mom wouldn't have had a setback").
- Family meetings needn't be a onetime event. Regular meetings cool tempers and ease tension.

When dividing tasks, remember that every family member has natural strengths. For example, some are great hand-holders; others excel at creating a website that keeps everyone in the loop. Those unable to attend day meetings may be key players at night. People often become more cooperative when they focus on working together and begin to see results. It becomes a team.

Set Up a Shared Family Calendar

At the Heath family meeting, siblings and their spouses created a shared calendar to keep themselves updated on their parents' needs and their own availability for visits. After each visit, each sibling e-mailed the others about the parents' moods and treatments, briefing the next visitor and helping the parents feel well loved.

An Internet-based care calendar allows all members of a busy, scattered family to access the patient's schedule and condition at any time, from any location. For a user-friendly calendar service, free for caregivers, go to Lotsa Helping Hands (www.lotsahelpinghands. com). The calendar is based on social networking models *but* is totally private. It takes only five minutes to set up but gives the subscriber (the main caregiver) a private and secure Web community. It can even remind subscribers to take out the garbage at specific pickup times.

Lotsa Helping Hands is a for-profit business that keeps the service free for caregivers by partnering with businesses who license their service, promote it to their employees and customers, and pay a licensing fee.

FOURTH TURNING: PLAYING GOD

thirteen

THE WHOLE WORLD IN MY HANDS

People who become superb caregivers—totally committed, highly skilled—tend to overlook a growing danger. It lies in doing too much, refusing help, and ignoring your own creeping isolation. Beware certain misleading mantras:

"I'm the only one he trusts."

"I'm the only one who knows what she needs."

"My mother doesn't want anyone else in the house."

Roles may be reversed. Child becomes parent to the father who taught you to throw a ball and drink a beer, or the mother who nursed you through countless fevers and failed crushes. Role reversal is even more jolting when illness strikes your spouse.

You may come to believe that you hold the life or death of your loved one in your hands, and to some degree, you do. But in assuming this exalted role, the primary caregiver begins to submerge his or her identity, risking a loss of healthy self-identity and social life. If you keep begging off dinner invitations, saying you can't leave your loved one alone, friends will stop calling. Depict yourself as indispensable at home and people will stay outside the wall you're building around yourself. Soon your life is defined entirely by the unending needs and demands of a person who is not going to make a lot of progress. The pitfall at this turning is that we often find ourselves "Playing God."

BLESSED WITH ANOTHER REPRIEVE, *we were back in Berkeley for Clay's first class on January 23, 1998. Once again the circle of care around him broadened. Aaron Latham lived with us for most of that semester while team-teaching with Clay. The two men had begun as mentor and disciple. Now they fused as teachers of the next generation.*

But could Clay talk?

He wore a lapel microphone to class. His students greeted him with surprise and affection. He rehearsed a little speech to put them at ease and began by choking it out: "I have a chawenge—excuse me—a challenge—in speaking clearly. Surgery on my tongue. So I need to use a mike . . . and re—rely on Aaron to speak for me, while I heal. But there's nothing wrong with my brain. I'm still Clay Felker. [It came out missing the "l" in Clay and the "f" in Felker.] Sorry. I can't say my name right—doctor says I should change my name to Izzy Cohen. My passion is still shaping your talent. Helping you think up and write and edit magazines of the future."

Disarmed by his courage and his commitment to return to them, his students helped to compensate for his limitations. Stoically, Clay found a way to hold back the oral secretions that flooded his mouth, clamping his lips to one side. It was another proof that if we believe in ourselves as normal, and pass off our limitations with a simple explanation, we are accepted as we are—normal is as normal does.

I THINK BACK TO *what "normal" dinner at home became for Mr. and Mrs. Felker during this phase of the cancer war.*

There are two place settings, mine with the usual plate and utensils, his with a pitcher and syringe. His feeding tube has become a permanent fixture. He will not eat by chewing and swallowing. He will eat by pouring and waiting.

The liquefied concoction in Clay's pitcher consists of organic vegetables, whole wheat pasta or noodles, chicken or fish, protein powder, and some olive oil for good fat, all simmered into a soft stew, then whipped in a blender and strained through a sieve. We go through this process three times a day. The preparation allows Clay's food to slide easily down a quarter-inch tube and enter his stomach through a perfo-

ration just below his beltline. Swallowing specialists warned him not to take any-thing by mouth—not even water. If food slipped down his windpipe and got into his lungs, it could cause pneumonia.

We don't go out much anymore. We entertain at home, buffet dinners for stu-dents and Sunday brunches for friends. Clay never eats at these parties. His dietician, no gourmet, says Clay's diet is nutritionally impeccable—no sugar, salt, saturated or trans fats; no junk food, burgers, fries, pizza, bloody red meat, or artery-clogging cheeses and ice cream. I flavor the brew with vanilla, a scent that stimulates the appetite.

He could live for years on such a diet. But could he bear a literally tasteless life? In any case, we will never again savor menus together while sipping wine by candle-light in romantic restaurants. But stop! I catch myself wallowing in self-pity—a fool-ish waste of precious time. Never give in to it. I remind myself that my job is to widen the margins of our lives.

THE NATURAL INCLINATION AFTER *the fright of a recurring illness is to pull back and remain inside our comfort zone. But life without the thrill of the new can become humdrum and gradually close in, sealing our identities as patient and caregiver rather than as people with untapped potential to continue growing. I believe it is important to push ourselves out, plunge into life again, take a trip, find a healing place that will reawaken the spirit and render the world fresh and thrilling again.*

It could be as simple as a drive to a different climate or scenery. I know a couple who live in a city apartment. Every six weeks or so, they take a train to a riverside village an hour away and enjoy a romantic overnight in a bed-and-breakfast. The village is the kind of place where the husband, who has MS, doesn't feel shy about slowly crossing the quiet street alone, and his caregiving wife can rent a bike and hap-pily wheel around traffic-free streets.

I had enough frequent-flier miles from making speeches around the United States to fly us to Europe for nothing. And I had been saving for a family vacation to celebrate his recovery.

"How about taking a barge trip down the Seine this summer—bringing the kids with us?" I proposed one night at dinner. It wasn't simple, but I knew it would ap-peal to him.

"I've always wanted to do that," Clay said.

"So let's get out of this hiding mode. Go out and live like normal people."

"How do I eat on a barge?"

"We'll figure it out."

Traveling—Fearless or Foolish?

I didn't want to dwell on the last time we went to Paris. Then, Clay was a giant of a mind and we had lunches and dinners with his counterparts among European editors and writers. Ideas flew like sparks from a fanned fire. We ended every night in hungry love.

I knew it would be different this time, but not how different. Waiting for a taxi at Charles de Gaulle International Airport, Clay could barely stand up, utterly depleted by the night flight and no food except for a can of Ensure. He had to tell me—and I know he hated the humiliation of it—"Don't leave my side." As I dragged both of our bags into the courtyard of our cut-rate hotel at 8:30 A.M., after traveling twelve hours door-to-door from our New York apartment, I chided myself for thinking I could take this sick man on a transatlantic trip and make it joyful.

But I was Playing God.

He went to sleep while I ran out to find a blender run by European current. It was fun foraging for Greek yogurt and organic eggs, oatmeal, and ripe fruit. I stopped at Le Pen to buy prettily colored journals for Maura and her husband, Tim, and Mohm and her husband, Sean, to record their observations of our trip. Both daughters checked in at another hotel for a day and night with their husbands and friends before their week's confinement with the oldies. I couldn't wait for their bright company. To be honest, I needed help myself. They and Ella, Dr. Pat, and my sister, Trish, were the hands that held me up when I faltered. Every caregiver needs caregivers.

Back in the hotel room, I mixed a hefty breakfast for Clay with all his powders and potions, neatly packed for the whole trip. What to do for an in-room lunch?

I made up my mind right then. We were not going to hide in hotel rooms. Just because my husband had to eat through a GI tube, we would not give up going out to lunch or dinner. We would make an adventure of it. At four that afternoon, I crossed the street to a baby bistro and peeked inside. The Rôtisserie d'en Face looked informal with high red banquettes, all the better to hide our unusual table manners. The menu offered simple French traditional fare, free-range chicken flamed on a spit in an ancient brick oven. Perfect. No fancy quail or pigeon with bones or rich, up-all-night sauces.

I asked to speak to the chef. A young man appeared, eager to please. Would he be kind enough to use our blender and grind up a meal of chicken, potatoes, and fresh vegetables for my husband who must eat through a tube? I showed him the tube with its tiny aperture. "He cannot take any food or wine by mouth."

A look of horror clouded the chef's face. "Quel dommage!" In France, not to engage the sense of taste is an unimaginable fate.

"Toujours? Ou temporairement?" the chef inquired anxiously.

I couldn't bear to tell the probable truth. "Temporary."

"Oui, oui, revenez après sept heures."

He was welcoming us to return after seven—I was thrilled!

"Oh, madame, which veg-e-tahbuls?" the chef called after me. "Haricots verts?"

"Anything you have." I did not remind him that my husband wouldn't know the difference.

That evening Clay dressed impeccably. He carried his strainer in a small shoulder bag. He clearly doubted that any busy chef would bother to reduce his meal to the consistency of a milk shake. He was wrong. He watched with his nose as well as his eyes while I was served a glistening breast of free-range chicken, mashed potatoes dented with browned butter, and the promised string beans. When a waiter arrived with a silver carafe containing Clay's liquefied meal, he beamed as though being served my version—a scene he would describe to our girls in loving detail the next day. Two waiters carefully blocked the view while my husband poured the perfectly strained meal into his GI tube.

For dessert, the chef sent out a pitcher of strained red berries and a cup of whipped cream. I coaxed Clay to let the cream melt on his tongue, just this once. Bliss softened his face. As we prepared to leave the table, a middle-aged French couple came over to welcome us to Paris. None of the other patrons paid us the slightest attention. It was a peak experience and reinforced the lesson: If you strive to live a normal life, or the nearest equivalent, and you carry it off despite deformity or handicap, most people will accept you as normal.

That evening changed Clay's whole outlook. He was not ashamed to make love to me. He felt whole again.

Thereafter, we were fearless about eating out. If we could do it in a French restaurant, we could do it anywhere. And we did. Once we were back home, I got used to stopping in to confer with chefs or restaurant managers before making a reservation. They were almost invariably intrigued by the challenge and happy to oblige. We ate out in cafés with friends, in museum cafeterias, or in back booths of restaurants that I reserved in advance. We were no longer prisoners of chronic illness.

STRATEGIES

Don't Give Up on Traveling

Vacations are as vital as fresh air and music to revive the spirit. Traveling can change your entire outlook on the world. Happily, more and more travel agents now specialize in "barrier-free vacations" for caregivers and their loved ones who rely on a wheelchair and other medical aids. Your travels can be as ambitious as a safari in South Africa, or as tame as a romantic cruise to the tropics. Cruise lines strive to accommodate passengers with special needs with everything from more-accessible cabins to pool lifts.

"Tell me where you want to go!" the vibrant woman on the other end of the phone challenged me. She was Jani Nayar at the Society for Accessible Travel & Hospitality (SATH) in New York City (www .sath.org). SATH trains local agents and service providers to combine your special needs with previously challenging destinations. *Clay would have loved this,* I mused. Jani's voice interrupted my thoughts: "South America? Egypt? You can go anywhere now. The world has opened up to people with special needs." She began by referring me to three travel agents who specialize in safaris for people who are disabled.

A 2002 study found that people with disabilities spent $13.6 billion on leisure travel that year. The study was repeated in 2005 and got similar results. Travel agencies, hoteliers, car companies, and providers of equipment (scooters, oxygen tanks, wheelchairs, and hospital beds) eagerly compete for this growing population of travelers.

- **Smooth Sailing.** Accessible Travel & Leisure (ALT), founded by three British wheelchair users in 1997, devises barrier-free holidays for people who have difficulty walking or mounting steps. Their website (www.accessibletravel.co.uk) is full of testimonials about carefree travel in places one would never imagine negotiating in a wheelchair. Venice, for one. Cobblestones? Hundreds of footbridges? High water for six months? No problem: ALT specializes in finding hotels abutting vaporetto (water bus) docks. From there, wheelchair users roll easily aboard ferries that glide smoothly to central Venice and St. Mark's Square.

- **Railroads.** Eurostar (www.eurostar.com), the under-channel train linking London and Paris, has a special fare for wheelchair users. It also accepts registered assistance dogs and special diets.

- **Airlines.** Most airlines ease travel for handicapped passengers, with priority boarding and bulkhead seating. Some have wheelchair-accessible bathrooms.

- **Travel Agents.** To find travel agents attuned to customers with special needs, try SATH (see above) or the website for

ASTA (American Society of Travel Agents) at www
.travelsense.org.

- **The Whole Story.** Candy Harrington, known as the guru of
accessible travel, has written a definitive guide entitled
*Barrier-Free Travel: A Nuts and Bolts Guide for Wheelers and
Slow Walkers.* This book has all the details about traveling
by plane, train, bus, or ship. Candy has also written *There
Is Room at the Inn: Inns and B&Bs for Wheelers and Slow
Walkers.* Visit Candy's website at http://candyharrington
.com.

- **Driving.** Car rental companies are also addressing special
needs of travelers. Avis Rent A Car launched "Avis Access"
for Travelers with Disabilities and provides a dedicated
twenty-four-hour toll-free number, 888-879-4273, for
customers with special travel needs, along with access for
those with a hearing impairment.

  However, long-distance travel is too arduous for some.
  With a change in attitude and some creativity it is possible
  to enjoy time-traveling in one's own home. With music,
  movies, posters, and props, spiced with the cuisine of the
  imagined destination, a caregiver and her loved one can go
  almost anywhere.

THE VIEW FROM MEREDITH VIEIRA

Whenever I watched Meredith Vieira clowning as the irrepressible TV
personality on *The View*, I wondered how on earth she balanced that role
with the role of caregiver for a husband with multiple sclerosis. It was even
more unimaginable when she agreed to replace Katie Couric as cohost of

NBC's *Today* show in 2006. This was a much more demanding job, and she admitted that contemplating such a radical change drove her into a fetal position.

I read that her eldest son, Ben, had pushed her strongly to take the job. "He said, 'Jeez, Mom, this is a no-brainer,'" Vieira told the press. I asked if I could interview her about how she composed her public life with the demands of caregiving for a seriously compromised husband. She eagerly agreed.

Vieira burst into my office with an explosion of friendliness. Pitched forward on her three-inch heels, she wrapped me in a hug. This is Meredith Vieira in person, very much like her comfortable morning TV presence, only more so—spontaneous, sincere, utterly real, with her honeyed voice and off-center smile. She is in her midfifties now, with two sons recently off to college, a daughter in high school, and a husband who has had cancer twice.

"My emotions are right about here," Vieira admits, pointing to her mouth. "I have to lock them up at work, but they are ready to spill out at any moment."

She had been up since 3:00 A.M., as usual, to read the news for two hours before commuting into Manhattan to cohost the number one network morning show from seven to nine. The minute she gets back home to Westchester, she kicks off the showy heels and wiggles out of the tight skirt and cashmere sweater and becomes a jeans and clogs kind of girl. Then her life becomes mostly about her husband, Richard Cohen, once a powerhouse news producer at CBS where they met and married in 1986.

She remembers him from their dating days as a tall handsome athlete who jogged with her in shorts even in Chicago winters. But there was another side to him that she couldn't put her finger on. She told him, "There is a certain sadness to you, and yet when we are together I never see it, except in your eyes." Richard readily admitted that he had been diagnosed with MS when he was twenty-five. He even took Meredith to meet his doctor. In the waiting room she found herself staring at two or three men, the same age as Richard or even younger, all of whom had MS and were in wheelchairs. "It could be worse," she told herself at the time.

"Did I look at Richard and ask myself, 'Do you want to see yourself ten or twenty years down the line with somebody who might be in that position?'" She shook her head no. "I was falling in love."

For the first six years after they married, her husband's slowly progressing illness was not apparent to others and he insisted they tell nobody. His disease began manifesting itself with brief episodes of weakness, followed by remissions when his mobility returned to near normal. "Now it is getting worse, and where it stops, we don't know," she told me. "He walks with a cane and has very limited eyesight."

I asked where she found the energy for the job of caregiving that would await her at home. Her husband needs help with walking, although he denies it, and has often taken dangerous falls. Her reply startled me.

"I don't define myself as a caregiver," she said. "My husband doesn't like the term—it makes him feel diminished." She acts as an emotional caregiver rather than providing day-to-day care. "Richard compensates very well." The way she lives with the certainty that her husband's condition is worsening is by blanketing herself against seeing the adverse changes as long as possible. "I couldn't tell you what year it was that Richard started using a cane," she admits. "It all kind of runs together for me. I guess I'm in some denial myself."

The first shock of cancer blindsided both of them. "We were catapulted into a whole other realm." Her eyes widened. "That's when I felt, 'Wow! Now how will I define myself?'" She could not remember the year of that fateful diagnosis.

Cohen told me it was 1999. He called his wife just before airtime on *The View* to tell her the doctor found "something abnormal" in his colon. She remembers his voice being preternaturally calm. They went together to a consult with the doctor. Vieira was mobilized as the good reporter with her notebook. "I wanted to make sure I got down every detail and asked questions that Richard might not ask." Questions like, "What does malignant mean?" And "If you take out this malignancy now, is that the end of it?"

The answer came less than a year after his first surgery for colon cancer. This time when Cohen called during a break on the set of *The View,* she cried aloud, "It's back!" It isn't like Vieira to be hysterical—she's a doctor's daughter—but until that moment she had never thought about her husband's mortality. "I thought in terms of his getting weaker, and having a harder time negotiating life on a day-to-day basis. But cancer said to me, he could die. I felt this tremendous sense of guilt. Did I not ask enough questions?"

This is a common reaction to the Boomerang stage. We so often blame ourselves for not making prognostications that even doctors cannot. The truth is, we can't know the future for cancer survivors, and often they are secretive about new symptoms or doubts of their own.

"It's part of his denial, he doesn't want to acknowledge the space that he's in," she surmises. Cohen almost never asks for help, Vieira reveals, and that is an ongoing problem for both of them. His second surgery was more radical. Cohen was heavily medicated afterward and found himself wrestling with hallucinations in the hospital. "He called me in the middle of the night, saying there were spiders everywhere," Vieira recalls. "He knew it was the drugs but he was scared, and he never acts scared about anything." She found a friend to stay with their children and dropped everything to drive into Manhattan and comfort her husband.

Frightened as she was, she felt good about being needed. "I wish I could have more of that role, but Richard rejects it. It took a lot for him to make that phone call. It had to be true panic that allowed him to pick up the phone and say, 'I need you.'"

Recalling that episode explained a lot about why Vieira does not define herself as a caregiver. "I felt like I could be part of the solution, even for a situation as temporary as hallucinations," she said. "The bigger issue is that I'm not allowed to play that large of a role as Richard's caregiver."

Whenever she hears about a new holistic approach for mitigating the impact of MS, he meets her enthusiasm with resistance. For years she has been urging her husband to see a nutritionist. He refuses. She was excited to learn about the philosophy taught at Can Do Multiple Sclerosis (www.mscando.org), a nonprofit organization that invites families living with MS to come together and learn about dealing with fatigue, cognitive issues, and how to maintain well-being for the caregiver and the children as well as the MS patient. "I wanted us all to get more involved and to make it a family illness," Meredith says. Cohen said he wasn't ready.

"Richard usually says, 'I could be following these so-called cures until I'm dead. I just want to live my life.'" His way of dealing with stigmatizing ailments is not to hide or allow chronic illness to define him but to insist upon fitting into society on his own terms. Although he is legally blind, Cohen has written two books by pressing his face right up against the computer screen.

Vieira was delighted when her husband found an outlet for his own fears and furies by writing about them. Cohen's first book, *Blindsided,* is a brutally honest account of his refusal to surrender to the ravages of chronic illness. It was only in his second book, *Strong at the Broken Places,* that Cohen reached out to talk to and write about other survivors of chronic conditions who refuse to see themselves as victims.

"Richard's writing that last book was a significant event in all of our lives," Vieira said. "Being able to talk about himself in the first person, who he is and how he thinks about his own illness, has connected him with a huge network of people with all kinds of chronic illness. And that has provided him with tremendous self-worth. As a caregiver, you can't give them back their mobility, but you want to save their self-worth. I've seen that blossom again in Richard."

He counters his encroaching dependence with defiance. This is both admirable and sometimes downright dangerous.

"I remember getting very angry with him when we were crossing the street with the children and he was on a cane, moving slowly, not steady on his feet, and he wouldn't even wait for the light to change," Vieira told me. "He would almost dare the cars to hit him." When he dismissed her protests, she had to draw a boundary line.

"Don't put us in the terrible position of worrying about your crossing the street," she told him. "Do it on your own time if you must. But this isn't demonstrating independence. This is being pigheaded."

Meredith had to adopt a philosophy that allows her to live with the risks her husband takes and the possible recurrence of cancer. "You can allow yourself to go down the worst possible path instead of the best possible path, very easily, because that's where your fear lies," she says. "I don't put my head in the sand, but I do allow the layers [of denial] to come off a little bit at a time."

At this stage, her naturally careless optimism began changing. "I'm sadder now—I feel it," she said. Clearly, a shadow continues slowly but inexorably to cast itself over future plans. But within less than a moment, she threw it off, shook her hair, and gave a husky laugh at herself.

To calm her emotions when they become riotous, she calls up someone in her girlfriend circle and says, "Let's take a walk." Sometimes she walks alone for two hours at a time on a long bike path, ending up at the Hudson River. Her other favorite respite is to sit on the sand at the beach. "These are when I have my prayer moments, when I get outdoors and outside of myself, feeling spiritual and connected to something greater than myself."

Signing up for a four-year contract with the *Today* show that ends in September 2010 puts her in a position to stop working before she hits sixty, if she so wishes. "It's a fantastic job, but we don't know what will happen with Richard from one day to the next. I don't know where we as a family will be at that point, and that will decide it. Maybe I'll want to say to Richard, 'Let's go visit Gabe or Ben or Lily at college,' or 'Let's go away for a month, let's just travel.'"

———

WHEN I TALKED TO Meredith a year later, she was in a different turning on the labyrinth. The signs of progression in her husband's illness were now undeniable. Richard still refused to acknowledge the uncoiling of control over his arms and legs. But Meredith's attitude had changed again. She could no longer share his denial and live with the frustration and barely concealed fear. The stress of walking on eggshells had reached a breaking point.

"When you're not sure what's going to cause more tension and what isn't, you can build resentment and anger and frustration that's often based on fear," she said. Of course, she acknowledged, the person with the illness is having the greatest internal struggle, "feeling it in a way you as the caregiver never will, and you have to give them time to come to peace and terms with the situation." But time was running out.

She had reached the center of the labyrinth.

Meredith was ready to accept that her beloved husband is not going to get better; he will become progressively weaker. She had to be the one who introduced the conversation about those alien objects—the walker and the wheelchair.

"That's been the greatest relief," she said. "Open communication. So much stress comes from one partner being ready to deal with the oncoming reality, when the other one is not. With an illness like MS, you have to look ahead and come up with a game plan so you're not caught high and dry. For the first time, I'm really looking forward—not in terms of fear, but wanting to get control."

We all want control. And of course, a progressive illness like MS is uncontrollable. But Meredith is now taking clear, practical steps to deal with the cards she has been dealt, and that helps her enormously in getting through the day. "I know now that, if Richard were to fall, if we have a walker or a wheelchair with us, I can get him from point A to point B, and that makes me feel better. I'm still going to be upset if he falls, but I'm going to be able to deal with it, instead of just sitting there helpless so that there are two people lost."

She also needed a mini-trauma to lift the veil of denial about her own need, after fifty, to take better care of herself. For years Meredith coasted along without getting a physical. Then, last year, she had a scare with a mammogram. A false positive reading put her through a biopsy. "Everything was fine, but it shook me up," she says. "It did sort of remind me that I'm not superhuman.

"When I get angry at Richard for doing something I think is irresponsible, I always say to him, 'MS is a family illness.' My not going for my checkups potentially affects us all, as well. So, that famous expression 'Do as I say, not as I do,' well, I have to do it, as well." She consulted a nutritionist who has been very helpful in supplementing her diet with nutrients she needs to combat chronic stress and support her immune system.

Even as Meredith feels more grounded by being proactive and planning for the future, she and Richard are making the most of the moments. Their best moments in the last year took place when they took their son Gabriel to college. They stopped in the city where they met, Chicago, and basked in a nostalgic replay of their lives together. "This was where I first looked upon him and thought, 'What a jerk, I'm gonna marry him!'" It brought tears to her eyes.

They were also watching yet another child spread his wings, the second of three. "It was one of those moments where we could toast each other and say, 'Hey, we did good.'"

As they move toward the In-Between Stage, their goals are changing, too. "I don't feel that urgency to travel that I felt before," she said. "All these places that we said one day we would go, it just doesn't have the same importance to me. I feel an urgency to be *with* Richard. The world can be your living room."

What is uppermost now is not travel. It's time. Time spent together.

fourteen

TAKING CLAY TO MONET

My idea in taking my husband to France was to surround him with beauty and gentle joys. To me, joy is an intentional happiness that does not depend on fickle events or weather. We can create joy by consciously appreciating the smallest gifts of the day, of nature, of the kindness of strangers, of every stroke of love. Unhappiness seems to me a bad habit caused by ignoring earthly delights instead of looking for them.

We drove to the west bank of the Seine and met the children and their husbands. "Maura!" Clay shouted on seeing her. She kissed him warmly. I could feel a momentary transfer of his dependence. It unwound a notch in the coil of my constant vigilance. I was tired of Playing God.

I wanted Clay to see and smell Giverny, Monet's living work of art: his rose-colored country cottage, vast gardens, and the ponds that inspired his grand lily panels. It would be a treat for all of Clay's senses, excluding taste. And neuroscience is increasingly impressed with evidence that certain aromas, colors, and sounds can stimulate healing, not to mention the pleasure of escaping the boredom of a sickroom!

We found the famously trellised Japonais bridge still flowering in late July with wan wisteria and the delicate swaying of willows—Monet's painting come to life. Clay became more animated than I had seen him in weeks. He would sneak up behind Mohm and make one of his corny jokes or point out to her the history lesson behind the paintings. We learned that both of Monet's wives died before him. Most *of his friends and even his son died prematurely, followed by his gradual loss of sight. The only certainty the artist could rely on was the yearly rebirth of his garden. It inspired him to go on, through the glaze of double cataracts in both eyes, to stretch the canvas of his mind to mural proportions and to finish his last ten years rendering the ever-changing light and shadows on his lily pond, until his death at the age of eighty-six.*

It gave Clay hope. And it told me to keep on tending my own garden—it would outlast my husband.

WE COULDN'T WAIT TO *see the former cement barge that would carry us down-river into medieval France. The barge had been remodeled as a lovely little riverboat. A serious young woman introduced herself as the chef. She studied Clay's regimen like a sacred text, and we developed a menu that would please everyone, agreeing that aromatic herbs would be a fine way to tickle his appetite.*

I also counted on the healing powers of nature, a truism first noted by the Greeks, who built temples to their god of healing, Asclepius, high up on hilltops overlooking the sea. In our high-tech urban hospitals, nature is shut out. Most patients look at brick or concrete walls. Even if there's a view, it's often blocked by the ubiquitous green curtains separating beds. Any sense of day or night disappears, replaced by the "sundowner effect." Studies going back to 1984 have shown that patients heal faster if their beds are beside windows looking out on the natural world.

The salon of the barge had large windows and a long white sofa, made for lounging and gazing out at the bucolic countryside. The kids quickly found a hot tub on the foredeck, where they all dunked before dinner.

We had talked often about Clay writing his memoir. That was my hidden agenda for the barge trip. This seemed like the right time to encourage him to review his life, which can illuminate the moments of deepest meaning and threads of continuity. He resisted; he was an editor, not a writer. "Then talk your story to the children," I urged. "Maybe you'll discover more of yourself through their ears."

His temperature was as volatile as his moods. Suddenly feeling feverish, he would retreat to the lower cabin. If I suggested a short walk after dinner, he might snap, "No! I can't take the chance of getting a chill again." I lashed myself for putting his health at risk, but dammit, why couldn't he try harder to enjoy the now—this very moment, this unrepeatable gift?

The second evening, as a red sunset daubed the silver poplars, the barge turned off the Seine into the narrow, gentle Yonne River. Suddenly, Clay reappeared on deck. "It couldn't be more idyllic," he said. From then on, he spent sunny afternoons sitting on deck telling stories about the country we were sliding through. One was about French villagers sabotaging German invaders during World War II—how the villagers sawed down poplars to fall across roads and block panzer tanks. Later Clay mused, "This lovely little river, the purr of the barge, the gentle countryside passing by—I've wanted to go on a barge trip for years. But it's even better than I imagined."

We were six people together, spanning ages from twenty-eight (Mohm) to seventy-two (Clay), six people at different stages, temperaments, and tempos, confined for all but a few hours of excursion a day on a barge smaller than a basketball court. It was a condensed replay of family life, with its cycles of delight and drama. The shadow of Clay's mortality made every moment indelible. But I felt this precious time slipping away.

"Clay, we have two and a half days left," I nudged. "This may well be the last time you ever have your daughters' undivided attention. Do you really want to leave them with only bits of your life? They want your full story. It's a gift that only you can give. They're waiting. You promised."

He said nothing.

Defeated, I climbed the stairs to the lounge to read.

Ten minutes later, Clay appeared. Gruffly: "Okay, let's get this over with."

Sharing Family History

The girls started with the question "What drew you from Webster Groves, Missouri, to New York, the Big Apple?" Clay warmed up quickly. A life unfolded.

"My earliest concept of New York came on a visit to my grandfather, Henry Clay Felker, in Joplin, Missouri. I read the whole series of Horatio Alger books. They always featured young poverty-stricken boys, immigrants usually, who sold newspapers on the streets of New York and had absolutely nothing but luck and pluck—that was the name of a typical Alger book. But through hard work, *they would be befriended by some rich older man who would help them make their way."*

"So why did you identify with them?" Mohm, the Cambodian refugee, wanted to know. "You weren't an immigrant."

"In a way, I was, an 'immigrant' from the Midwest when I first came to New York. And I didn't have any money in that summer of '46."

"Weren't you at Duke?" Mohm asked.

"I'd been drafted out of college."

"You were in World War II!" That her stepfather had a connection with ancient history came as thrilling news to Mohm.

"The first thing I did when I got to New York City on the day I was discharged from the navy was to take a train from Bainbridge, Maryland, to Penn Station and tell a cabbie to take me to the street of jazz—Fifty-second Street off Sixth Avenue." The words were racing out of his mouth with surprising ease. "I ducked into a club called The Four Deuces and headed straight for the men's room and literally ripped off my navy blouse and pulled off my bell-bottoms and changed into the one civilian suit I had from college, a gray flannel pinstripe."

"What was the hurry?" Maura asked.

"Because I wanted to be part of New York."

I butted in. "Tom Wolfe likes to tell the story of your beginnings in Webster Groves, Missouri, with his own twist."

Clay chuckled. "Tom insists I was born with a dominant New York gene. He pretends he interviewed my sister and she told him that my first sentence as an infant was, 'What do you mean you don't have my reservation!'"

"When did you put out your first publication?" Mohm wanted to know.

"My first publishing venture—I was about eight years old—the Greeley Street News *was a neighborhood paper I printed on a hexagraph and sold for five cents."*

Maura's turn: "Where did you get the inspiration for the New Journalism?"

"In the stacks of Duke University library." His face was flushed with pleasure as he recalled one of those incandescent discoveries of youth. "I pored over the hundred-year-old journalism of Horace Greeley's famous newspaper, the New York Tribune," *he told us. "Greeley saw news as narrative. I read story after story about the Civil War written by soldiers—kids—boys who were living it,*

and writing about it with the vivid detail of novelists. It was so much more gripping than straight news stories."

Clay's storytelling that night revived his essence: the insatiable curiosity about how things work. It was not sociology, it was Felkerology. He was the teacher and his writers were the social archaeologists, digging up the underground culture of Wall Street, the culture of power-brokering in politics, the cop culture, the Mob culture, the new youth culture—New York ran the first inside story from a hippie commune and another from inside the head of a radical student bomber at Columbia. Clay insisted upon saturation reporting. His writers had to get inside their subjects' heads, under their skin, behind their eyes, and evoke their unique perspective through dramatic scenes and actual dialogue as vividly as a good novelist or short-story writer. That was how Felkerology helped to shape the New Journalism.

Recalling the thrill of experimentation with narrative journalism, Clay came fully alive that night. Before any of us knew it, church bells chimed the midnight hour. Suddenly, he faded. I helped him downstairs to bed. He felt hot. I put a cold cloth on his head and took his temperature. It was over 100. He called for Maura and Mohm. We surrounded him, Mohm holding his hand, Maura's hand on his head, and I curled beside him. They thanked him. He squeezed his eyes and whispered "Thank you" back.

"My three muses," he murmured.

———————————

STRATEGIES

Encourage Storytelling

Everyone has a story to tell . . . not everybody has someone who will listen. "Caregivers are so focused on how they're feeling, they don't remember they can still have a meaningful relationship with the person they're caring for," I was reminded by Amy

Trommer, a dementia-care trainer at the Alzheimer's Association in New York City. "Even people who have been married for years can discover information about their loved one they never knew and be able to share that information with the person as the disease progresses."

Caregivers are often too busy or don't know how to listen without correcting the person's story. It's not important to get the facts straight. What matters is to draw out what the patient remembers most vividly and cherishes about a story. Don't expect all the recollections to be sweet. Regrets will surface, too. Be prepared to be surprised, even embarrassed. Inhibitions fade as we get older.

If you freeze up when it comes to playing the interviewer of an elder, you can easily find books that offer prompts for questions to ask and space to jot down the answers. That leaves you with a record to remind your loved one where he or she left off, so you can pick up their life story in your next session.

In his little gem of a book, *Aspire!,* Kevin Hall urges us to understand that words are what connect us to one another. "They are the essence of who we collectively are. We should never underestimate the power of the right word spoken at the right time. Especially when a person's brain uncoils with the advance of Alzheimer's disease, every single word becomes so much more valuable."

He tells the story of a friend, Jim Dyer, whose wife and soul mate, Renie, was two years into her disease when Jim began listening more intently and taking notes on what she said. Over the next five years, he accumulated eight thousand words, every one of them a treasure, which he cataloged in a journal. As time went on, Renie seldom spoke at all. Occasionally, she would communicate in a language all her own. But Jim noticed that his wife seemed satisfied just by knowing that someone was listening.

One Thanksgiving, although surrounded by family and friends,

Renie could not be coaxed to say a word all day. Later, her son wheeled her over to the piano she used to love to play. She listened to her grandson play. Hall writes, "When he finished, everyone in the room heard Renie say two words in loud clear English—the two most important words she could have said on that day—'Thank you.'"

A volunteer trainer at Hospice New York told me that a large component of their training program is how to enhance listening skills. Some patients are only barely able to verbalize. It's important to be able to capture and interpret those words. They can be the touchstone for both the patient and caregiver to talk about their lives. By taking them away from the mundane details of illness and care, it can deepen their relationship.

Alzheimer's patients often find it easier to paint memories or emotions that they are no longer able to talk about. Alzheimer's trainers talk about how to stimulate conversation by journaling with the patient, or using photographs.

It's best not to correct Alzheimer's patients when they get facts wrong about people or places from the past. Don't upset them. Just go along. Simply ask them to tell you more about the person or place they have brought up. You may be able to fill in gaps of the story. By staying calm and patient, you can still have a meaningful connection with your loved one. And that's the goal.

The Alzheimer's Association has worked with StoryCorps (www .storycorps.org), a nonprofit organization that honors people's lives by recording their stories. National Public Radio airs StoryCorps segments on NPR's *Morning Edition* program and on the NPR website. Another resource is *Listening Is an Act of Love,* a book by Dave Isay, founder of StoryCorps.

At the Zen Hospice Project in San Francisco, each caregiver cultivates the "listening mind" through regular meditation or spiritual practice to help them develop awareness, compassion, and balance so they can respond to the needs of the dying and hear their stories.

"As hospice workers, one of our central tasks is to be available when stories are ready to be told," says Frank Ostaseski, founding director of Zen Hospice Project. The idea is to support dying people to recount their lives. Volunteers record the stories and send them to friends and families. The abbot at San Francisco Zen Center, Tenshin Reb Anderson, advises the hospice volunteers to simply "stay close and do nothing." Ostaseski said that's the best advice he's ever gotten. "We sit still and listen to the stories."

Why are stories important?

Stories are powerful and sometimes life-changing. To encourage family members to recount their version of their own past, even decades later, may change their perspective and the caregiver's as well. Telling their story can help them make sense of their life and imbue their existence with new meaning. Storytelling may also heal wounds and inspire forgiveness and reconciliation. It can explain motives to resentful children, a priceless legacy. Most important, it can dissolve regrets and allow the storyteller to die in peace.

Coming Out of the Cocoon

Friday, July 28, our final day. While packing, I idly flipped on CNN. Breaking news. Monica Lewinsky is glimpsed through a car window being driven into the arms of Ken Starr, the special prosecutor in the Clinton sex scandal. In her lap she holds a blue dress. She looks like a triumphant tart. The anchor salivates: "It could be the first physical evidence that she and the president had a sexual relationship!"

We were all disgusted. Our middlescent president's tacky affair had smutted up our pristine holiday. "It's showdown at the OK Corral," said Maura. We went around the breakfast table guessing whether Bill would come clean, tell the truth, and apologize to the American people. I suggested he was a born prevaricator. I was sickened to think of Hillary being dragged through the ultimate degradation and wondered how long she could lie to herself.

Clay came to full attention as the editor. He planted exactly the right story idea. "Write another piece on Hillary. Now! For Vanity Fair. *Then do a book."*

He was back as my full partner. My mentor, my inspiration, my champion. It was the way we first came together, as editor and writer, and the way we loved best being together. I couldn't wait to get back home to start researching a biography of Hillary.

As we disembarked the barge, it was Clay whose voice was dominant again: "Dinner! Our place! Rôtisserie d'en Face."

Hard as it was to plan this trip, I was proud of pulling it off. The memories would be among our most vivid. And the storytelling had revealed to us a Clay we had not known, the young, insecure "immigrant" from the Midwest hell-bent on becoming part of New York.

But the trip only reinforced my illusion of Playing God. On our dreamy voyage down a gentle French river far from real life—surrounded by a loving family, protected by an expert captain, served by a skilled chef—I had lulled myself into believing that yes, I could control our lives. Keep the monster at bay. Save Clay for another day. We would live like normal people. Forever.

Why Doesn't He Appreciate?

That fall I sent Clay back to Berkeley, with Saint Ella as his caregiver, while I stayed behind to work on the piece about Hillary and the Clinton marriage. We needed the money. And I needed a short break. After the peaceful barge trip, I had come to a boil of frustration and resentment at returning to the yoke of responsibility for making and taking Clay to appointments with a round of doctors to be checked out before he returned to teaching. We heard no worrisome news, but something wasn't right.

"I'm so afraid Mr. Felker's going to die," said Ella within minutes of my return to our Berkeley home in October. I was shocked at her words. Her cheeks were wet with thick tears. "Sometimes, when you're away, I get up at three in the morning and tiptoe up to his door to look in—I'm so afraid some night he might just slip away." She heaved her sobs into my shoulder, and I sobbed with her. "You got to slow down, Ms. Sheehy," she begged. "I love Mr. Felker, he's such a good man, but I

can't help it. I just feel like with all his weight slipping off him, his pants hanging heavy down in the bottom . . ." she broke off. "I can't bear to lose the both of you." She doubled over in weeping.

I cradled her head on my bosom. We switched roles for the millionth time. Now I was the consoling friend, and she was the distraught wife. Some days we switched a dozen times.

Then came the reality of facing Clay's condition. Shoulder bones poked out of his back like handlebars. Radiation burn had left a purple bruise on his throat. The tension of holding back the constant flood of oral secretions gave him a permanent scowl. When he met new people at a party, they were often intimidated or repelled.

While I was away this time his personality had changed drastically. Gone was the tender, openly loving, less defensive man who had returned from the barge trip committed, he told me, to show how deeply he loved me. The current Clay was sick, solitary, angry. He hated his dependency and saw his powers shrinking by the day.

During one of our coast-to-coast phone calls, Clay raged at me for "abandoning" him. He was furious that I planned to give our annual Thanksgiving party. "I told you, I don't want any more parties," he snarled. "When you try to help, you just screw things up." As time passed, he repeatedly called me stupid and selfish. I wanted to lash back. Sometimes I did.

Clay told Dr. Pat he knew he wasn't expressing affection or giving back much. "She saved my life, literally," he said. "I tell her I love her, but she doesn't seem to hear it." He said he was using all his energy just to get through the day. He had nothing left by night for himself, never mind for me.

Dr. Pat advised me to accept what he said. "Focus on taking care of yourself. Men pull in when the stress threatens to overwhelm them."

Ella wisely warned that if I responded to Clay's outbursts, it would eventually make me sick, too. "Just don't think about these phone calls," she advised. "Be like President Clinton—deny everything. If he can do it, so can we." We both laughed.

STRATEGIES

Protect Yourself from Patient Backlash

When people are really sick, they often revert to old defenses, such as denial or blaming everybody but themselves. Those defenses are familiar and take much less effort than learning new coping behaviors. When I pushed Clay, it just drove him into a defensive crouch, leaving us worse off than before. I had to learn a new approach.

I later discovered from scientific literature why seriously ill people often seem ungrateful or even hostile to those helping them. Apparently, the brain area that normally focuses on other people and the outer world shuts down when we become really sick, allowing another area that focuses on internal organs to become more active. This rechanneling of attention and energy is seemingly primed by the immune system as it mobilizes all defenses to repel invaders.

"We become exquisitely sensitive to internal signals from our throat or stomach or lungs, and acutely aware of every breath or twinge, and we lose interest in anything beyond the self," writes Esther Sternberg, author of *Healing Spaces*. Dr. Sternberg, an M.D. and immunologist, has done extensive research on brain-immune interactions for the National Institutes of Health. When we are really sick, she says, the burdened immune system literally erases all memory of our surroundings.

So how is the caregiver to react? A lot of elder abuse stems from the caregiver's repressed anger over being unappreciated.

Confide in a friend or a therapist or a spiritual counselor. Pedal it out on the treadmill. Slam it across the tennis net or down the bowling alley, but don't take it out on the patient. It will only thicken his or her shell. A longer-term solution is to find a creative outlet to express the full force of your anger—writing in your journal, dictating into a tape recorder what you really feel, or transposing those heightened emotions into music or songs or poetry or a play or a book.

fifteen

GUESS WHAT, WE'RE NOT GOD!

As the primary caregiver, you are the CEO of a start-up in the business of saving a life. Everyone looks to you to pull it all together. The better you are at rising to the occasion, and the longer you carry the lion's share of responsibility, the easier it becomes to feel like you're God. Paradoxically, this is the pitfall for the most devoted of caregivers.

In the back of my mind was the notion that I saved my husband from death by cancer and now I must save him from its return. I was vigilant. Hypervigilant. I had become very good at cultivating personal relationships with doctors and nurses who then bent over backward to treat my husband promptly and well. I coaxed him to try Reiki and chair yoga. I even got him to go on a Dean Ornish retreat, where the famed cardiologist persuades men, with scientific evidence, that the greatest healing medicine is love, given and received. Clay found it helpful and hopeful. His blood pressure decreased significantly.

When your caregiving efforts seem to work and your loved one improves, you may begin thinking your luck has turned. God has linked you to some higher power, real or imagined. It's very good for your ego. But I believe something deeper and more desperate may be going on. The more you sense your actual powerlessness to restore your loved one's health, or at least to keep him alive, the harder you strive to hold on to the illusion of control.

Then you hit the downside. When things don't go well, it must be your fault.

How many caregivers fall into the same trap? Frantic over our inability to control a disease process, we revisit childhood fears and revert to our most primitive coping mechanisms—just like our loved ones. It is easy to slip into catastrophic fantasies.

If and when we do accept that we cannot control our loved one's life course, we may swerve to the other extreme and feel ineffective, helpless, guilty. We are in danger of being consumed by what-ifs and remaining in crisis mode, a state of hypervigilance. Is this frenzy necessary? As Mark Twain once said, "I have been through some terrible things in my life, some of which actually happened."

The Codependency Trap

I was creating a codependent relationship. It left Clay ever more dependent on me, rather than less. I had to change my part in it. I had to give him back the power to make the decision to keep himself alive.

I went back over my journals written during Cancer War Two. A few yellow pages torn off a pad held a rich insight given to me by a therapist I worked with during Clay's treatment in Boston. She explained how projection works. "Your husband projects onto you the person who will make him feel better, help him through the day, the person in whose presence he can feel relaxed and emotionally supported."

What was wrong with that?

"Nothing . . . as long as you have no other life." I remembered her deadpan expression.

I told her that I had another life, as a journalist and author. It was my identity, and such as it was, my contribution. I wanted to continue to be part of the American conversation.

"Clay has to find his emotional voice," she counseled. "You've been propping him up emotionally for years. He needs to find out what he really feels. The more you play the nag, the less he'll do for himself!"

Remember this: You are not responsible for the course of a loved one's physical or mental condition. This is how I put it to myself as I dropped off to sleep each night: Let go, let God take charge. Life is like an ocean, sometimes calm, sometimes choppy, sometimes stormy. When the waves swell and become overpowering, resistance ensures defeat. Instead, relax and ride with the swells; pray and know

that sooner or later your feet will touch bottom. You will regain your equilibrium.
You will return to shore. And calm will return to the sea.

THE CONSEQUENCES OF PLAYING GOD

Debbie Burger, the alpha female (in Chapter 4) who runs her own roofing business in Oakland, California, had an *aha!* moment when I described the fourth turning of playing God. "My mom fell and broke her back, and my dad first got pneumonia right around the same time that my husband was diagnosed with Parkinson's disease," she recalled. "For the past nine months, I've been running back and forth between hospitals, first with my dad, then with my mom—literally back and forth, rescuing them from the brink of death. Constantly chasing down nurses and doctors to see what was going on. I saw my dad's pneumonia getting worse, my mom becoming more immobilized.

"There was a seminal moment for me when I realized that I was going overboard. The doctor came in after a long weekend, and I jumped down his throat. 'Why haven't you returned my calls in three days!' The doctor glared at me. 'You need to back off,' he said. 'You need to go take care of yourself, and you need to let us take care of your parents.'"

Debbie felt as if she'd been slapped. I asked her if she recognized this experience as what I call the Playing God phase. "Yes!" she said. "My whole role, my whole Playing God persona, my devotion, my expertise—all that had been yanked out from under me. Until then, I'd been full of self-praise. All during that weekend when the doctor was gone, I kept thinking: 'If I hadn't been here while the hospital staff was screwing up, my parents might have died.'"

She thought again. "You begin to feel it's your responsibility to pull them through each emergency and then get them well."

Debbie had reached a caregiver's deep end, the edge where desperation drives us to demand that we call the shots, run the show, pull the strings, and control the uncontrollable. It was the doctor's clear insight that pushed Debbie back on her heels and prompted her to call her caregiving friend Irene and say, "We have to go on a retreat—I'm getting crazy."

Irene Garcia-Sabourin, who was fighting for the life of her husband with Stage IV colon cancer, knew the place Debbie and I were talking about. "By the time you get to that place," Irene said, "it's like, oh my God, now everyone's looking to me to make every decision. You paint yourself into a corner."

We talked about how Playing God is a profound metaphysical stage. "You get caught up in the desire to control and it turns into rage—because in fact, we're all so helpless in the face of aging and disease," Debbie said. But all you do is alienate people. And by trying to force a result, you don't allow for other possibilities.

"Before I went on retreat," Debbie continued, "I was obsessing about my parents getting a flu shot: If my mom doesn't get a flu shot, her next cold will kill her! What if she gets the flu while I'm away! Then I caught myself. I had put Mom in hospice care a week before I left. She has caregivers around the clock. I pay for them. I don't have to be constantly vigilant. If something goes wrong, I didn't screw up, I didn't kill my parents. At some point, you have to let go."

Debbie had given herself that week's getaway from caring for her mother. While Debbie was at the ranch, her eighty-three-year-old mother got an infection, from which she died a month later.

"All the guilt came rolling over me," Debbie said. "But I was able to flip it. Without that break, I could not have stayed by her side, lovingly, during those last suffering weeks we went through together. I needed some distance to get a broader perspective. As caregivers, it is so easy to put ourselves in the God role and feel we are able to manage things that are really beyond our control. We can't do that and stay healthy."

We must have a sixth sense that tells us when the end is near. It's impressive to me that so many caregivers I have interviewed describe taking short vacations that turned out to be about a month before their loved one passed on. Perhaps we instinctively take time out to mobilize our physical and spiritual resources so we can be fully present for the last good-bye.

Debbie had an epiphany during that week on retreat. She had arrived at the ranch feeling a spring coiled up in her gut. "It was so tight I was afraid that if I let go, it would explode and I would fall apart. At the ranch I realized what the coil was. It was a huge burden of guilt: whatever I did, it was never enough. Getting away gave me the perspective that I was doing the best I could, and the best you can do has got to be good enough."

The breakthrough for Debbie and Irene Garcia-Sabourin came through finding each other. Each had husbands who were prematurely ill and parents who were rapidly declining. Now they sustained each other. As Irene described their sisterly bond, she said, "Debbie and I assured each other that we would make it through. We could be heroic in our role as caregivers, but we could also cry. We could openly admit we were angry at what we were going through, and somebody understood."

When the two women take a weekend getaway together, they explore the power of prayer. They share their difficulties and then have a conversation with God. "We both have a comforting realization," says Irene, "that God knows what we are feeling."

A gift of incalculable worth came to Debbie during the weeks when she sat vigil with her dying mother. She found boxes of letters that her mother had saved, every letter the two of them had exchanged. She was flooded with memories about her childhood in Africa. Her mother had started a book about it, but once she broke her back and became an invalid, she had not been able to complete it. Debbie took the letters to her mother's bedside and said, "Mom, I am going to finish this for you." She was transformed from a sallow, hollow-eyed old woman to one who glowed with joy.

This endeavor became Debbie's lifeline to come back. "I finally gave myself permission to do something I had been afraid of for thirty years. I found the story inside of me that I had been writing in my head all that time." To make time for this act of loving and grieving, she would flesh out her mother's book. But it soon became her own book. Debbie took an early retirement from her company, retained half of her ownership, and turned over the operations to her partner. She was also preparing for a future with a husband who was fighting Parkinson's disease and who might have only five more years of being self-sufficient.

"So I'm leaping into the void," Debbie said with a bounce of girlishness in her voice. "I'm setting off on a new career as a writer that may or may not be successful, but there's something very exciting about taking the risk and jumping off the cliff. It's joyful!"

STRATEGIES

Take a Reality Check

What are your expectations?

- Do you expect your loved one to get better? Or do you expect the worst? Imagining the worst possible scenarios only builds anxiety. It is important at such a point to talk to a therapist or spiritual guide or a well-grounded friend, who will hopefully make you aware of what you are doing. Most people, if they learn to catch themselves in this kind of destructive mind chatter, can flip their thinking back to the reality of the present.

- Who can give you a medical reality check? You will spare yourself much stress if you ask somebody familiar with your loved one's disease—a neutral professional, or better yet, another caregiver—to give you reality checks on a regular basis. This will allow you to be more effective in helping where you can do so best.

- What does your loved one expect from you? It's important to clarify that your primary role is not to be doctor or nurse or therapist, but to be an advocate with the professional care team and to offer consistent emotional support. The emotional part is vital and often quite subtle. For example, when Debbie Burger gave her mother the reasons she had to get away to a health ranch to repair herself, the older woman surprised her by freely giving her blessing. The giving helped her mother feel empowered.

- Has your loved one begun to come to terms with loss and frailties? We don't do any favors by constant cheerleading or supporting their fantasies of a full return to their old selves. Dr. Fisher had to warn me against telling my husband he could go back to normal swimming after his radical surgery. As it turned out, he could still swim, but he had to relearn how to compensate for new restrictions. If you're the one with unrealistic fantasies, ask your primary doctor to talk privately with your loved one and set realistic goals between them. If no doctor is willing, try passing on the facts as you understand them to a pastor or therapist or a best friend. Let that person have the conversation.

- Do you see your loved one's recovery as your sole responsibility? If so, consult a best friend, pastor, or therapist.
- Can you accept the truth? It's simple: nobody can or should handle this job alone for long without adequate help. If you seem unable to let go, you absolutely must ask a social worker how to spell yourself. Without help, you're likely to get sick and ultimately fail to meet the impossible goal you set for yourself.

Set Boundaries!

Parents and spouses who are ill can become master manipulators. They know how to play off each member of the family against the others to get what they need or want. The person they feel most comfortable with is the person who always gives in. Don't let that happen to you. Set some rules—give-and-take. And introduce other family members, friends, or care helpers early, before your loved one and your siblings and relatives get used to you being the family hero—the solitary caregiver.

sixteen

WHEN A COUPLE IS
DIVIDED BY DEMENTIA

"It was one of those things that happens to somebody else," says Keith Wolfard, a firefighter who was accustomed to rescuing people in his work. He is tall and solid as a hickory tree, with a grand flourish of thick gray mustache that droops to his chin. A guy's guy. Never in his wildest dreams did he imagine, as a man, that he would become tapped as a full-time caregiver in his own home.

They were only in their fifties, Keith and Daphne, enjoying a blissful second marriage. Daphne was fiercely independent, ever ready to prove she could reel in game fish bigger than herself. With his own strong hands, Keith built them a beautiful early retirement home deep in the tall firs of rural Oregon. He didn't want to acknowledge his wife's creeping dementia. When Daphne's friends alerted Keith to her abnormal behavior, the couple made the rounds of doctors. No fewer than three physicians dismissed the idea that she had the dreaded disease, Alzheimer's. The couple relaxed and tried to forget about it.

Doctors often resist listening to caregivers when they describe symptoms of concern in a family member. Keith finally had to make a trip to Oregon Health Sciences Hospital where Daphne could have a complete diagnostic workup by a team specializing in the disease. It took a spinal tap to reveal the protein associated with Alzheimer's. She had the disease. But the upside of early discovery and treatment was that it slowed the progress of unraveling in her brain for another seven years.

After the devastating diagnosis, Keith set up a New Normal routine for them. As Daphne's disease progressed, he came to accept that "I had to create new New Normals for us every day." Being a rescuer both by nature and profession, he devoted himself to "saving" his wife.

Keith was still able to work his part-time job as a long-haul trucker. But over the next seven years, he refused any help, except occasionally from his daughter. "I'm a big strong healthy guy, and hey, as a firefighter, I'm used to stress," he would tell concerned friends. "I saved people and I dealt all the time with death and dying."

With strangers he could protect himself with emotional detachment. "With someone you love who has Alzheimer's, it's entirely different," he said in retrospect, staring at a photo of his pretty wife. "It's emotionally draining. The person you looked forward to having a good full life with, enjoying the things we all look forward to, you're seeing now deteriorate before your very eyes, slowly, very slowly." Keith was losing the love of his life, her zigzag deterioration marked by fading awareness, interrupted by sudden clarity, even giddiness, and then back to the slow, insidious dimming. The ambiguity of it all was torturous.

Fearing his own destruction as a husband and a rescuer, Keith mounted that familiar defense—Playing God. Those of us who make this turning in the labyrinth of caregiving do so with the best intentions and utmost compassion, but also out of fear. We work so hard to fix the problem—we commit so much of ourselves—that, in effect, we fear that if we fail to save our loved one we will lose ourselves. Thus we're driven to work even harder, take even more responsibility, becoming our loved one's sole rescuer. He or she inevitably becomes even more dependent, reinforcing our own delusion.

Ahead of us lies a great fall: the cold truth is that no matter how hypervigilant we may be, we cannot control implacable disease.

Keith's fragile world shattered on the awful day he lost Daphne when she literally lost herself. Unable to get home from his trucking job in time to take his wife to a doctor's appointment, he asked Daphne to drive herself and said he'd meet her there. But Daphne never appeared. Keith began dialing her cell phone. He took comfort in knowing that he'd placed her phone in her glove compartment with an automatic recharger.

After several hours, she answered! With huge relief, Keith asked where she was. Daphne couldn't say. "Can you pull into a gas station and get its address?" Daphne didn't respond. Hour after hour, he asked the same questions. Finally, he asked Daphne to repeat his words. She scrambled them.

"Something had gone wrong in her brain. She couldn't even comprehend my questions."

As Keith recalls that moment, his eyes tear up. The disease had finally rendered him and the police and the cell phone company powerless to help. Dr. Pauline Boss describes how caregivers in Keith's position must learn to live with things they cannot fix. "It is especially difficult for people accustomed to averting the greatest tragedies," she says.

Lost for eleven hours, Daphne finally pulled into a gas station near midnight as a cold front sliced through the area. The attendant filled her tank, but she could not produce her cash or credit cards. He thought she was drunk and called the police. She was forty-five miles from home.

This was the Boomerang, a forced turning in the labyrinth of caregiving. The disease had resurged, wrecking all their efforts to adapt to it. Once Keith had Daphne back in his arms, he knew she needed twenty-four-hour supervision. Her behavior changed; she became easily angry and combative, like a terrified child. Her own daughter recoiled from these changes in her mother's personality, very common in the later stages of Alzheimer's.

GRIEF AS FEAR

Fortunately, this episode punctured Keith's fantasy of Playing God. He now recognized that he had to reach out for help and find ways to nurture himself.

He was already grieving the incremental loss of his wife. It was the kind of grief, closely related to fear, that C. S. Lewis describes in his elegiac book *A Grief Observed*. Watching his wife die of cancer, Lewis writes: "When I speak of fear, I mean the merely animal fear, the recoil of the organism from its destruction; the smotherly feeling; the sense of being a rat in a trap."

Keith now did everything for Daphne: he fed her, brushed her teeth, took her to the bathroom and cleaned her. As he sank deeper and deeper into grief, he gradually discarded almost everything that defined his previous life. "I felt my whole focal point was my wife's care, and I kind of let things slide for myself."

He rarely let Daphne out of his sight. He stopped working, stopped going out to the garage to pursue his passion for restoring old cars. He even begged off the annual "wild hog" motorcycle trip with his Harley buddies. When anybody offered to help, he insisted that he was a big strong man who needed no help. Soon he became a "rat in a trap," isolated in the early-retirement home he had built for two happy people. Following Daphne around all day to make sure she didn't fall or burn herself, he would peer out the windows at the fir needles piling up in the driveway, rejecting even his former pleasure in manicuring the grounds that he and Daphne had so lovingly planted.

Keith and Daphne were now on different paths. He was moving close to the center of the labyrinth of caregiving where, if our loved one clearly cannot recover, we must begin the hard work of recovering ourselves. Daphne's path was a slow but inexorable decline. Keith's only hope was to find the thread that would lead him back to life, through human connections and a return to his passionate hobbies.

REENTERING THE OUTSIDE WORLD

Keith took the first baby step by hiring a home health aide for a few hours every day to look after his wife. He then found the "Powerful Tools for Caregivers" program (first mentioned in Chapter 4) that saved his own health and sanity. PTC is an education program that teaches caregivers the skills and confidence to better care for themselves while caring for someone with chronic illness.

"There are two objectives," says Donna Schempp, senior program director at Family Caregiver Alliance. "One is having a life after you're a caregiver, and one is having a life while you're being a caregiver. If you don't take a break, all your good work is going to be for naught."

Keith was crazy about old cars, and a weekend car-swap meet was coming up that he'd always loved attending with his Harley buddies. He told his PTC classmates: "Daphne's disease has finally reached the point—I knew it was coming but wasn't ready to admit it—that I have to reenter the outside world."

When the aide called in sick the day before the car-swap meet, Keith called a nearby foster care home. The director encouraged him: "Why don't we try to bring Daphne up for the weekend and see how it works out." Keith packed a few things for his wife, made sure to include her favorite stuffed animals, and sat with her at the foster home until she felt comfortable.

Once he reconnected with his buddies, "I did let myself go to a degree," Keith told me. He was a guy again, shouting, laughing, drinking beer, crashing late, and then, suddenly, it was Sunday evening. He rushed back to the foster care home. The director met him at the door.

"It went fine," she assured him. "We've made the transition already. You know it's going to have to happen at some point. Maybe this is the time to make that decision and make it happen now."

All at once, he had rounded the circle and was smack at the center point of the labyrinth of caregiving. He had to choose: go down in despair, with his wife, or begin the baby steps of the sixth turning, Coming Back. I asked if he had actually reached that point.

"That sounds right," he said. "But I still wasn't ready. With professional help, I could see that sooner or later I was going to have to let go. I knew that somebody else would have to provide Daphne with the care she needed. And no question: she was in better hands there, dealing with professionals who do it on a daily basis. But I still struggled with the sense that I was abandoning her."

Keith did leave Daphne in the facility, but it was no abandonment. He visited Daphne every day, taking her out to lunch or for a long drive. But he needed the rest of the day to begin reclaiming himself and remembering what nourishes him. He spent mornings cleaning the house and yard; he tinkered with his precious antique cars; he got up earlier and earlier. He learned, to his surprise, that when he is gone, Daphne does not miss him; she isn't fully aware of his absence.

"But when I go there to see her, she lights up like a lightbulb."

This was the beginning of Keith's retirement from Playing God. As we talked about our shared experiences, we both felt more hopeful that we could move beyond this turning. I promised to revisit Keith six months later and we'd compare notes on our journeys. I will pick up Keith's story in Chapter 21 in The Sixth Turning: Coming Back.

Meet Keith Wolfard online. Go to my website www.gailsheehy.com/ caregiving.php.

STRATEGIES

Revise Your Attachment

The deepest sadness is to grieve for the loss of a loved one who is still here. But we must begin at some point to accept that there will be no great reversal. We can only save ourselves by "revising our attachment," as Pauline Boss puts it in her book *Ambiguous Loss* (Harvard University Press, 2000). "We don't cut ourselves off from a loved one, even after death, but we have to learn the most exquisite of balancing acts: how to remember what was and honor it, and at the same time commit to going on."

With Alzheimer's disease, of course, she or he will never fully return to you. That is the torture of dealing with the forgetting. Your loved one doesn't remember when you last came, or that you were just there; but you do. It is imperative that you reach out to people who do light up when they see you. That means going out for coffee or dinner with people who are fully present, even as you continue to visit and touch the person who has dementia. Dr. Boss says short visits are better than long stays. If the caregiver is depressed or anxious, the patient picks it up. "Caregivers must connect with people in the healthy world so they can be less anxious and angry and lonely when they visit the world of dementia."

Powerful Tools for Caregivers

I cannot recommend highly enough the "Powerful Tools for Caregivers" (PTC) training program. As I discussed in Chapter 4, this program was developed in Portland, Oregon, by Legacy Caregiver Services, part of Legacy Health System, a regional health center; and it is free. The pioneers, Kathy Shannon and Leslie Congleton, were two caregivers determined to aid family members with cognitive decline. Committed to helping others in the same situation, they began publicizing the program across their state. Fortunately, Oregon is the most progressive state in health-care initiatives for the elderly. As mentioned earlier, more than eleven hundred class leaders in twenty-eight states have been trained to teach the program. It works for caregivers in all kinds of situations, not just Alzheimer's.

The six-week PTC program is held weekly for ten to fifteen caregivers. They're taught how to balance their lives and make tough decisions. Specifics include how to use community resources, manage stress better, communicate effectively, and cope with unruly emotions such as anger, fear, and despair.

Confidentiality is assured. "In many ways the classes resemble intimate support groups or private therapeutic counseling sessions," says Miriam Callahan, project coordinator at the Caregiver Resource Center in Buffalo, New York, which offers a PTC course. The privacy allows tears, confessions, and soul-searching.

One key tool is the "Action Plan." Participants pledge to do something very personal every day for a week. It can be anything pleasurable that completely removes them from caregiving—bike riding, swimming, listening to music, working on cars, doing yoga, having coffee with a friend. The results can be quite poignant. One woman managed to go to the end of the block, buy a cup of coffee, and walk back to find that the world hadn't ended and that her mother was still alive. Later, she was able to walk around the block every day and then to the library for one hour, while an attendant took care of her mom. She took pleasure in reading a book and sipping a coffee. Like man's first step on the moon, it was a beginning.

For information about PTC and to find a leader in your area, call Jean McFalls at 503-413-8018 or e-mail caregiver@lhs.org. PTC is offered collaboratively by many nonprofit organizations such as AARP, Area Agencies on Aging, Cooperative Extension services, and parish nurses. Participants receive *The Caregiver Helpbook*. Oregon classes include some in Chinese and Spanish.

To obtain information about Legacy Caregiver Services, based at Portland's Legacy Good Samaritan Hospital & Medical Center, go to http://legacyhealth.org. Or call 503-413-7706 (Oregon), 360-487-1188 (Washington).

Connect with Other Well Spouses

Isolated caregivers can share experiences with peers via the Well Spouse Association, a welcoming support group for men and women with diverse caregiving profiles, ranging from newcomers to thirty-year veterans to widows and widowers eager to give back hard-won lessons. WSA provides local support groups, publishes a newsletter, and offers chat rooms on its website (www.wellspouse .org).

Is It Really Alzheimer's?

Here is a shocking estimate: 33 percent of American women will die with dementia. But before you clutch, you need to know that many will die before dementia surfaces as a real problem. And not all dementias are Alzheimer's; aging brings many other milder cognitive changes, to say nothing of memory loss caused by everything from depression to mismanaged medications.

Alzheimer's itself is very difficult to diagnose and is often missed by doctors who say, "She's old, what do you expect?" To get a clear diagnosis, you must have a diagnostic workup and see a neurologist. Some states have free diagnostic centers.

When overused, some popular sleeping medications can

exaggerate memory lapses and produce symptoms similar to those of Alzheimer's. Dr. Jairo Rodriguez, a certified clinical nutritionist in New York City, often sees patients over fifty who complain of an amnesia-like sensation. "When I ask, they're usually taking a prescription sleeping medication on a regular, long-term basis. My clinical experience with patients taking 5 or 10 mg of Ambien per day is that it can enhance a predisposition to memory loss. If a patient also drinks alcohol, both create a depression in the central nervous system. Over time, the combination can create a huge effect." Is it reversible? Yes, Rodriguez says, but it may take several months.

Dr. Mary Sano, a neurologist and research director at Mount Sinai Alzheimer's Disease Research Center in New York City, has studied the disease for most of her life. "Beware using any psychotropic drug," she told me. "Ambien is in the same class of drugs as Librium and Valium. They all blur cognition. Even worse is occasional use in the elderly because they have no tolerance to it. Ambien has a record of creating more memory loss."

The good news is that recent research shows the actual incidence of Alzheimer's is going down in the United States. As levels of education and health care rise, the risk of dementia apparently decreases. Older people today are more cognitively stimulated, they spend more time communicating via computers and reading, which keeps the brain active and delays dementia.

The best diagnostic tools for Alzheimer's combine taking a good history and looking for evidence of cognitive impairment, says Dr. Sano. Getting reports from family members or close associates about changes in behavior in the person's everyday life could be convincing enough, unless it's a young person. Impaired memory is the earliest clue. A diagnostic evaluation is worthwhile if your loved one has been showing symptoms of short-term memory loss and confusion over the past six months. With some behaviors, a doctor can tell you right away, "Don't worry." If a person says, "I go into a

room and forget what I came in for," that happens to all of us as
we get older. Perfectly normal. But if a person says "I lost my car
three times" or a family member reports that Mom's electricity has
been shut off because she forgot to pay the bill, those are signs of
cognitive changes.

The local Alzheimer's Association can tell you where to go for a
basic screening, or ask your internist. If the doctor does a cursory
test and brushes off the family's concerns, the family that persists
will certainly be referred to a specialist. Mary Sano advises starting
with the health professional who knows the patient best. "It would
be the rare doctor who would ignore a family member who called to
say, 'I'm worried about my mom.'"

Fifth Turning: "I Can't Do This Anymore!"

seventeen

TRAUMATIC TRANSITIONS

Following our healing barge trip in France, we were blessed with a seven-year reprieve between health emergencies. From 1998 to 2005, Clay seemed to gather energy. He had the rare good fortune of finding a role in which his passion and experience fit like a second skin—call it the Guru Stage. As founder of the Felker Magazine Center at UC Berkeley's Graduate School of Journalism, he was attracting talented young editors and writers in their twenties and thirties who were eager to put themselves to the test under his leadership. "They're on fire with the idea of having a magazine, just like I was," he told Charlie Rose in a PBS interview.

On Thanksgiving of 1999 Clay was feeling renewed after a full forty-session course of hyberbaric treatments, lying in a closed oxygen tank to revive the deadened tissue in his throat so medication could be absorbed. Mohm and her husband had flown out to Berkeley and were helping to set the table for a holiday feast with a few friends. (No Thanksgiving party, according to Clay's wishes.) It was two days before my birthday. The phone rang. My hands were wrapped in baking dough for a cranberry upside-down cake and the chanterelles for Alice Waters's turkey stuffing were sautéing too quickly, so the phone slipped out of my hands. Clay handed it to me.

"I wanted to wait until your birthday to tell you," Maura stammered, "but I couldn't wait—I'm pregnant!"

Joy swelled all over my body and tears squeezed from my eyes. Clay had recovered enough of his voice to be understood and enough of his life force to be loving again. Both my daughters now had graduate degrees. And now the most delicious news of all—I would be a grandmother.

The week after Thanksgiving, I gave birth to my thirteenth book. Hillary's Choice *was published on November 29, and I was off on a whirlwind book tour. It was a very good year. We had made a full circle of life, and nobody had died from it. We go on.*

On 9/11, Clay was in Berkeley, asleep and unaware of the annihilation at Ground Zero. That national passage shattered the expectations of all Americans. Our "homeland" now shared a vulnerability to mass terrorism with most of the rest of the world. As soon as possible, Clay flew home to his beloved New York. It was late at night in a pouring rain when we made a walking pilgrimage down to the smoking ruins. A bagpiper wailed in the gloom. Press passes allowed us up close. A New York City transit manager was crawling around the pile looking for any sign that his wife was still alive. The steaming phantasmagoric ruins seemed to hiss no survivors.

A few weeks later I set out to explore the human side of the catastrophe for Vanity Fair. *In Middletown, the New Jersey suburb that suffered the largest concentrated death toll at the World Trade Center, I saw a microcosm of how we as Americans would deal with this national tragedy. Over the better part of the next two years, I lived half of every month in Middletown. Visiting with grieving families, including four women who became known as The Jersey Girls, was both exhilarating and depressing. During this period, Clay took care of me for a change. He always called when I was in Middletown to urge me to take a warm bath and drink hot milk and call a therapist to unload the sorrows I was absorbing. Then I'd fly out to sunny Berkeley and sit on our deck and write. It turned into my next book,* Middletown, America: One Town's Passage from Trauma to Hope.

In 2004 we were blessed with a second grandchild, this time a baby girl who, from the moment of her first choice of "blankie," preferred pink. On a personal level, this New Normal was shaping up as possibly the best ever.

But during this long escape from darkness, another cancer lurked in wait. In early 2005, lymphoma attacked Clay in the shoulder, directly below the site of his two courses of radiation. He immediately began chemotherapy, laced with the antibody Rituxan. We decided to stay in California for the duration. Our trusted oncologist, Dr. Coleman, directed the treatment by one of his former colleagues, Dr. Jeffrey Wolf, at Alta Bates Hospital in Berkeley.

The year 2005 marked our fourth battle with the Big C. We would beat it, of course. We were hardened veterans by now.

Chemo—Killing to Cure

But this time the treatment was chemotherapy. I had to suspend work on my next book, a subject, ironically, that was the last thing on my mind: Sex and the Seasoned Woman. My job now was to shepherd Clay through the next four dreadful months with several frantic trips to the emergency room. He kept right on teaching.

The chemo was brutal. It played havoc with his heart rhythms. Then strange new symptoms appeared. Clay now felt as if he were walking on Jell-O. It turned out that one of the chemo agents commonly used for lymphoma at the time, vincristine, leaves most recipients with neuropathy, a partial deadening of nerves in the legs or feet that makes balance precarious. (They don't tell you about this beforehand. Most of the newer agents used in chemotherapy for lymphoma also commonly leave some degree of neuropathy.)

He couldn't take the stairs in our idyllic house in the steep Berkeley hills. We had to give it up and move to a ground-floor condo in Oakland. But the condo had a sunny window wall overlooking a golf course. Before moving, I selectively dug up slips of my favorite flowers and shrubs and even a few dwarf maples and baby bamboo trees. Clay and I created a pocket version of our old terraced garden on our new condo terrace. We sat out there in the cool of sundown, listening to the trickling of a fountain and watching the deer gather to lay down on the velvety fairway.

When the chemo ended, Clay was assured of "prolonged survival."

One evening, as Clay stood looking down at the kitchen counter, his knees unbuckled and his torso went rigid. His eyes blurred, his body sank to the floor, and he uttered a slurred command—"No nine-one-one!" Of course I called 911. Seven minutes later, three giant firefighters loomed in our doorway lugging all the paraphernalia necessary to stop a stroke in its path. What they ended up doing was no more than laying Clay flat, raising his legs above his head, and injecting warm water into his bloodstream.

"Positional hypotension," the medical officer pronounced.

"Hypo, not hyper?" I asked.

"Hypo is when blood pressure drops rapidly. In older people with poor circulation, blood pressure can plunge just because the person changed position too quickly—got up too fast, say, or leaned over a sink, compressing the blood supply in the neck. Suddenly, not enough oxygen gets up to the brain and the person begins to lose consciousness."

"I feel dumb calling you out just to give him a hot water injection."

"No, you were right. If we didn't get him flat and his legs raised, he could have had a stroke. The hot water was just to get the blood moving to his heart and brain faster."

"Clay, are you okay?" I was anxious.

"Fine!" To prove it, he sat bolt upright. The EMS men barked at him to remain flat until they took his pressure again. He thanked them but begged not to be taken to the hospital. No chance. We spent the evening in the emergency room.

Round-trips to the Emergency Room

After that, I thought I knew how to avoid the ER. Whenever Clay got that glazed, unfocused look and wooden soldier body, I would repeat the ministrations of the firefighters, as efficiently as one repeats a familiar recipe.

Since I couldn't get back to New York to work with my editor, I hired a freelancer. Monica Bauerlein was not only balancing a job as coeditor of Mother Jones, she came to our condo with her newborn in a sling. One day when we were deep into editing, we heard a loud thump from the bathroom. Clay was sprawled on the floor, unconscious. Monica and I couldn't lift him. She ran for the phone.

"No, wait, I can fix it!" I called. But before I knew it, the sirens were screaming. EMS was rushing in. Clay was being rolled into the hall on a gurney. The busybody septuagenarian who fancied himself the building manager suddenly appeared. He had a curdled look.

"This is the third time you've had an ambulance blocking our garage. We can't have you here anymore!"

Another traumatic transition. Clay was unable to finish out the semester, so we left for New York in April. He vowed to return for the fall term, and to keep hope alive, I ignored the busybody and continued to pay rent on the condo for the next year. Back in the city we began to establish yet another New Normal. Clay set up a vigorous rehabilitation program. He refused to consider a wheelchair.

Then came a bizarre night at Lincoln Center Theater. Clay and I were seated in a tight, hot corner of the topmost row, wedged against a wall, for a play about a murder. When Clay fell asleep, his head folded over his neck. An hour in, his body stiffened and I thought—Oh, God, how do I lift a two-hundred-pound man over six other seat-holders at the climax of Act One?

My frantic attempts to bestir him failed. I had to pass a whispered plea down the aisle to summon the firefighters. Ssshhhhhhh was the hiss that met my plea; the New York culturati were not interested in a real-life tragedy, only in the murder about to take place onstage. My heart began beating again only when two burly firefighters cantilevered Clay's dead weight over the heads of the peevish patrons. Once the firefighters laid him flat and raised his legs and I rubbed his feet to encourage circulation, he quickly revived.

We would never again go to a play or movie without a wheelchair.

Fateful Conversations

Clay was speaking as little as necessary. At our dinner parties, he now dropped out of the quick and jaunty badinage, not wanting to break the tempo. The brilliant intelligence in his eyes would dart from one speaker to another, the only reminder of how his voice and ideas used to dominate any dinner table through the sheer force of his intensity about getting to the heart of a story.

Over a private dinner one night, Clay casually answered my equally casual question, "So, how did the CT scan come out?"

"Fine. No change."

"Did you discuss it with Dr. Coleman?"

"Not yet."

"But that's fabulous news!"

"Yuh."

He didn't want to show me the report. "I can't trust you." He scowled. "You'll attack me." Attack him? His reaction made no sense to me. And the test didn't explain why he had trouble breathing and talking and swallowing. We both knew some inexorable organic process was going on, it wasn't good, and *nobody was touching it. The only test that can be trusted at times like this is intuition.*

I couldn't wait to talk to my soul sister, Dr. Pat. After a sleepless night, I found her at six in the morning in the bare antiseptic setting of a New York hospital examining cubicle, where she was waiting to deliver a baby. I knew Pat kept in touch with Clay's doctors. I asked her why was Clay having more trouble than ever speaking and swallowing his secretions.

"His trachea—his windpipe—is beginning to narrow," she said in her even professional voice. "It's the radiation effect. Tissue necrosis it's called." She sat opposite me in a metal chair, drained of sleep, draped in her pallid green scrubs, and invited me to spill my scattered fears. Then she pulled them together and shaped them into one sharply pointed question.

"You chose this man," she began. "You engineered his return to life and a new dream on the West Coast. What you're really asking yourself at the deepest level is 'Do I want to stay with Clay during his long, not-yet-dying years?' Recommit at the peak of your flaming fifties, when you're at your most delicious, sexiest, toned, terrific, wise, energetic, and still climbing in your career? Do you want to put in the next ten years with a man you love who is older, aging faster, and not healthy— knowing you could be seventy when he goes, in descent yourself, and alone? Clay's no fool. He must know at some intuitive level that's the question you're playing with. That's why he's attacking you. Most women couldn't even ask it of themselves."

A long pause. I stared at her solemn face, her clear blue eyes and pale freckly skin—a mirror of myself, ten years younger, another survivor, both of us self-made successes but vulnerable to the losses of aging like everyone else. Then she said something that made her eyes spill over with tears.

"Generosity becomes you. I'm a beneficiary."

The decision that would shape the rest of my life was boiled down to a few simple words. In that brief, soul-baring conversation, I knew that my proper destiny was to stay with Clay and fight. To see the war through. I have always been a fighter. So was he.

My insight: As a little girl, I was pitted in swimming races from the age of five against boys much bigger than I. With the starter's gun at my back and my father's obsession for winning seared into my mind, I bent over so far in my preparatory racing dive, I could feel the condensation of the water on my goggles. I swam crazy fast. As if the only alternative to victory was death.

I usually won. I was used to winning. Why would I give up on this man?

Clay was my soul's partner. For so long, he had been the strong one who encouraged and mentored and supported my efforts to become a good writer. I was now needed to be the strong one, his channel to joy and hope. I would just have to work out how to meet my own separate needs.

I needed to reassure him that I was not going to leave him.

When You Least Expect It

The Fourth of July in 2006 began as a carefree holiday weekend around the swimming pool of our country house in Long Island. The sun was high, the grandchildren giddy, and I wasn't Playing God. Happily off-duty, I didn't register Clay's cough as the giveaway of another Boomerang.

He had gone back to bed for most of the morning after a violent expectoration of his liquid breakfast. I didn't connect all that with his grumbling over the previous weeks about feeling "too full." I should have guessed. His body was no longer absorbing a normal amount of food.

When the sun was too hot even for the children, Clay suddenly appeared on the lawn, staggering toward the pool. Maura and I rushed to help him. His skin was the shade of asphalt. Breaths rattled in his throat. He looked at me with an uncomprehending plea.

"Clay," Maura commanded, "we need to get you to a hospital—now!"

He hated ambulances. Foolishly, we walked him straight to the car, rolled up the windows, turned the AC on high, and sped off toward the country hospital, a good hour away with holiday traffic. The temperature was well over ninety when the AC conked out. Clay needed to vomit. One block from the Sag Harbor police station, we pulled over and called 911: "We have a man in his seventies who can't breathe." A policewoman in off-duty shorts and flip-flops appeared on a bicycle. Soon after, Clay was sliding gratefully into the cool womb of an ambulance.

The young summer intern in the ER frowned over his stethoscope. "This man is drowning."

His lungs were bulging with fluid and aspirated food particles. I felt the stab of bad-mother guilt. I'd been guarding the grandchildren from falling into the pool and letting my husband drown.

A national holiday is no time to come down with double pneumonia. The only available docs were young summer temps at a country hospital one hundred miles from our physicians in New York. The local pulmonary doctor was on vacation. Sophisticated equipment was unavailable. It was vital to move Clay to a higher-grade medical center, but the computer balked. It couldn't verify his Social Security number. The administrative office was closed for the holiday weekend. Clay's condition deteriorated.

It was almost thirty-six hours before we finally got Clay into another ambulance and sped two hours to a hospital in New York. He was admitted to the ICU. Now we were playing a much higher level of the life-or-death game.

I AM ON DUTY 24/7 and living in the present tense. The first move to master: Catch the Doctor. It requires getting to the ICU before 7:00 A.M. Doctors peek in on their patients before any family can get in their way, look over the charts, and decide whether to come back sooner or later. They are paid for this look-in.

The supervising doctor on Clay's case is the pulmonologist Dr. Bushra Mina, also known as the intensivist, meaning he supervises all those in intensive care. He is exotic. Egyptian. Slim with a swaying walk, he dresses immaculately in Burberry shirts in hot colors with cool ties. I can't keep my eyes off him. He is the only man I see for days who is not supine, inert, with an elephantine trunk of tubing draped from his nose. The intensivist can walk and talk and exert full motor control, which reminds me of my husband's better days.

The next game to master: Identify the Alarms. There are four levels. The steady bleep, like a car alarm. The bus honk. The evacuation squawk. And finally, the "paper out" alarm on the heart monitor. This sometimes goes on all night, like a low-grade torture technique rendering sleep always just beyond grasp. One imagines the doctor being concerned when he looks at the chart the next morning and sees the patient had zero heartbeat for the last ten hours. But doctors don't react. Only patients and their caregivers are subjected to the constant alarm. It becomes white noise to all others.

There are probably worse places to be on a Saturday night than running an ICU alone, but the Saturday night nurse is in no mood to pay attention to a mere family caregiver. When I run to report that the evacuation squawk has been going for five minutes, she blows me off.

"I have an emergency."

"We do, too; he needs suctioning so he can breathe."

"I'm busy now. I'll be by later."

"But his blood pressure is 200 over 105."

"I told you, I have an emergency."

How many emergencies top blood pressure that breaks 200?

I seek out the intensivist. He comes; he sees; he conquers the problem. He is brilliant. I need an intensivist.

After a week I understand why most nurses and aides never look up. ICU patients are not long-stayers, some of them not long-stayers on this earth. They're usually sucking life from a respirator or have tubes sprouting from their mouths or throats, so they can't talk even if they want to, which most of them don't. They mainly zonk out. Some hallucinate, others sleep during the day if they're suffering from sundowner effect. The staff has little incentive, if any, to get attached to patients. It could be heartbreaking.

The black-and-white pocket TV on the wall gets only CNN, the Food Network, and Channel 54, the in-hospital system. That one favors heavily stringed celestial music, as if welcoming patients to the Other Side.

Week two, Sunday morning, 7:00 A.M. Just off the red-eye from a speech in California, I take a taxi straight to the hospital. The Saturday night nurse is the only one covering this side of the ICU all weekend. No aides. No intern or resident in sight. She blocks my path.

"Who let you up?"

I pull rank. "I'm an ICU wife. I can come whenever I want."

I notify her that his blood pressure is topping 200 again.

She repeats: "Who let you up? Visiting hours don't start till eleven."

I say, "He really needs to be checked."

"I'm busy with another patient."

I try again. "I want to help you to do your job."

Unconvinced, she walks away.

Once Clay is moved out of ICU, our trusty financial adviser stops by with a power-of-attorney form. Pleased that he thought of this obvious precaution, it still feels like a violation. I can only imagine how Clay feels as he contemplates losing his mind and turning over all decisions to his wife. In his unsteady fingers, the pen skitters across the page.

Friends come to visit. They are shiny and all dressed up for a night on the town. They bring the tabloids and read aloud the scandal everybody's talking about at East Side dinner parties—Mrs. Astor's son is being called a mom abuser by his own son.

"It's shocking to see Clay like this," says one of his old friends. "You must have someone with him twenty-four hours a day."

Feeling guilty, I call the in-hospital nursing service and go over the options again. For a CNA, a certified nurse assistant, who can only be a companion and help with a bedpan, it's $264 for a twelve-hour shift. For an RN, a skilled nurse who can give medicines and monitor all the machinery, it's $780. Can I interview her and find out if she has experience taking care of this kind of patient? I ask. Not possible. Hire blind or not at all. I hire a CNA. Next morning I arrive at seven. Clay's blood pressure is over the top again. He asks for a pad and writes: "Private nurse fighting with night nurse."

Turf war over who's supposed to suction him. I decide it's better to stay myself until he falls asleep at 11:00 P.M., even if I get bounced by the Saturday night nurse.

After two weeks in the ICU, Clay is stable enough to move to a regular floor under the care of the intensivist. We had no idea he would remain in the hospital for another month. The medical care for his lungs and heart was attentive and superb. The problem is, in many acute care hospitals today little attention is paid to maintaining a patient's muscular-skeletal strength.

———————————

STRATEGIES

Move, Baby, Move!

When older people are hospitalized, their bodies can decline very rapidly. After two weeks, many can't stand up independently. They need two helpers to get out of bed and into a chair. But hospital rules insist these helpers be hospital employees. They can't be family members or privately hired aides—the people already present in the patient's room. Probable result: the patient stays in bed, becoming more debilitated, dependent, and discouraged.

Hospitals are cutting back on physical therapists (PTs), leaving patients immobilized in beds, losing strength and flexibility. Atrophy doesn't await old age. It can start affecting any inert person of any age in a week. Seniors are extremely vulnerable. "Each new hospitalization creates more problems for the older adult," says Mary Naylor, a gerontology expert at the University of Pennsylvania. "We've tracked a two-to-three-day stay and found it contributes further to their health decline. Even while on bed rest, patients need light exercise. And those short of breath and medically unstable also need some exercise to prevent the long-term consequences of immobility."

I sneaked in a young physical therapist and passed her off as Clay's niece. He welcomed her. She was a professional, not a nagging spouse. She helped me lift him to standing so we could encourage him to try walking with support. This was essential: he was about to be tested to determine his readiness for rehab. As Clay teetered a bit, the PT was moved to mention an alarming parallel: "Do you know why they shoot horses that break a leg? They can't get up. When they don't stand or walk, they don't work their lungs. They get pneumonia and die."

I urge caregivers to visit the hospital armed with light weights and elasticized bands. Every day, give your loved one mild exercise and stretching. Better to do it in short sessions but more than once a day. Make it a routine; we humans respond to routine. Along with cheering up the patient, miniworkouts aid breathing, prevent muscle cramps, and get blood moving around the body, carrying the oxygen and nutrients needed to speed healing.

Dealing with the Discharge Planner

Suddenly it's a Thursday afternoon and you're told that the patient is ready to leave the hospital. You are visited by the discharge planner. This is not the empathetic social worker who settled in the patient. The discharge planner is, in effect, the bouncer. These folks report to the business side of the hospital. Their primary job is to get the patient out as soon as possible.

You may be caught totally by surprise, as we were. You protest, "But I'm not ready to take him home," which may be entirely true, but it won't get you anywhere. What can stave off a premature exit are six magic words.

"It would be an unsafe discharge."

The insurance company or Medicare dictates how soon the patient should be discharged from the hospital. It's all based on the diagnostic code assigned to the patient on admission. The code for the condition that brought the patient into the hospital entitles him to a certain number of days. If he is discharged earlier, the hospital makes more of a profit; if he overstays, the hospital loses money. And if he develops secondary complications or picks up one of the rampant infections that flourish in the petri dish of a hospital, the caregiver may have to fight to get a decent extension.

Discharge is based only partly on the patient's degree of wellness. There is a business calculation: How soon can the patient be moved out without risking a backfire and possible lawsuit? Readmissions are much more profitable than long-stayers. Not surprisingly, we were told over and over, "If he relapses, just bring him back to the ER for reevaluation." The clock starts running again with each readmission, and both hospital and doctors are reimbursed once again.

But you and the patient have more clout than you probably know. If you believe the patient is still too sick or unstable to be moved, you and the patient are entitled to ask to see the patient advocate. Every hospital is required by law to employ patient advocates who will listen to your concerns, respond to a complaint, and help to resolve conflicts. The patient advocate may go to the doctor, who may okay an extension. If not, advocates can assist you in finding home-health-care and/or community services to help you get set up at home.

NEVER allow a discharge into a weekend: If problems develop, you will not find it easy to connect with the doctor or a nurse or social worker familiar with the case. And commit these words to memory, should the need arise: *It would be an unsafe discharge.*

Twenty-four Steps

When the discharge planner came to see me, at the end of Clay's six-week hospitalization, she handed me a crude mimeographed sheet of facilities for rehabilitation with no guidance on how to sort through the subculture of aftercare options. Acute rehab? Subacute rehab? Or would he be consigned to "long-term care" in a nursing home, where little attention is paid to the possibility of ever coming out again? I had only two days to investigate the choices.

Who would decide Clay's fate? I wanted to know. It's a joint decision based on an evaluation by the attending doctor, the hospital's physical therapists, and the medical director of the receiving facility.

The intensivist tipped me off that the number of steps the patient can take would have considerable bearing on where Clay would be sent. Under twelve steps and Medicare won't pay for rehab. The patient would be consigned to long-term *care in a nursing home. For subacute, he has to make twelve to fifteen steps. The price of admission to the Harvard of acute rehab—the Rusk Institute of Rehabilitation Medicine at NYU Langone Medical Center—is twenty-four steps. We had one day to rehearse.*

I will never forget sneaking into my husband's hospital room the morning he was to be evaluated. He looked so weak and tired after another long battle against double pneumonia. The physical therapist and I had worked him up as far as six steps. It was 6:45 A.M.

"Morning, sweetheart. It's showtime!" I held up his favorite running shoes. He smiled.

"Today the PTs are coming to test you to see if you're strong enough to recommend for the acute rehab program at Rusk Institute."

"What do I have to do?"

"Twenty-four steps."

"Get me out of bed! Practice."

He walked and rested, marched in place, then collapsed. We listened to jazz. By one o'clock, when the evaluation team appeared with their clipboards and opaque expressions, Clay swung his legs over the bed and pulled himself up on the walker. Then he pushed past the team and straight out the door, leaving them openmouthed.

Thirty steps! He was in! It was as great a thrill as watching my first child walk.

THE RUSK INSTITUTE WAS *a revelation. Clay was still a sick man, but the dedicated professionals at Rusk were not going to let that inhibit them. Pam Singer, a social worker with a corona of silver-threaded black hair and a heart of gold, took me under her wing and introduced the round of experts who came to work with Clay, on the spot, at his bedside, until he was able to go to the workout rooms. Pam became my advocate.*

Dr. Jung Ahn, the brilliant Chinese-American medical director, consulted closely with me and kept close watch over Clay's medical problems. Soon, he was moving around all day from the walking track, to writing, to exercising his tongue and learning how to swallow, coached by one of the finest speech pathologists in New York, Dr. Barbara Leader. If he had a hypotension episode while overexerting himself in the PT room, the Duke-trained therapist would release the back of his wheelchair and get him flat until his blood pressure returned to normal.

Clay did not want me to stop being a wife and a writer and turn into a nurse. He insisted I get back to work. I found a college-educated nurse's aide from Gambia, Isatou Sawahnee, who trained under Ella Council to learn how to prepare Clay's tube feedings. Tall and stately with her hair wrapped in a brilliant turban, she would turn up in the morning with containers and surgical gloves and stand by Clay's bedside like a centurion, pouring his breakfast into his tube. Dr. Ahn was horrified at first. No one had ever brought in food from the outside—the risk of bacterial infection! But once Isatou demonstrated for the nurses her meticulous process and the superb nutrition and caloric intake we had worked out, the staff gathered around and asked her to teach them. In the late afternoon I would relieve her and give him dinner and provide the evening's entertainment. Clay was buoyed by all the attention and by demonstrable proof that he was making progress at last.

Misplacing Clay

Pam Singer helped to take the trauma out of the next transfer of care—the step-down to a subacute facility. After I had visited three nursing homes on the Upper West Side of Manhattan, one of which was a horror, and one of which refused Clay, I was relieved that he was accepted at the Jewish Home Lifecare facility on the edge of Harlem. (He wasn't Jewish, but neither were most of the residents and floor staff.) He was promised a private room with a window and assigned a wheelchair. I brought in a portable DVD player and lots of family pictures for the bulletin board. There was a pleasant library, a café for snacks, and a concrete garden with a few trees and a fountain. It was a mild September. After confinement in hospitals, it felt like being let out of jail. Medicare would pay for his stay for up to ninety days. We were certain he'd be able to go home in a few weeks.

At last, I had a Saturday to myself to do catch-up errands. Around four, I called Clay to say I'd be a little late bringing his dinner. No answer. I called the nurses' station. His room was empty. They couldn't find him. I had a delicious fantasy that he'd gone AWOL. But levity vanished when nobody could tell me where my husband was. Shifts had changed. I had to track down the nursing supervisor on an emergency number to get someone on the floor to look up his case file. A cryptic notation was read to me:

"One-ten P.M. Patient unresponsive for five minutes. EMS called. Possible acute stroke."

I froze. Why hadn't I been there! Acute stroke? Why didn't they know to lay him flat and elevate his legs? A letter from Clay's cardiologist was in his records at the Jewish Home warning about possible episodes of positional hypotension with instructions not to send Mr. Felker to an emergency room. Why didn't they call me?

"Where is he?"

"No note."

No note? A man is just shoved into an ambulance and carted off into a megalopolis with forty-two hospitals and no note is made of where he was dropped off? I trembled with rage and a gnawing fear. I called Pam Singer, the wonderfully supportive social worker from Rusk. Together, we divided up the likely suspects and began calling hospitals. No luck.

Hours passed. It dawned on us that if he were lying in an emergency room, the hospital would not have a record yet of an admission. The two of us made the rounds in person from ER to ER. That night, seven hours after Clay had been transferred out of the nursing home, I walked through a downpour and into the main entrance of New York Hospital on the East Side, far from the nursing home. Yes, Clay Felker had just been admitted from the emergency room.

Relief was brief. Outside his room, my heart racing from running down the hall, I pulled up short. How to prepare myself for what I might see? Acute stroke? I leaned against the wall and closed my eyes and tried to meditate. Breathe. Let go. Let God take over. The buzz and bells of a big-city teaching hospital faded in and out of my consciousness. I felt a hand squeeze mine. A nurse. She looked up his chart and told me it was not acute but transient. He was conscious. I could go in.

His eyes found mine and slowly focused. A flicker of recognition slowly triggered a faint smile. I moaned, "Oh, darling, you're you."

His eyes begged to know, why? He had no memory of what had happened. Neither one of us would ever really know. A neurologist I reached by phone told me he wouldn't have the results of a brain scan until the next day. He was reassuring. A nurse found me a chair and relaxed the rules. I could sit with my husband overnight.

How could I ever leave his side again?

But through that long dark night, I had to keep batting away the persistent thought:

I can't do this anymore.

STRATEGIES

Don't Succumb to Caregiver Guilt

"I can't do this anymore—and I don't know where to go for help."

This is the most common hotline message received by San Francisco's pioneering Family Caregiver Alliance (415-434-3388). Donna Schempp, program director, says all successful caregivers need to know three key things: where to find help, how to arrange breaks, and how to cope with runaway emotions. Not surprisingly, the most unruly emotion is anger, triggered by fatigue, frustration, and resentment. I particularly admired the caregiver who told me: "After three strokes, my husband still refused to go to a nursing home. So I asked if I could take his bed."

It's perfectly normal to doubt you can carry on. It's so predictable that your real problem is not doubt but feeling guilty about it. Don't! Even Rosalynn Carter admitted to me that she faltered after years of being responsible for her mother. Former President Jimmy Carter and Mrs. Carter, a partner in all his activities, set ambitious goals for themselves after their White House years. They visited more than one hundred and twenty different nations on behalf of the Carter Center to promote peace, health, human rights, and mental-health care. On top of her busy travel schedule, Mrs. Carter oversaw her mother's care when she became ill. She had to be moved, first to assisted living and then to nursing care. When she came home, she found that her mother was both overmedicated and taking the wrong medicine.

"I felt awful. Horrible. All caregivers feel guilty. Especially those doing long-distance caregiving. Every time I came home from a trip and went to see my mother, she'd say, 'Where are you going next time?'"

After her mother died, her brother had a stroke. "Of course, I was the one to take care of him," Mrs. Carter told me. "And the first time I came back from a trip, he said, 'Where are you going next time?' And I said, 'I can't do this anymore!'" Mrs. Carter, then eighty, smiled gently. "But I did it. You do it because you have to. But there is no reason to feel guilty."

Transits Without Trauma

No one should be in a hospital alone. Be there as your loved one's advocate as often as possible. You provide eyes and ears to help correct or prevent mistakes. Your presence gives him or her strength, reducing the helplessness that bed-bound hospital patients often feel. Share the vigil with other family members or friends.

Moving to Rehab? *Plan Early!*

Ideally, hospital patients headed for rehab centers have a discharge plan worked out by a team—the doctor, nurse, social worker, and family caregiver. In reality, these moves fall apart fast. Stay firm: get all the guidance and details you need.

Take care in choosing the kind of rehab program—you can't change later! You have two basic options—top rehab for top dollar, or good-enough rehab for less money.

Acute Medical Rehabilitation: These hospital-based programs have round-the-clock nursing. They are reserved for patients strong enough for intensive training—three hours a day, six days a week of physical therapy, occupational therapy, and often speech-language therapy. A social worker oversees treatment and partners with the family caregiver. Doctors are readily available.

Acute medical rehab, like Rusk, can cost up to $1,700 a day, with a maximum stay of two to three weeks. The insurance company does a precertification. If Medicare determines, along with the patient's doctor, that a patient needs acute rehab, a designated period of time will be covered. Updates are done every five days.

Subacute Rehabilitation: These programs are based in nursing homes, which comes as a shock to most people. Nursing homes contract with a physical therapy company. Subacute rehab is intended for patients not physically strong enough to take the intensity of acute rehab. It's an hour of therapy a day. Patients are not under the direct care of a physician, and if any medical problem arises, they are likely to be sent to an emergency room. Always post your contact numbers on the patient's medical chart and make sure special instructions are posted—even on the wall!

Typical cost: $700 a day, covered by Medicare up to ninety days. It's important that the caregiver visit the available programs and check out the care before accepting the transfer. Subacute staffs tend to be overworked and underpaid. Caregivers often hire a private aide to check on the patient.

Encourage your loved one to make the most of rehab. This is a very valuable recovery period. The rehab team usually appreciates the family caregiver's input, especially in providing details about the patient's home situation, so the team can help you prepare and order the right equipment. Don't feel pressured to take your loved one home if you are not ready. You may need time to rearrange your life, work, and finances.

High-Voltage Warning

Your hospitalized loved one may suddenly become angry, uncooperative, impossible. Hospitals are hardly rest homes. Most throb with noise, stress, congestion, and inexplicable information— all guaranteed to depress the sunniest newcomer. The most resentful patients tend to be people accustomed to being in full control on the outside. Suddenly out of their element, they often lash out just when they need you most. Take pity, not umbrage. The meaner they act, the more scared they probably feel.

Going Home Smart

Well before your loved one leaves the hospital, learn as much as you can about his or her regimen. You'll be in charge of home care. Ask a nurse or aide to demonstrate procedures, list needed items, and suggest equipment adapted to your specific home layout.

To ease rough passages between care settings, go to Carol Levine's brilliant website, www.nextstepincare.org. It's a free resource supported by New York's United Hospital Fund. Called Next Step in Care, the website has advice and information to help caregivers ensure smooth patient transitions. Levine is a veteran caregiver, author, and winner of a MacArthur Foundation fellowship. She has created booklets covering all transition stages, from hospital to rehab to home care.

The most popular form on Levine's website is the Medication Management Form (pdf, 120KB). It will help you to review your family member's list of medications and revise the list every time a nurse or doctor makes a change of drug or dosage. It's helpful to post this form on the wall or bulletin board so any aide or visiting medical person can review it.

Another popular form is Your Family Member's Personal Health Record (pdf, 92KB). This is designed to help you keep straight your family member's history of medical conditions and treatments—a story that can be hard to piece together when you see a new doctor! It includes space for you to include the patient's advance directives and insurance coverage. See www.nextstepincare.org/left _top_menu/Caregiver_Home/.

Create an Online Calendar

For computer users, an Internet-based care calendar is most efficient. It allows all members of a scattered family to access the patient's schedule and condition at any given time, from any location. As explained at the end of Chapter 12, Lotsa Helping Hands offers a free Internet calendar service for caregivers that is totally private. Subscribers need only fifteen minutes to create their own Web-based community, which functions as their secretary, coordinating all dates and tasks they share for their loved one's care. For more information see www.lotsahelpinghands.com.

Ask the Purpose of Every Test

Record the answers in your notebook. This information may be vital for insurance purposes or whenever new specialists show up for a consult. Carry a list of your loved one's current medications with dosages. Confirm names and dosages of all new medications the hospital prescribes. Update these lists before the patient leaves the hospital, so the medications can be replicated at home or in rehab.

eighteen

READY TO EXPLODE

As a Filipina woman, Felicitas Rocha* was conditioned to suppress anger. "I just bottle it up," she told me. "It takes me so much pushing to show my anger, I just become overemotional and clam up."

But she was now ready to explode, so frustrated that she actually felt like driving into the desert and never coming back. Anything was better than one more day of thankless caregiving for both her ungrateful husband and her debilitated mother.

Felicitas was one of my frontline barometers, a canary in the coal mine of caregiving. For months, we talked by phone, tracing her rising tensions. Finally we met in person. I suggested we drive together to never-never land—the California desert—"a Thelma and Louise trip." She loved the idea.

We rented a vintage Thunderbird convertible and drove like the wind. As the sun began setting, we pulled up short in a barren spot. Felicitas spilled her anger. "I just wanted to run away. Did you ever have that same feeling?"

"Of course. But I had a job that gave me an assignment that took me out of town."

"You were lucky to have a little breather." Then she became the advisor: "As a caregiver, you have to take care of yourself first."

I laughed. "Felicitas, when did you learn that?"

"Only in the last couple of months. I read it in a benefit book."

---

*Pseudonym.

"Where did that get you?"

"They have a call-in department, an 800 number. Then you get another 800 number. Nothing ever happened."

"That sounds par for the course."

We leaned against the coolness of the car and let the rays of the falling desert sun stroke our faces. Felicitas broke the silence. "Gail, did you ever have the same kind of problems when you were a caregiver for your husband?"

"Yes, I did. One day my husband fell on the bathroom floor. Fainted from a sudden drop in blood pressure. I called 911. When the EMS rolled my husband's gurney into the elevator, our building's busybody showed up. He complained that this was the third time we'd had an ambulance block the garage. He said, 'We can't have you here anymore!'" I told Felicitas that my reaction was a bitter private prayer: "Please, God, grant me a mild heart attack right *now,* so the EMS will put me in the hospital bed next to my husband—and I can finally get some rest. Amen."

Felicitas and I laughed and cried at the same time. That's the essence of caregiving—mixed emotions all the way to the edge. But stop right there: caregivers can help each other—don't give up!

YOU DON'T HAVE TO DO IT ALONE

Felicitas' retirement years had once looked bright and secure. She had worked for forty years and retired at sixty-two from a large insurance company in Newport Beach. With an empty nest, she and her husband moved to Palm Springs in 2002, where Felicitas plunged into a second career as a realtor in a red-hot California housing market. The couple finally bought their dream home.

"We took out a loan from one of the largest national subprime lenders—we got sucked into that," Felicitas says, choking back remorse. "After the first year, we paid higher rates every month while sales disappeared in my real estate business."

The couple was swept along in America's mass psychosis—the notion that real estate is a money machine and property values keep rising as faithfully as the sun. When the bubble burst, forcing the Rochas to give up their house, Felicitas' happy future vanished. Life became one crisis after another.

Her husband had already had two open-heart operations. In the year they lost their house, he had more surgery, this time for prostate cancer.

For the next six years, Felicitas soldiered on, making do in modest rentals, nursing her husband at home and taking in her mother when she broke a hip. She was now desperate to resume working as an independent Realtor, but she couldn't do so at home. Her husband and mother were constantly competing for her attention. He was not only jobless but feeling powerless and disrespected—no longer the man of the house. "I stopped dreaming already," he told me. "Live only day to day."

Felicitas confessed: "I feel so inadequate. I'm not really prepared to take care of my mother's many chronic illnesses. My husband keeps hounding me to cook. Why should he cook, he says, when there are two women in the house? I want to concentrate on my job, earn money for my retirement. It's obvious: there won't be anyone to take care of me!"

Felicitas began having chest pains and dizziness, clear symptoms of heart disease. She felt panicky and often hyperventilated. Her husband kept saying, "Oh, it's nothing. It's going to pass." For five years, she never saw a doctor. She supervised her son's cataract operation but put off any appointment for herself. Why?

"I wasn't thinking of myself, just taking care of others."

One day her head began spinning. She couldn't stand up. *It must be a heart attack,* she thought and got herself to an emergency room. It was vertigo. A routine exam uncovered the physical toll on her health: high blood pressure and prediabetes.

By the spring of 2008, Felicitas couldn't speak a sentence without crying. She was juggling work and full-time caregiving for two dependents. Finally, she began calling the 800 numbers listed on her insurance policy. She received an application and a survey to fill out. Nothing happened.

After months of desperation and frustration, Felicitas happened to read a newsletter, "Renew," put out by Evercare Health Plans. She saw the promising words "You don't have to do it alone." Felicitas called and pleaded to talk to a mental health counselor. She reached a call center in Oregon and was given yet another number. This time, she did get a human voice. The officious voice on the other end of the phone said, "It will be a two-week wait."

"No!" Felicitas wailed. "I have to talk to somebody today or tomorrow at the latest."

"Why, are you having a lot of problems?"

"Yes, I'm contemplating leaving my husband of forty-four years!"

The gatekeeper came to life. "Yeah, that will qualify you—either contemplating suicide or killing somebody or leaving your husband of forty-four years."

Felicitas had cracked the code. She got an appointment for the next day and spoke to Kathy Hawk, a registered nurse at the Minnesota office who is a care manager.

"Yes, we do have a program called Solutions for Caregivers," Kathy confirmed.

"Oh my God, I need help!" Felicitas cried. "I want to leave home!" She gave a thumbnail sketch of the burdens of caring for both her immobilized mother and her unappreciative husband.

When Kathy immediately responded, "We can help you," Felicitas dissolved in grateful tears. "I can't believe somebody understands me."

Kathy said, "I will send you a registered nurse who can assess your needs as a caregiver."

"But you're up in Minnesota," Felicitas sputtered. "I'm out in the desert, in California."

"We can find you resources locally."

Felicitas remembers, "It lifted a whole ton of bricks off my shoulders."

Once Felicitas broke the seal on her anger, she was able to begin taking care of herself, and even able to laugh at her tragicomic situation. That alerted others to help her. Working remotely with Kathy Hawk, her Evercare manager, Felicitas discovered that because her husband and her mother were Evercare Health Plan members in California, they were each entitled to a home-care aide for forty hours a year. Hawk scheduled nursing assessments and found local resources for the family's needs. They included transportation to medical appointments, physical therapy, an adult day-care center for Felicitas's mother, a primary-care physician, and the two home-care aides.

Felicitas arranged with the local agency to spread out the home care over the year, about four hours a week. Her husband is the cook in the family but tires easily, so the agency housekeeper, Jessica, helps him with the food preparation. Felicitas discovered SilverSneakers, the leading fitness program designed for older adults by Healthways and open to Medicare members of managed care organizations. Exercises are done on a chair to music. Her mom loved it.

Most valuably, Evercare's manager Kathy Hawk became a trusted advisor and advocate for Felicitas, helping her navigate local resources and sorting out what various health plans would cover. She talked to the exhausted woman about the importance of maintaining her own health and wellness. She reassured her that her choices were excellent and surely the best for her family. Kathy says she can hear the difference in Felicitas' voice. "It's like talking to a different person."

Meet Felicitas online. Go to my website: www.gailsheehy.com/caregiving.php.

STRATEGIES

Does Your Company Offer a Care Manager?

Evercare Solutions for Caregivers is a national care management service. Evercare advocates like Kathy Hawk offer expertise and support, helping clients navigate confusing choices, pinpointing those best geared to a loved one's specific, ever-changing needs. You can buy the program directly from Evercare. You may possibly obtain it through your employer's benefit plan. Call 866-896-1895.

For information on Evercare's Solutions for Caregivers program, see http://evercarehealthplans.com/solutions_for_caregivers.jsp.

If you are self-employed or unemployed, call 866-463-5337 (Monday–Friday, 8:00 A.M. to 6:00 P.M. EST) and say, "I understand there's a benefit program called Evercare Solutions for Caregivers, and I need help."

COOLING DOWN STRESS

"As a minister I have buried more caregivers than care recipients," says the Reverend Gregory Johnson, cochair of New York City Family Caregiver Coalition. Givers clearly need care themselves. "But you can't take care of them until they realize they're family caregivers."

Dr. Esther Sternberg specializes in rheumatoid arthritis. Her career choice was sparked by watching her grandmother and mother give up their own health to be caregivers for dying husbands. Dr. Sternberg built her defenses early and high: "I felt the need to have as much control over death as I possibly could." As a medical researcher at the National Institutes of Health, Dr. Sternberg made profound contributions to stress studies by proving how intimately the brain and the immune system talk to each other. This achievement did not protect her from the same fate as her female forebears. Only months after her father died, her mother was diagnosed with breast cancer and late-onset rheumatoid arthritis. Dr. Sternberg began making frantic flights from Washington, where she lived, to Montreal to care for her mother. Those trips collided with prior commitments to give speeches around the country and produce a book on deadline. Worn out by hypervigilance, she was soon stricken with the very disease she went into medicine to treat.

Dr. Sternberg set out to heal herself from inflammatory arthritis by examining ancient Greek truths about harmonious living and testing them in today's frantic environment. She wrote a book entitled *The Balance Within: The Science Connecting Health and Emotions.*

"We have all experienced it," she commiserated with me. "But we push ourselves for weeks or months on end to make a deadline or to take care of a sick relative, and invariably we push our bodies too long and get sick."

Dr. Sternberg outlines the body's response to different kinds of stress:

Short-lived stress jump-starts the body's positive responses. In one swoop, hormones surge, adrenaline squirts into nerves all over the body and heart, gut, muscles, and skin respond. Our attention focuses, vision clears, and suddenly we can do everything better—running, seeing, thinking, and so on.

But if extreme stress persists (i.e., becomes chronic), it leads to extreme exhaustion, turning on a steady flow of cortisol. That chemical shuts down immune-cell response, leaving us less able to ward off infection. With a little calm and quiet between crises, the nervous system normally has time to recover and be ready for the next assault. With sufficient rest, people feeling burned out can regain all necessary hormones and normalize cycles.

How is this relevant to caregivers? Dr. Sternberg cites studies of nurses, teachers, and air-traffic controllers. "A major component of psychological stress that promotes later physical illness is not being appreciated for one's devoted work. Nurses, teachers, and air-traffic controllers are among those at highest risk for burn-out. They are faced daily with caregiving situations in their work lives, often with inadequate pay, little help in their jobs, and too many lives in their charge—just like family caregivers."

STRATEGIES

The Laughing Cure—No Joke!

The cheapest and most effective antistress medicine is a good belly laugh—and that prescription comes straight from the Mayo Clinic. A hearty laugh fires up and then cools down your stress response and leaves you feeling more relaxed. Laughter takes the focus away from guilt and fear and other negative emotions. The long-term benefits of laughter, as measured by the Mayo Clinic, are pretty amazing. It stimulates your organs, releases natural uppers called endorphins, produces the body's own natural painkillers, and turns on the spigot of neuropeptides, which fight stress and potentially more serious illnesses.

- Get DVDs of the funniest movies of all times. Three recommendations: *My Cousin Vinny* (put my husband in laughing stitches, even when he had surgical stitches), *Monty Python and the Holy Grail,* and any DVD of Lucille Ball shows.

- Many people love the Three Stooges reruns or those of *Seinfeld*. The Marx Brothers are a laugh medicine of long standing.
- Treat yourself to a night at a comedy club with friends. Memorize jokes for later retelling. It's the equivalent of carrying around a supply of Tums.
- Have a bang-up party or game night in your own home—why not! *You're* not sick. And laughter is contagious.

nineteen

MIND JOBS: CARING FOR A LOVED ONE WITH COGNITIVE DECLINE

If you're called to care for a loved one with cognitive failure, all bets are off. You're committed to braving darkness on a long journey without any certain end point. You face the biggest of all monsters, terror of the unknown. Even the most loving child or spouse may hesitate to sign on as the 24/7 minder of a mindless person.

WHEN HE FORGETS WHO YOU ARE

Sandra Day O'Connor grew up seemingly carefree as a cowgirl on a cattle ranch in Arizona. She was still carefree when she sailed through Stanford Law School, broke barriers against women lawyers, became majority leader of the Arizona state senate, and at fifty-eight endured a mastectomy for breast cancer that she discussed publicly without qualms. But in 1981, when President Ronald Reagan asked her to become the Supreme Court's first woman justice, she had doubts—big ones.

She was a midlevel state judge, happily rooted in sleepy Arizona with her husband, hardly accustomed to hobnobbing with Washington egos and debating constitutional law. She knew it was not her experience that brought the president to her door: "He was hoping to get votes from women, I assume, and rightly so," she commented publicly.

Her husband insisted she accept the honor. John O'Connor gave up his partnership at a Phoenix law firm and joined the new justice in Washington, gladly shunning any law practice that might conflict with his wife's position. In her first year on the bench, Justice O'Connor was battered by liberals as too conservative and hounded for media interviews as a historic first. She couldn't sleep. She lost so much weight that her clothes hung limp on her tiny frame. Her husband was her hitching post. He brushed aside her doubts and gave her unconditional love and support according to the book *Supreme Conflict* by Jan Crawford Greenburg.

What sustained her throughout her Court tenure was a future dream—a vision of going home to Arizona once she and John retired, of aging securely together, golfing with friends, playing with grandchildren.

Fate had other plans. In the early 1990s, her brilliant husband was stricken with Alzheimer's. The couple coped with the slow unraveling of his mental acuity for the next fifteen years.

By the year 2000, a momentous election year, Sandra Day O'Connor was arguably the most powerful woman in America. With Justices Scalia and Thomas swinging decisions to the right, O'Connor had found her role as the centrist coalition-builder on an increasingly polarized Court. She became the ultimate swing vote. Her vote halted the Florida recount and handed the office to George W. Bush over Senator Al Gore.

Her intention had always been to remain on the Supreme Court until she herself was in "really bad shape" before retiring. She loved the job. But in 2005, she was caught off guard by two health crises. Chief Justice William Rehnquist, a fellow Arizonan, was desperately ill with cancer, yet not ready to relinquish his robes. He knew his old friend Sandra was seventy-five and also weighing her options for if and when to step down. He confided a personal decision that foreclosed her choices.

"I don't think we need two vacancies" on the Court at the same time, he decreed. She would have to retire right away, or be prepared to serve two more years in case he should die beforehand.

Her husband's neurological disease was now progressing rapidly. It was impossible to handle long-distance. Two of their grown children lived near him in Arizona, but they certainly couldn't provide constant care. She faced an excruciating choice: resign immediately to supervise her husband's care, or stay in Washington for another two years during which he might die.

Her heart ruled. She stepped down in 2005 "to take action" in caring for her husband. Retirement would be her New Normal. In the first year, she wrote a children's book based on her own adventures as a cowgirl. But the Alzheimer's behavioral changes that pain so many families soon destroyed O'Connor's dream. She decided John O'Connor had to be moved to an assisted-care center.

ANOTHER NEW NORMAL

"He knew this was sort of the beginning of the end," his son Scott O'Connor told a reporter for Fox News. "It was basically suicide talk."

Sandra Day O'Connor remained silent about the pain of these private decisions until 2007, when Arizona TV revealed that her husband had struck up a romance with a fellow Alzheimer's patient at the same care center. Mrs. O'Connor continued to visit him and found him sitting on a porch swing with his girlfriend, happily holding hands, oblivious to his previous attachment to the white-haired woman with the tiny frame, his wife.

When O'Connor bravely testified before Congress to advocate for more funding for Alzheimer's families, she revealed that Evercare had provided a care manager and counseling that helped her to understand and accept the changes in her husband. Subsequently, her son Scott told the local Gannett-owned TV station, "Mom was thrilled that Dad was relaxed and happy and comfortable living here and wasn't complaining."

The trailblazing jurist openly regrets having to leave the high court so soon. In the end, hers was the ultimate act of courage, to use her experience to highlight publicly a common if seemingly intolerable twist in this heart-wrenching illness, hoping to erase some of the stigma. (John Jay O'Connor III died in 2009.)

THE RELUCTANT CAREGIVER

The intense-looking woman at the woman's support group meeting couldn't hold back any longer. She raised her hand. "My husband has been diagnosed with early Alzheimer's. He's only fifty-eight. Our marriage was rocky even before this. I'm struggling, not with how do I take care of him, but do I want to take on this role at all?"

It was a stunningly frank expression of the flight response. The woman had one foot out the door before the meeting finished. I caught up with her and introduced myself as a fellow caregiver for a husband. She confessed that she'd felt ashamed of admitting to such feelings and wanted to disappear. We made a date to have coffee the following week.

Lorna* is a recovering born-in-the-1950s corporate wife who punched all the approved tickets of her generation: raised two children and two step-children, followed her husband through countless moves to regional offices, cared for each of his parents until they died, and served as the caregiver for both of her own parents. She buried all four of them. Then suddenly she was fifty—effervescent, full-bodied, funny, feisty, and hey, still attractive! She was ready to fly.

What held her back? That was the problem, it had no name.

She suspected for several years that her husband was showing the signs of some sort of early dementia, but he flatly refused any medical consult. "Who gets demented in their fifties!" he demanded. "You're crazy. It's all in your mind." He had retired early and was studying to become a musician. He claimed as his midlife privilege the right to be a little eccentric.

Failing to get a doctor to take her concerns seriously, Lorna had found another way out. After many long round-trips between their southwest home and New York City, she landed a make-do consulting job. This was her cover. She had to move to New York for her career, just as her husband always expected her to move to further his career. They would adjust to a commuting marriage. This would be their New Normal, and they would avoid divorce.

But as their successful yearlong experiment was nearing completion, and the lease on her husband's apartment came to within a month of expiration, Lorna grew alarmed. He wasn't hiring movers or calling storage facilities or Goodwill. More worrisome, he couldn't seem to follow the detailed instructions she would e-mail. She had to take a month off and fly out and execute the move without his help.

Tonight, a year later, Lorna is tucked into a banquette at a café near her studio apartment in Greenwich Village. Her husband moved in with her six months ago. He doesn't look like there is anything wrong with him, but she

_____

*Pseudonym.

admits that living together in such a small space has been rough. As we dip French bread in oil and sip Pellegrino, Lorna recounts what it's like to go to the theater with her husband.

"We take the same subway we have taken the last twenty times we have ridden to Times Square," she recounts. "But as we step out of the subway, he looks a little bewildered. And as we get closer to the escalator we always take, I say, 'This must look familiar.' He admits, 'It's like the first time, every time.'"

If she hands him their theater tickets, he gets nervous. He takes out his glasses and looks at the address, they walk twenty feet, and he stops again to put on his glasses and check the address. After this happens three or four times, Lorna's impatience is hard to miss. Her husband says, "I know I forget things and there's something wrong, but I don't have Alzheimer's!"

What, then, she keeps puzzling, is the storm in his brain that keeps washing out names and addresses he has tried to memorize only moments before? He can't say. "I keep waiting for him to convince me that I'm wrong," she sighs. "But when I lose patience and confront him, 'What's wrong with you!' he stares at me blankly as if I'm speaking a language he doesn't understand."

To compensate, her husband began tidying up around their studio. No sooner did Lorna put a dish in the sink than he would step up to wash it. "One day when I was feeling really nasty, I said to him, 'I don't care if you never do another dish, I just want you to TALK TO ME!'" His body froze like a robot. He looked at her but with confused eyes. He stopped doing dishes.

Lorna faults herself for being impatient with him, then admits she cannot control her rage anymore. She blurts her most primitive wish: "I hate to admit this, but I believe my husband has Alzheimer's and I don't want to do this!"

She pulls out the folded scrap of paper on which she jotted the words of the neuroscientist who did a recent brain scan. Her husband refuted the scientist's conclusion. "No! I do not have Alzheimer's." It was all a plot, maybe to get his money, or to give Lorna an excuse to follow through on her occasional threats to leave him.

"He can't see what effect this is having on me," she moans. Of course, that is the cruelest part of the disease—he cannot see how she feels. For him, the New Normal is a sinkhole of dread. Desperate to escape her own fears, she thought of taking a plane somewhere. Instead, she decided she would just go to a hotel and chill out for a while. She packed a suitcase and rolled it around the neighborhood, debating whether to put herself in a nice hotel or a crummy hotel to save money. She decided on a mid-level establishment.

She left a voice-mail message for her husband: "I'm going away for probably three days. You can call me if you absolutely have to but I hope you won't—I really need a break." Even though the hotel was only three blocks away, she had no sooner bolted the door than she felt like a different person. "The relief was physical," she said. "I'm going to do it again."

She weighed her options against her conflicted emotions: "After the depth of affection and connection that I have developed with him over the years, I can be very bold and say mean things, but I probably won't really be able to detach from him completely; maybe we will just live separately. Maybe I'll get his daughters to help and just be one of his caretakers."

The stalemate was finally broken when Lorna found a woman psychiatrist who was open to partnering with her as her husband's caregiver. The psychiatrist gently persuaded him to get a full cognitive workup at a major medical center. Lorna was freed to explore a new job, one that offered less money but paid off in social purpose.

"I've stopped obsessing about my husband," she told me recently, looking excited about the start date for her new position. "Today, it feels like a return to balance, which includes children and grandchildren and the prospect of new and exciting work." Then she mused warily, "But after going through this phase, I wouldn't predict anything about the future."

twenty

COGNITIVE COMEBACK:
A CREATIVE BREAKTHROUGH

With no drugs on the horizon that effectively prevent or cure Alzheimer's disease, there hasn't been much hopeful news to cushion the dreaded diagnosis. But the true story I tell here illuminates a breakthrough in *connecting* to people with Alzheimer's—through art. It's a story that needs to be passed on to every caregiver who fears that Alzheimer's has robbed the mind and soul of a beloved, forever.

Berna Huebner never gave up on her mother, Hillie Gorenstein, even as she struggled all through her eighties against the progression of Alzheimer's disease. An artist, known as Hilgos, Hillie lived near Chicago with her husband. Her daughter lived in Paris. Berna faithfully sent pretty French postcards to her mother, hoping to inspire her to continue painting. But on one of Berna's bimonthly fly-ins to check on her eighty-six-year-old mother, Hillie made a definitive announcement:

"I'm closing up shop."

Hillie quickly slipped into the fog of listlessness, punctuated by agitation. She lost interest in communicating and basically detached from the world. With great reluctance, the family had to place Hillie in a nursing home. But Berna wouldn't give up. On another of her fly-ins, she asked her mother a simple question:

"Mother, would you like to paint?"

Her mother lifted her head. The lights were on in her eyes. The few words she uttered were the first to make sense in many months:

"Yes, I remember better when I paint."

BRINGING MOTHER BACK

That was the insight Berna needed. She became determined to bring her mother back from her detached state. She asked for help from her mother's geriatric psychiatrist Dr. Larry Lazarus at Rush Presbyterian Hospital in Chicago. He suggested she get in touch with her mother's former school, the Art Institute of Chicago. Students were happy to come and paint with her. Berna hired student Jenny Sheppard as her mother's lead art coach.

But Alzheimer's excels in perversity. Hillie refused to go near her easel. She became more agitated and given to wandering. When she became aggressive with the nurses, they had to sedate her. She retreated still further.

At the age of ninety, for the first time in many years, she did pick up a brush. For a full hour, with Jenny at her side, Hillie's mind and her gaze were concentrated on making a painting. When she put down the brush, she spelled out the experience in the title for her work:

"The Hidden Hour."

Berna interpreted that phrase to mean that her mother had found a channel to reconnect to her creativity in a new and secret way. Then for the next six weeks, she again refused to paint. The nursing home sent word to Berna in Paris, "Your mother's lights are off. No need to paint with her."

But Berna kept calling Jenny and the art students to go in and work with her mother. One day Hillie beckoned to Jenny and smiled. "I've never had anything like this before," she said, happily. "Let's just keep it that way, you know?" The art students became her memory vessel and her family. When Hillie was ready to paint, she would walk around uttering the signal, "Quick-QuickQuick." Staff and students would set up the art table. Jenny would offer her the brush. And the magic reconnection with her old world would be renewed.

"This is my touch time," Hillie would murmur as her fingers ran over the art paper. She smiled when the students would touch her, and she touched back. In retrospect, Berna could see that her mother had retreated to a developmental age of about four to six. "But she could still recognize me and her grandchildren. And she developed a real relationship with the art students—whom she hadn't even known before she had disease." That was a revelation to Berna: "So even at that advanced stage, there is still some growth possible in human connections."

From that time onward, Hillie painted and sculpted, danced and played catch, and painted some more. A lot more. She was by then in an advanced stage of Alzheimer's. But her personality and her sense of identity as an artist were revived. She always seemed to know who her daughter was. Whenever Berna appeared to prod her to paint, Hillie would say the same thing. It sounded like a teasing acceptance of the reversal of mother-daughter roles:

"Watch out, here comes the real one—the boss."

Hillie Gorenstein lived almost to the age of ninety-four. She left hundreds of paintings. She dictated a note to her two children saying she had enjoyed a long and wonderful life and that if her story could be of help to the medical world, she would be pleased.

Berna Huebner has turned the story, with the science behind it, into a remarkable documentary titled *I Remember Better When I Paint*. Featured in the film is Rita Hayworth's daughter, Yasmin Aga Khan, president of Alzheimer's Disease International. Yasmin told me that her mother's agitation in late-stage Alzheimer's was calmed by both music and art; not entirely, but significantly. The film offers new hope to families and caregivers as they advocate for ways in which their communities can help cope with Alzheimer's.

CREATIVITY NEVER DIES

Unbeknownst to Hillie or her daughter, the phrase "I remember better when I paint" was becoming substantiated by hard science. Researchers were discovering through brain imaging that Alzheimer's disease normally spares, to a very large extent, the parts of the brain related to emotions and creative expression. Creativity is possible almost to the end of the disease. Emotions often become more vivid and unrestrained.

Neurologists are beginning to recognize the benefits of nonpharmacological therapies—simple creative stimulation like group painting sessions with young people as mentors, and group outings to art museums and music concerts. Even in your own home or your parents', you can break out crayons or water colors, shakers and drumsticks—just as you would do to focus the chaotic energy of a four-year-old—and tempt creative expression.

The most innovative care facilities have already found that creative activities can evoke remembered experiences and awaken creative impulses in residents with cognitive impairment.

Dr. John Zeisel, an early practitioner in nonpharmacological treatment of Alzheimer's, believes that "art, music, and physical therapy can change the symptomology of Alzheimer's disease." A sociologist who has taught architecture, Zeisel has created a homelike setting for a small number of residents with cognitive impairment and called it The Hearthstone Way (three residences in New York, four in Massachusetts). I visited the treatment center on Manhattan's Upper West Side and was astonished to find myself in what looks like a gracious colonial home. The handrails are not institutional metal; they are wooden chair rails. Wide halls are carpeted wall to wall. And the walls are a constant reminder of each resident's past, hung with "memory boxes" the residents compose by selecting the photographs that most vividly recall their cherished experiences.

At Hearthstone, people are people, not patients. They have stimulating activities all day long. They start with exercising and later discuss TV news. They fashion wreaths for the seasons, with tasks broken down into minitasks, according to Montessori methods. They gather in a living room around a fireplace to enjoy an aromatherapy session, maybe using the creams and lotions popular with their generation. These sessions awaken the most basic of human senses—smell.

And most popular of all, the residents paint. With young mentors to work with them, the painting connects them to colors and shapes that evoke past experience, and gets them talking.

Zeisel, author of the book *I'm Still Here,* says, "If people are coached to do activities that are not task-based, it enables them to feel and express feelings they may not have been able to do even in their healthy life." When people with Alzheimer's connect to art, it allows the caregiver to connect with them. Families find it's a revelation to see that a loved one's emotions are still vivid and opinions are still intact, even strident.

STRATEGIES

Stages of Alzheimer's: A Guide for Care

Friends often tell me, "My mother has started acting just like an adolescent—she's always talking about her high school boyfriends," or "I hate to admit it, but my father seems a lot like my four-year-old these days." These admissions are painful, but in them are the best clues for how to connect with your family members at whatever stage of cognitive decline they are experiencing.

People who develop Alzheimer's disease go through a reversal of the predictable stages of becoming an adult.

Dr. Barry Reisberg, a pioneer in Alzheimer's research, spelled out for me his theory of retrogenesis. "Alzheimer's disease reverses normal human development," says Dr. Reisberg, a psychiatrist and clinical director of the Aging and Dementia Research Center at New York University Medical Center. "The cognitive changes are accompanied by functional losses, with a very strong relationship between the two. When adult test measures don't work anymore, if you give a patient test measures designed for a child or infant, they work very well."

What is so positive about this research is that it can be translated into a scientifically sound basis for care—and caregiving. People living with Alzheimer's are fully human at all points in the evolution of the disease, Dr. Reisberg emphasizes. They have the same predictable human needs, at different points, as a teenager or a child at the same stage of development.

Stage 1—This is normality. People are free of subjective complaints or objective evidence of memory impairment.

Stage 2—Subjective cognitive impairment. People notice they're forgetting names and misplacing things. This usually begins about fifteen years before mild cognitive impairment.

Stage 3—Mild cognitive impairment. Dr. Reisberg coined this term. "We showed many years ago that mild cognitive impairment begins about seven years before obvious dementia," he says. People have increasing difficulty doing complex occupational jobs, like writing reports or doing volunteer work that entails executive tasks, or planning social functions like putting together a big party. Most people simply withdraw: "I'm getting older, I'm not up to it."

Stage 4—Mild dementia. People have difficulties with complex activities of daily life: writing checks correctly; paying bills on time; shopping and coming back with the right things; preparing a holiday meal for family in the usual way. People just back off, so it is not always evident. People can still manage many activities and live on their own. This stage lasts about two years, on average.

To be aware of how the stages of dementia are a reverse mirror of the stages of adolescence and childhood helps the caregiver to find natural channels to engage with the family member—just as they might with a teenager or child. It makes it easier to understand and accept the person's capacities as well as their needs. If you hire care aides, you can encourage them to do creative activities with the person, rather than leaving the individual to just stare at a TV. It will make the aide's experience more satisfying and the patient more emotionally balanced.

For example, in stage 4, when people have trouble with finances, think of them as at approximately twelve years of age. They have the same need to demonstrate independence as twelve-year-olds do. But they also need help with their finances so they don't sign the wrong document or write the wrong figure on the check.

Stage 5—Moderate dementia. People lose the ability to pick out the right clothes for the day or season; they have to be prompted or corrected. Memory for basic facts such as one's address of many years ago, or the current weather conditions, or the name of the current president, becomes compromised. People react in different ways to their thinking and memory problems. If they are living on their own, they may become angry or suspicious. The moderate dementia stage lasts about a year and a half.

Stage 6—Moderately severe dementia. First clue: People begin to have trouble putting on their clothes properly. They may have trouble adjusting water temperature when they shower at home, where they may have done it for years. They go on to develop incontinence: urinary first, then fecal. If there are no other health complications, people spend about two and a half years in this stage. Speech ability declines.

Stage 7—Final stage. Functions previously acquired in normal development such as dressing, bathing, and continence have already been lost in reverse developmental order. Speech is limited to only a few words. Some people make up words, some repeat words and phrases over and over: "Johnny, Johnny, firstborn son" or "terrific." Most are quiet. Ultimately speech becomes limited to a single word, if that: "yes" or "okay."

Loss of the ability to walk invariably follows the loss of speech or occurs at about the same time. If the person survives, they go on to lose the ability to sit up, to smile, then the ability to hold up or move their head. People die at all points in stage 7, which can last seven years or more.

Are there ways to delay the progression of this disease? I asked Dr. Reisberg.

"At the moment, no preventative measures for Alzheimer's have been proven effective," he said. But sometimes small strokes and blood vessel changes in the brain and elsewhere are the prelude to Alzheimer's dementia, and these changes also accompany the progression of the disease. Possible preventions for stroke include controlling vascular risk factors, meaning high blood pressure. Exercise, mental activity, and a healthy diet, sometimes referred to as a Mediterranean-style diet, all appear to be possibly useful in forestalling dementia.

A person at stage 6 needs the same kind of care as a two- to five-year-old child. Children at those ages don't just sit and read alone, but if you give them crayons or paints, they'll go right to drawing. If you leave four-year-olds in a day-care center without supervision or structured activities, they will run up and down and eventually start hitting others. It's the same for stage 6 Alzheimer's patients in senior day-care centers, says Dr. Reisberg. They will pace up and down and, if left with nothing to do, may eventually become aggressive, angry, and even combative. But if they are given something creative to do, they become curious and engaged.

SIXTH TURNING:
COMING BACK

twenty-one

BREAKING DOWN, BREAKING THROUGH

This is a critical turning point. It is the middle of your journey. You know you have reached it when and if you become aware that your loved one is not going to get well or return to you whole. He or she will become more and more dependent and needy. This is a time to pause in sadness and reflection. Losses weigh heavily. But it is also a time for inner work on ourselves. It is here that caregivers who survive begin the effort of coming back to life.

We need to begin releasing our loved one. So much easier said than done. Letting go is a slow and painful process. With any rebound, of course, we will seize upon the sign of hope that full recovery is still possible, and there may be lengthy reprieves. Beginning to anticipate the decline of our loved one, however, allows us to begin imagining the possibility of our own comeback to life.

I wrestled with writing about this turning, because it was in many ways the hardest passage in my caregiving journey. Just thinking about it recalls those mornings that I would awaken in a jolt of panic, heart pounding, pins and needles in my hands and feet, and a surge of uncertainties flooding my semiconsciousness: What's going to happen to Clay? What will be left of my life?

I later understood, intellectually, that I had come upon the center of the labyrinth. I was not ready to accept. I admit it. After nearly fifteen years of habitual efforts to pull my husband back from the edge of death or descent into depression, I felt overwhelmed by fears of losing him and falling into financial ruin. And that fear was real. As a consequence of my denial of his decline, I had been spending with abandon to support the same lifestyle we had enjoyed before his illness.

We had given up the dream house in Berkeley; we were unwanted in our condo sublet in Oakland; and the truth was, Clay did not have the strength to go back to teaching. After ten years, our golden California dream was fading fast.

Our apartment in New York doubled as an office for me. How could I take care of him at home without either giving up my career and income or continuing to spend down our dwindling resources by hiring caregiving help?

The cost of hiring aides to help me care for my husband 24/7 would be staggering. At the peak it could amount to $15,000 to $20,000 a month. Yet I could not bear the thought of abandoning my husband to a nursing home. Most people feel the same way. What then? It was a conflict that obsessed me.

To keep hope alive, I foolishly continued to pay rent on the condo for another year. I was holding out the fantasy that Clay would improve and we would resume our beautiful bicoastal life.

I was stuck at the center of the labyrinth.

LOOKING DOWN AT MY body in the shower one morning, I saw another circle forming. On one side of my waist was a band of red splotches. It itched and burned and spread a little every day. I ignored it. No time for doctor visits for me. I couldn't afford to be sick.

"Wrong," scolded Dr. Pat. She badgered me to come in for my annual gynecological exam. Alarmed once she saw the half circle on my waist, she announced in her best gotcha voice, "Shingles, my dear." She asked if I'd ever had chicken pox. Yes. "Well, that viral infection goes dormant. But an immune system that is weakened by chronic stress can wake it up. You must start taking care of yourself!"

Good advice, which I pass on. I had dismissed self-care as selfish. Nonsense. Self-care is survival. It is not thinking about yourself more, it is thinking more of yourself.

Feeling the Fears

Our society instructs us not to feel what we're feeling if it's uncomfortable. Feeling bad? No problem! Escape into entertainment, alcohol, drugs, casual sex, big-time spending. My usual defenses were no match for the current pressures, leaving me fearful and pugnacious. I often exploded. It was like walking around with a live hand grenade for protection, often wounding the very people who were trying their best to help me. You're not supposed to be angry when you're a caregiver, but at some level, who isn't?

The downward spiral into self-pity was all too tempting. By assuming the lion's share of responsibility for my husband's medical support, I had been bleeding my own financial security. The time and money it took to jump whenever Clay had an emergency severely curtailed my earning capacity. I was constantly canceling speaking engagements and refusing journalistic assignments. My business expenses on two coasts had exceeded my income for two years running.

But that wasn't all. The IRS was breathing down my neck. I owed back taxes on a sprawling nineteenth-century farmhouse on two acres of prime real estate on eastern Long Island. This was my first and only house, the house that Passages bought, back in the 1970s when it was cheap. I was fiercely attached to it. This was our real home, never "decorated," but filled with treasures of our trips to other parts of the world; nothing valuable in dollars, everything priceless in memories. The tax bill was a recurring nightmare. If I didn't make a major life change soon, the IRS would put a lien on my home and the government would dispose of it and I would be caught in the vortex that takes down so many long-term caregivers.

I had grave decisions to make, and I had to make them without the help of my life partner. How do you get out of a hole? You stop digging.

Seeking Serenity

I confessed to Dr. Pat that I had bottomed out. Her diagnosis was that constant caregiving had displaced my religious upbringing. I did exercise religiously, but I was definitely out of spiritual conditioning. Without a lively faith, I was being overtaken by the fear.

She suggested I try a twelve-step program.

Grateful, but skeptical, I walked thirty blocks down the street from Dr. Pat's office to a twelve-step meeting in a large church. I expected a huddle of mournful souls reciting grisly accident reports on the train wrecks they had made of their lives. I had heard such accounts, secondhand, when my mother entered Alcoholics Anonymous for her recovery.

One step into the nave changed everything. Greeters lined the walls. They were *all cheerful, annoyingly cheerful. They laughed easily at themselves. They all talked about taking positive steps toward living with gratitude and feeling more joyous and free than before they found the program. They clapped for anyone who announced progress.*

I was shocked to find my own behavior described in some of the stories. Like me, the narrators had attacked their problems guided only by a ferocious self-will. When that didn't work, fear overtook. Or resentment, or both. I realized I had become powerless over my fears. In the fever to "save" my husband, I was losing the ability to manage my own life. I needed to find a way to restore my faith.

This was a spiritual program, but no church affiliation was required. We were encouraged to entrust our wills (or egos) to God, who was introduced with the shrewdly tolerant phrase "as we understand him." Doesn't everyone long for a power greater than ourselves to whom we can turn over the dilemmas and disappointments of life? I had always believed in God, but I sense his/her presence in diverse places—not only in church and prayer but also in art, meditation, love, nature, ethics, nonviolence.

The God I hoped to meet was the source of serenity, the missing force in my life. To my delight everybody else at that meeting had the same idea. At the conclusion, we all held hands and recited the universal serenity prayer by Reinhold Niebuhr:

> God, grant me the serenity
> to accept the things that I cannot change;
> the courage to change the things I can;
> and the wisdom to know the difference.

"The wisdom to know the difference" was not just a catchy slogan. It sounded like something God would grant if I met him/her halfway, by accepting the things I could not change—my husband's life trajectory and my own limitations. That was the road to serenity. But first, I would have to quit Playing God. I was full of compassion for my husband, yes, but my caregiving was spiked with more than a pinch of egotism.

I had to find the courage to change the things I could—especially myself. In the twelve-step group everyone learned how to open up and shamelessly examine our defects and draw support from our fellowship The best laughs are at ourselves, and we had many laughs at those meetings. The days went better after gathering in the early morning with my fellow pilgrims.

Finding My Joy

It was June at our country house when I felt the first sign of regeneration. Nothing much grows in the dark, and I had spent too much time in the dark of sickrooms. Spring explodes all at once in eastern Long Island. Rebirth runs riot. I began smelling blooms.

My special treasure was my Shakespeare garden, cultivated over the years with carefully selected bulbs and seeds to reproduce the flowers and herbs mentioned in the bard's plays and love sonnets. The year before, I had planted a row of Madonna lilies, and forgotten them.

One morning that June I found the lilies sprung tall, as if reborn overnight. They were almost life-size, marching uphill with white buds clasped like praying hands. I began visiting the garden several times a day to meditate, if only for a few moments at a time. Meditation was my release into the sunlight. Early one morning, sitting on a bench opposite the lilies, I opened my eyes to something magical. The Madonnas had all opened their ivory trumpets and were pointing to the sky. I could have sworn they were playing Bach.

I fell to my knees in the dewy grass, first laughing, then feeling the need to pray. Give thanks. Epiphany is a too grand a word. All I know is what I suddenly saw—an older woman standing atop a little hill, serene, just a shimmer, beckoning me to join her. Who was she? No surprise: me, years and years ahead. A tiny peek into eternity.

Yes, I would have guidance on the path of Coming Back. I would go out to the garden every day to pray with the Madonnas and listen for their music. My husband would say, "Big Momma is in the garden, and all's right with the world."

I began waking up earlier to meditate and go through my gratitude list. These efforts seemed to complement each other. My anxiety eased. Flights of negative thoughts slowed. My sister, a devotee of mindfulness meditation, passed on a lighthearted explanation of why meditation is a necessary complement to prayer. "To pray without meditation is like calling up God to tell Him your problem and hanging up before you get the answer."

Each time I meditated, I would ask my higher power to help me outgrow my drive to control things. I needed to become less willful and more willing to have the patience and wisdom to say: Thy will, not mine, be done.

I tested all this on a burning question: How could I keep my husband out of a nursing home? My mind sampled one solution after another. None worked. In the past, I would have gnawed on that bone until it was reduced to pulp. Now I focused on what I needed to do in the next twenty-four hours and delegated everything else to my higher power. Then I would wait for an insight, or inspiration, to bubble up from my subconscious.

It was in the shower many days later that the insight flashed like a neon sign: SELL YOUR HOUSE. Eureka! I felt a rush of pleasure and relief.

It wasn't long, however, before relief turned to regret. The house was our sanctuary, the place where I wrote books, where Clay biked and swam, where our grandchildren bounced on a trampoline, where our friends lolled around the pool on lazy summer weekends. Selling it felt like checking out of life.

BEFORE GOING TO THAT *extreme, I needed to revisit old pleasures. It began with appreciating the simplest things in life, like my grandson. Declan was then five and lived in Brooklyn. Being my first grandchild, he was the eternal springtime of my life. In the country I had taught him to fish and play tennis, but now it was winter. I began spending magic Fridays with him. We cooked together, howling with laughter when whipping cream got away from our beater and splattered all over the kitchen walls. We licked it up. We made music together. We didn't even need instruments. We clanged cups and glasses with knives and drummed on the table and sang old Beatles songs. Children live in the moment. My grandson always took me back to the moment.*

It struck me as paradoxical that we humans are most afraid of dying. Yet we often seem to be racing through life as if trying to get to the finish line. We can pray all we want, but we will never be given a better past. We can anticipate the future all we want, but we will never be able to control it. Meantime, we squander the present, this very moment—the one reality within our grasp.

Hungering for creative work, I rejoined a New York playwriting class given by Milan Stitt, a veteran playwright and teacher who ran the graduate playwriting program at Carnegie Mellon University. For several years, I had been developing a play about a couple faced with cancer and the impact on their marriage. It was much more than a cathartic exercise. Playwriting had been my secret passion since I was seven years old and put on the first of many live soap operas on my back porch.

Milan welcomed me back to his apartment with a cheery "Hi, pumpkin!" My fellow workshop students crowded round with hugs and squeals. How could I have stayed away for two years? It was all wonderfully healing. Whatever you did, Milan believed you could make it better and he made you believe it, too. He arranged for a staged reading of my play before a ticket-buying audience. I was thrilled. The next day he told me, "Now you're ready to write your play."

Giving Up My Passages House

Once my life began moving in a healthier direction, aided by a growing circle of care and support, I felt strong enough to surrender my greatest treasure—my house on Long Island. I gritted my teeth and put it on the market. Ironically, nobody wanted it. The house was in bad shape. Renovation was not in our family skills kit. We were all liberal artsy types who lived off ideas and worked in our heads, not with our hands.

One morning as I was walking out of a village coffee shop, I stumbled over an exceedingly long leg.

"Sorry," said a giant gray-haired man. He had sad, deep-set eyes, but a smile played around his lips; he had tripped me up on purpose. I shrugged and went to my table. He came over and showered me with apologies and bad jokes. He designed and built houses, he said. I stared at my newspaper.

Then he told me he was a recent widower. That got my attention. He had cared for his partner for two years after her stroke. He did it full-time, walking her up and down Main Street until her life ended, six months earlier. How did he know I was on the same walk? He didn't. Was this the secret hand of my higher power?

I told him I had to sell my house, but I worried that it wouldn't pass inspection. He lit up. "Why don't I come over and take a look at your place and see what we could do to increase its value."

My smart financial friends had warned me not to gamble my only savings on the hope that rehabbing the house would bump up its value and make the sale worthwhile. Not in a falling market. So I said good-bye to the widower and unlisted him in my mind.

A couple of weeks later, he bumped into me on the street, again on purpose. The widower introduced himself as Richard.

"Any offers yet?"

I had to admit there were none.

"How about I come take a look at your house?"

As we walked the property together, I began to see it with fresh eyes.

"You have a quarter of an acre here that's all junked up with dead shrubs and vines and old tree stumps," he said, whacking at the tangle with a machete. I noticed his strength for the first time. He was a world-class skier and former president of the national ski association. Seventyish, I guessed, but with a body that looked like it had been carved out of hardwood.

"I could clear all this out and then buyers would see a vista straight into the woods," he tantalized me. "It'll raise your price by half a million." For emphasis, he performed an excavation of an old tree stump with his bare hands.

"Very impressive, Mr. Bunyan," I said, "but I couldn't pay you very much."

"Don't worry about it. Whatever you can, when you sell." He would be my property manager, he said. To have anyone managing anything for me sounded tempting.

The next morning I awoke to the loud sound of a chain rattling and the groan of an overtaxed engine. Looking out the window, I saw my new property manager hauling out the stump of a thirty-foot arborvitae with his truck. He cut the dead monster into three neat pieces. Over the summer he worked miracles on the house. He hired day workers to acid wash the stucco and repair the roof and spackle and paint inside and out. He rewired the electrical system and replaced faulty water pipes and dove to the bottom of the pool to plug leaks. Once the house was virtually inspector-proof, I had a solid offer. The buyer put down a hefty deposit. I thought I was home free.

By midsummer, when my days and nights ran together in the pallor of a midtown hospital where I was watching over Clay for weeks in the ICU, the house sale fell through. The potential buyer had never "cleared" her check for deposit. It was a crushing blow.

When I went out to Long Island to arrange another showing, the molten sun of late summer was almost too beautiful to bear. I walked every inch of the beloved grounds of my house, weeded the Shakespeare garden, and clipped the faded roses to save for potpourri. I ached all over.

Richard appeared, now as a friend, and rescued me from despair by taking me to his favorite spot, the walking dunes. It was late on a lazy afternoon, but the sun was still strong and the beach was deserted. The warm sand on my bare feet, the spanking breeze, the sparkling water, and the whitewashed sky without limit suddenly jolted my senses awake. How could I have forgotten the joys of nature? The delight in feeling like a woman? There are parts of being fully human that must never be given up.

We would find another buyer in no time, Richard assured me. Meanwhile, he said, I must claim at least an hour a day to take my mind entirely off what wasn't happening with the house and what was happening with Clay. It was my own mantra coming out of his mouth!

A Triangle of Care

I discovered that I could take Clay out of rehab at the Jewish Home on weekends and let him enjoy our country house, provided I had all the equipment in place to keep him safe. (I had to pay the Jewish Home for the privilege of taking the patient out; Medicare won't cover it if the bed isn't occupied!) Richard offered to set up a hospital room in the country house. Soon, Clay was sitting in his favorite chair in the dining room, a dominant presence again, supervising the inner repair work on the house. We ate lunches together, the three of us. I no longer felt isolated.

A unique bond formed between these two men, both grown old enough that their macho urges were tempered by the rise of tenderness and need for connection. As a widower, Richard needed to fill in the hole left by his partner's death. He was a rescuer by nature. In me, he admitted, he saw another "damsel in distress." Helping Clay and I helped him, he said.

How would Clay respond to Richard? He had always been possessive and proud of being my protector. His mind was fully functional, but his body betrayed his efforts to help me. His sadness, even shame, was palpable. He needed to know that I could survive without him. He sized up Richard and responded to him man-to-man in a nonverbal way. Clay would get up and lead him around the house, pointing silently at ceiling cracks that needed patching. He let it be known that he appreciated what Richard was doing to help me.

Richard wouldn't let me forget that daily hour for restoring myself. He knew all kinds of secret places to watch the sun rise. In the stolen hour before the world wakes up, he would drive me to his favorite creeks and coves, slide a canoe into the water, and we'd paddle, silently, listening for the birds to call and fish to jump. Finding a sandy spot, we'd sip coffee from a thermos and squint at the horizon for the first halo of sunrise. We shared a worship of nature on those sunrise sojourns. It was enormously healing.

Thanksgiving that year was never truer. Elaborate arrangements had to be made to take Clay to the country for three whole days. It rained like hell.

On arrival, I couldn't get Clay out of the car without the danger of the two of us sprawling in the mud. Richard raced over and picked him up and carried him inside to his makeshift hospital room. Neither of them said a word. They didn't have to. Faced with the limitations of aging, people form attachments beyond the ordinary, and that summer and fall we three helped one another survive.

The family all came and we cooked the most traditional turkey dinner. Sitting in his chair by the window, Clay spoke with his eyes. His mind had always been engaged day to day, but he was seldom emotionally involved. He saw himself as an outsider, extraneous to all that was happening. The transformation on that Thanksgiving was remarkable. He wasn't the tense, controlled man who had to work to maintain his dignity in the rehab hospital. He was a very central, organic part of all that happened. Presiding over the family, he experienced himself as belonging again.

In the middle of carving the turkey, I stopped. This was Clay's role.

I turned to him. Richard and I pulled his chair closer to the table so he could carve. I handed him the great knife. I bent to kiss him. Richard told me later, "I saw Clay's eyes glow. The muscles in his face relaxed, he smiled like a happy child. Warmth and love radiated from him as a presence that filled the room." Richard wiped away his tears. "I loved him, too."

By the end of November—weeks before the IRS threatened to put a lien on the house—I had a solid offer. This time I was smarter; I asked that the deposit be nonrefundable. This buyer was a friend and she agreed. The house would be sold.

Now I had to focus on moving out of the condo in California and emptying the big Long Island house by January 2, the day the new owner would take possession. Two days later, on January 4, Clay would be discharged from the Jewish Home, ending the ninety-day rehab stay provided by Medicare. If he failed to leave, I would have to pay $450 a day out of pocket. That's $13,500 a month.

In my frantic rush to meet all these deadlines, I spent New Year's Eve alone in my half-empty country house, sorting and packing the last vestiges of artworks, furniture, and memorabilia accumulated over thirty years, plus the archives of two

*long journalistic careers—all searing reminders of happier days. I had little to
celebrate.*

    *I survived. My Passages house became history. My husband came home. And so
began my next three months of bird-dogging Clay's slow, stuttering return to nearly
full mental capacity. I have to be honest—those three months were grim. All too
often, I heard my inner voice screaming words every caregiver will recognize: I can't
do this anymore!*

    *But I was coming back to myself. It took another year, with help from the
twelve-step program, my grandson's wisdom about living in the moment, giving up
what I could no longer afford, renewing former passions, and accepting the
kindness of a stranger who brought me back to nature. These godsends took me a
long way toward mastering my fear of losing Clay.*

    *This was the toughest turning of all. But although I did not recognize it at the
time, it put me on the path of Coming Back.*

STRATEGIES

Reconnect with Your Transports to Joy

    How long have you been going in circles? Have you lost track?
Are you exhausted but can't sleep? Facing financial meltdown?
Alone and afraid? Do you lurch from crisis to crisis, chained to your
loved one's progress or retreat—one step forward, three back?

    When it's clear that your loved one will never get well, you have
reached the center of the labyrinth of caregiving. You will probably
feel conflicted—relieved yet resistant. Some days seem black with
despair, others shot through with promise. This is a turning point
that presents you with a crucial choice: go down with your loved
one, or make a conscious effort to come up for air and reconnect
with your transports to joy.

It's not easy. You can't just walk away from your loved one. A long vigil may still lie ahead. But you must move. You must begin Coming Back *before* you begin saying good-bye.

This sounds impossibly hard, I know. But the alternative to Coming Back is losing your self. When you oversee the deterioration of someone you love, the process keeps washing away the "me" that once comprised half of "us."

"The longer this erosion of self goes on, unless the caregiver makes an effort to come up for air on a daily basis, the harder it is for him or her to return to those dreams that were shared with the individual." This is the expert observation of Dr. Jonathan Mueller, a neuropsychiatrist at the University of California, San Francisco, who has studied families caring for Alzheimer's patients and developed the widely used cognitive screening test Cognistat. "At some level the caregiver feels anger and resentment, but it can't be expressed to the loved one, so it spills out elsewhere."

Coming Back requires going out into the real world for at least a quick sampling every day, and for a daylong break at least once a month. This is the time to rediscover old friends, hobbies, and passions put on hold. Your moves can be big or small, as long as you *act.*

Ask yourself: In another life, what were my personal lifelines? Music? Sports? Painting? Causes? A book club? A football pool? Coaching? Collecting? Restoring something old? Learning something new? Cooking, writing, woodworking, fixing up old cars?

Ask yourself: What kind of garden can I cultivate? It needn't be an actual garden, just something beautiful you grow with loving care. It might be tutoring a poor kid with a bright mind or a superb pitching arm. It might be helping to create a new town library or a sports field or an arts center. I myself began making patchwork quilts out of the sweaters and shirts that my husband could no longer wear. It was a way of passing on something of him to our children and grandchildren.

All these are means of gradually giving yourself permission to begin letting go. Many caregivers find this unburdening easier when they seek (and receive) spiritual support from a higher power. But everyone in this situation deserves to feel cleared for takeoff, for reentry to the living world. You will continue caring. But at this turning, it is essential that you look out for the well-being of the caregiver—and that's you!

What is the key to reviving a sense of joy? Ask yourself: When and how can I stop trying to control what I cannot change?

KEITH WOLFARD'S COMEBACK

Keith Wolfard is the firefighter in Oregon whom we met in an earlier chapter. He knew all about the darkness at the center of the labyrinth. Just as I had, Keith struggled to accept that the person he loved most in the world would never come back to him whole.

Keith had sped through the happiest years of his life on his Harley, his waist hugged by the arms of his younger wife, Daphne. Now, after seven years of pretending that Alzheimer's wouldn't take Daphne from him, he had to face reality. Daphne was no longer Daphne. Still only in her fifties, she had been replaced by a combative, cursing screamer. "I came to the realization that it wasn't her that made those words come out."

Once Keith made the painful decision to put Daphne in a residential care home, he began the hardest part of his journey. He had turned sixty-two and he was working his way back out of the labyrinth. He told me he felt both guilty and good about it.

By placing her nearby, he was able to take mornings for himself, breathing the fresh air of rural Oregon, working on his yard, and rebuilding his beloved antique cars. Afternoons were reserved for visits to Daphne. When I revisited him, he was polishing his fiery red Harley and looking forward to taking Daphne for a bike ride. It was one of the small joys he could still share with his wife.

Daphne emerged from the facility clutching a stuffed white dog and looking tentative. Her face was still beautiful but without definition, like a pencil sketch of a fiery Irish lass with the color missing. When she saw Keith, the pinch of tension between her brows softened. A smile spread all over her face. Grateful still to be recognized, Keith wrapped her in his arms.

She also recognized me. I told her how lucky she was to have such a strong and healthy husband who couldn't wait to see her. She looped her arm around Keith's waist and said, with the fervor of a child, "Mine!"

Gently, he slipped on her motorcycle helmet and helped her to straddle the bike. He held her hand and asked if she wanted a ride. "Yes!" She was fully alive in the moment. And Keith was again her rescuer. Off they roared, with Daphne beaming, seemingly secure that as long as she hangs on to her husband, she was safe.

A couple of hours later, Keith left Daphne at the facility and rode back to his empty house, brushed away some tears, and walked outside to smell the fir trees. After a while, he chopped firewood to release his feelings. I asked how he saw his life. "I'm not sure about the future," he said, "but we're doing okay right now."

He was beginning the long journey home to himself, without abandoning the love of his life. This is the fragile balance we must try to maintain as partners in life begin to take separate paths.

twenty-two

CARING FOR THE *UNLOVED* ONE

It is common practice to refer to the person you are caring for as "your loved one." But I don't have to tell you that adult children aren't always buddy-buddy with parents. What if The Call summons you to take care of an *un*loved one? Particularly between mothers and daughters, the wars can persist even beyond the grave. Consider this vivid story I heard (names withheld at request):

For fifty years, nothing had changed between Daughter and Mother. The harder Daughter tried to please her, the more critical and demanding Mother became. From the time she graduated out of pigtails, the daughter's hair was always wrong; her grades, embarrassing; her taste in boys, pathetic. Mother did not mellow in her later, widowed years. The daughter served as Mother's caregiver and unpaid limo driver, listening to her bitch and moan while being hand-delivered to hit shows, cocktail parties, doctors, lawyers, hairdressers, and, who knows, gigolos.

Mother had ruled out mortality, at least for herself. In recent years she had acknowledged, sort of, a "trembly problem" (Parkinson's), and "little heart flutters" (congestive heart failure), and a pesky need to hide under her skirt her "little evening bag" (colostomy). Daughter seethed but held her silence. After all, Mother was sick. Daughter just tuned out.

Today was different.

Driving Mother to the beach, Daughter kept hearing the dragon lady's complaints. Suddenly, she could bear no more. With hot rage, she shouted,

"I'm sick to death of your put-downs! This time I'm leaving you at the beach for good! NOW SHUT UP, YOU UNGRATEFUL OLD HAG!"

Stunned by her own outburst, Daughter looked over nervously to the passenger seat. There sat Mother, wordless, safely sealed inside her jar of ashes.

STRATEGIES

Necessary Reconciliations

Imagine loving our parents differently. Can you? Even if years of estrangement have separated you, there is always time to meet again and pick up from now. It is not necessary, and not plausible, to go back over wounds that have become embedded in each of your psyches, expecting a different result. And now, by virtue of years lived apart, you are both somewhat different people with different perspectives.

Go on. Take a chance. This is one of the potentially richest passages of your life. Why not create a reconciliation ritual?

A friend of mine was moved to do so, after decades of estrangement from her mother, when she visited Salisbury Cathedral near Stonehenge in England. Her mind was suddenly flooded with vivid memories of a happy vacation she had spent there with her parents when she was very young. That visual imagery played over and over in her mind's eye, until she wrote a simple note to her mother describing her memories and thanking her for a happy time. The note opened a window. She and her mother spent a weekend together, shopping and trading stories, normal things that mothers and daughters do together. But the daughter learned that her mother had been abandoned as a baby and shunted around foster homes. "She had never felt loved."

The daughter worked with the deacon of her church to create a reconciliation ritual—an offertory of healing with hymns and dancing, bread and wine. In the presence of family and friends, mother and daughter spoke words of love.

WHEN THE CAREGIVER IS ABUSED

It isn't only parents who can become impossible as they wrestle with the decline of their own health and independence. The next story, about Mary Tinker, reveals a hidden aspect of caregiving for a spouse: it can turn into domestic abuse.

It is an easy trap to fall into, and even harder to see a way out. Why? A suffering person can be highly manipulative, playing on the caregiver's compassion and guilt. And the wife who does everything humanly possible to keep her husband alive may come to be seen, and to see herself, as heroic.

Mary's husband was accustomed to letting her deal with the unpleasant realities of life. He didn't believe in insurance, for instance, so Mary hung on to her full-time job at a senior center to provide health insurance for him and their two young sons. He didn't believe in going to doctors, so he brushed off Mary's pleadings that he pay attention to his chronic stomach pains.

It took two years before she was able to drag him to a doctor for a colonoscopy, whereupon he was diagnosed with advanced colon cancer. Mary knew her husband did not have long to live. But how long? Privately, the doctor told her he would live for two years max. It turned out to be four.

Mary anointed herself as the sole caregiver. She quickly established herself as the only person her husband trusted to provide his constant care, from cleaning his open wounds after surgery to staying in constant touch with his doctors to hear news he didn't want to know.

I asked Mary why she wouldn't accept any help. Her answer was "I have a strong sense of commitment."

Mary was a prime candidate for Playing God. It may feel powerful, especially to a woman who has little self-esteem, but over time the caregiver begins to lose herself. "I wasn't aware of my desire to play God," she admitted. "Yet we so often find ourselves going down that path, wanting to believe 'I am the one who can do it better. No one else is going to do it the way I do.' It's a trap."

Playing God can take a devastating toll on a mere human. No earthling can control the trajectory of disease or elude the eventuality of death. Taking on that responsibility invites overwhelming stress and is destined to end in failure and a residue of guilt.

Mary had dropped out of high school to marry at eighteen and was in her midthirties when she took on this second full-time job as her husband's caregiver. For four years she and her children walked on eggshells around an angry and increasingly abusive man. Their older son, age ten at the time, became the brunt of his mental and physical blows.

Mary's husband was jealous that she was the well one. One night, when they were lying in bed talking, he blurted out, "Why me? Why not you?"

Her husband's resentment is typical of many older, sick, or frail people. As they forfeit their independence and lose control over their bodies, they may become desperate to control the person caring for them. It's a consolation, but it can become perverse. Mary's husband also tried to demonstrate his control by spending money recklessly.

Mary was alone in worrying about their dwindling funds. How would she be able to support herself and the two boys once her husband passed on? His callous response was "You've got a lifetime to clean up whatever mess I leave behind."

She could barely clean up the mess he was making of their lives in the present. Carrying a full-time job and a full-time caregiving role, while being hypervigilant to protect her sons, Mary was constantly fatigued but could rarely sleep—not even on a Sunday when God takes a rest. "You get to the point where crisis just feels routine," she says. "You're caught up in the day-to-day drudgery of what has to be done, and the guilt of not getting it done."

Her blood pressure shot up. Having totally neglected taking care of herself, she wound up in the emergency room with huge welts covering her body from head to toe. The doctor said he'd never seen hives like that before. It was only one of her body's stress reactions. Soon after, she began losing her hair. When the stress of caregiving is acute, nonstop, and pro-longed, the aftereffects can last for many years.

"It still hasn't all grown back," she told me, running her fingers through sparse salt-and-pepper tufts. And this is fifteen years later.

At the end of her second year of Playing God, she hit the wall. "I felt like 'Why can't we just get this over with?'" Mary began entertaining fantasies of divorce. She wrestled with herself because, believe it or not, her husband was a minister. As a woman of faith, she felt guilty about exposing a minister as a child abuser.

When her husband caught on that she might be ready to leave, he threat-ened that if she filed for divorce, he would kill her. "Because," he said, "I have nothing to lose." The raw truth of that statement was terrifying. Her hus-band had guns and he knew how to use them.

She waited until the next time her husband had an emergency admission to the hospital and was kept there. This was her chance to serve him with divorce papers. On discharge, her husband was taken in by his sister. Mary wouldn't have him back. Now, she had to find her own way back to life.

MARY'S EMERGENCE

The next three months were a revelation to Mary and her boys. Living in a stress-free situation, they were able to revive their enjoyment of simple pleasures. They went hiking together. She took the boys to ball games. They'd curl up at home with popcorn and watch a movie, just the three of them, with no fear of shouting or violence.

This is tantamount to "respite," a break from long-term caregiving that all support organizations consider essential for the health and sanity of long-term caregivers. For Mary, it was a rehearsal for finding the confidence to take on the role of a widow with young children. She became comfortable in her own "shelter" and began to invest in her own future.

Remembering the sheer guts it took for her to remove her children and herself to safety, Mary still dissolves in tears. She had to have many conversa-tions with God to believe he knew her heart, and to convince herself that this was not a vindictive act. She wasn't abandoning her husband, she was saving herself and her family. His sister was readily available to take over his care.

Mary's story points up the absolute necessity for the caregiver to take care of herself. Even after her husband died and she was out of danger, Mary was plagued by nightmares. Although her house was peaceful, she often dreamed that he was still in control, their finances were shrinking as he overspent, and abuse was always around the corner.

She had begun seeing light at the end of the tunnel only when she accepted, "I can't take this anymore," and started putting one foot in front of the other on the long but rewarding path of completing her education. She was able to envision a future self who had completed high school and college and earned the advanced degree that would qualify her to become a health professional. That would allow her to help other caregivers to draw boundaries and survive. "I felt engaged in life again," she says with pride. "I had a goal for a career path. I knew this is what would sustain us when he was gone."

The most creative step Mary took to comfort her children was to begin writing a journal about her emotional state during the crisis. In the journal, she addressed her preteen children as if they were grown, explaining the thought process that led to her decisions. It consoled her to know that as adults, her sons would read about her conversations with God and, she hoped, understand her actions. Perhaps more important, the journaling allowed her to trace her own journey, and forgive herself.

FOLLOWING HER HUSBAND'S DEATH, Mary's mother fell ill. At first, she found herself slipping back into the same role. But she had changed. By now, she knew the pitfalls of Playing God. She also knew the ropes of caregiving and how to confront barriers in the health-care system.

"By the time I got to the third doctor with no clear diagnosis, I was fed up with their pat answers," she told me. "I took charge. I put my advocate hat on. This doctor was there to provide a service for us. I wanted his attention. So I was very . . . *direct*. I told him straight out, before he had a chance to say anything, that I didn't want the stock answer: 'Your mother is just getting old.' That didn't mean that she was disposable. I wanted him to do a thorough examination and find out what was at the bottom of this drastic change in her health."

The root of the problem was all about a medication that was interfering with her thyroid. Once the dose was adjusted, her mother was back on track within a couple of days. If Mary had not advocated, her mother would probably have deteriorated rapidly and died prematurely. "I'm sure that does happen in many cases."

Our "new" Mary now has the confidence and experience to offer strong advice for other caregivers: "When caregivers are passive, busy medical practitioners just take the easiest path. Don't take the initial, simple answer, because most times that will not get to the base of the problem." Particularly with older people who have multiple interactions with drugs and symptoms, she counsels, it's essential that the caregiver go into the doctor's office prepared to give a clear account of all the symptoms and the time frame over which they have developed. Mary spoke with assurance:

"Caregivers are professionals. They need to be treated like professionals. When they're interacting, whether it's with a physician or a pharmacy, they need to see themselves as professionals. My mother's doctor actually started to respect me more. He wanted my input. It was a total turnaround of attitude, both with him and with the rest of the staff."

Mary's comeback was a long but happy period, when she pursued a bachelor's degree—"That was huge!"—and went on to get a graduate degree. "It not only improved my self-esteem, it's opened tremendous opportunities for me. I was able to move into a career that I love." Today, in her midfifties, she is a highly credentialed and respected care manager working at the Council on Aging in Silicon Valley. A public-private agency, COA provides care managers to help families keep their loved ones out of the hospital and cared for in the home with community services. Mary's natural gift for helping others now has a creative outlet.

She counsels caregivers to avoid Playing God: "Your health has to come first. You must get respite. You can't take care of someone else if you're coming to your wit's end. It's so easy to let that happen and not realize when you're reaching burnout." She winds up with the very encouragement she wished she had had:

"Join a support group and let others who have been through this journey convince you how vital it is to take care of yourself. Otherwise your health may suffer irrevocably."

After twenty years of caregiving for members of her family, Mary lets nothing interfere with her two weeks of vacation in Hawaii. Her sons are grown and married. She recently moved her mother into her sister's house. "For the first time in my adult life, I have found myself totally free, and am I enjoying it!"

I asked Mary, "Why do you think women so often allow their loved ones to use them and abuse them when they're sick?"

"We tend to think—inside ourselves—that we're failures if we don't do it all." With the benefit of hindsight, Mary fires back at her own ignorance: "It's a bunch of bunk! We don't have to do it all!"

SEVENTH TURNING:
THE IN-BETWEEN STAGE

twenty-three

BEYOND CURE, WHAT NOW?

"Your husband has entered the cycle of slow dying."

The words were unexpectedly blunt coming from the intensivist, the lung doctor who had never given up on Clay. This was late spring 2007. Clay had been circling in and out of the hospital, repeatedly attacked by lung infections. Twice, Dr. Mina had taken Clay into the bronchoscopy unit and tried valiantly to dredge the infection out of his lungs. But Clay no longer had enough strength to cough up the knots of secretions that kept reinfecting him.

"How long?"

"He could live another year like this. Maybe two."

I blurted: "I don't know if I can take that."

"What's the alternative?" the doctor asked.

"You tell me."

"The next time he gets an infection or pneumonia, don't send him back to the hospital."

Give up? Quit? Surrender? Again, I was the bird who flies into the glass window—I hadn't seen this coming.

"Where do we go now?"

Dr. Mina had no answer. At this stage of half-life, doctors have no more answers. Unable to effect a cure, they feel defeated.

The next day, Clay's physician quarterback, the internist Stuart Orsher, told us that he had one more rabbit to pull out of his hat. A surgeon could do a laser fix that might open up the narrowed aperture at the top of Clay's trachea so he could cough out the infection. Clay declined; he knew the necrotic tissue in his throat would never heal.

I asked Dr. Orsher to step outside Clay's room. It was time to be totally frank. "Haven't we reached the end of what medicine can do to reverse Clay's path?" I asked.

Dr. Orsher huddled close and spoke like an old friend. "Clay should have been dead years ago. He almost died several times this year. You've given him ten extra years of life. Nobody has gotten the care and attention you have given this man. That's why all the doctors who have worked on Clay make every effort to keep him alive—because we've seen the devotion between the two of you."

It was a surprisingly human observation, and I was deeply touched. But we were beyond rabbits now. I had to speak the word most doctors will not. "Is Clay ready for hospice?"

The doctor avoided my eyes. Like Dr. Mina, he was as torn as I was. He mumbled, "Why don't you investigate it."

Clay was not actively dying. But he was beyond curing. This is serious chronic illness. This is a new turning in the labyrinth.

This is where we as caregivers must begin releasing our loved one. Letting go of the all-out fight to bring him or her back to health. That doesn't mean giving up. There is an important difference between denial and hope. Ruth Cohn Bolletino, a New York psychotherapist who specializes in working with cancer patients and others with life-threatening illnesses, makes a clear distinction in her book How to Talk with Family Caregivers About Cancer. *"Denial is the refusal or inability to believe the reality of what is happening. Hope, on the other hand, is the belief that whatever the present situation, there is a chance that things can change for the better."*

People with serious chronic conditions that recur but also recede may still have a clear and hungry mind, or a body that yearns to move around, however that can be made possible. With the right environment and realistic treatment goals, they can still enjoy and participate in life, despite limitations. There are still family barbecues to be savored, conversations with God to be had, memoirs to be written or last lectures to be delivered, or grandchildren to be savored.

But what to do in between?

NOBODY WANTS THE CHRONICALLY ILL

Who are the chronically ill? It's your sister with MS, your dad with nerve damage from cancer treatment, or your spouse with the early signs of dementia after a mild stroke. It is estimated that more than 133 million Americans live with at least one chronic illness. Given the state of art in medical and pharmaceutical treatments, most life-threatening diseases now turn into chronic conditions. The growing ranks of cancer survivors have a chronic illness. Heart disease often becomes a chronic illness. So do diabetes, stroke, respiratory illness, and all the progressive degenerative diseases like MS and Parkinson's, and, of course, any form of dementia from mild to Alzheimer's.

Often, it is not the primary disease that the chronically ill are battling. It is the aftermath of treatment. The body is gradually weakened from the long fight, together with considerable inactivity. Clay's doctors were telling me that he very likely would not die from cancer. It was the death of tissues and cells in his body from the assaults by radiation, surgery, and chemotherapy that had weakened him. He would most likely die of pneumonia. This is a very common scenario.

As routine functions like walking and eating, or moving around without constant fear of falling, become consistently problematical, the demands of caregiving can become all-consuming. People with chronic conditions like these don't belong in emergency rooms and cannot be cured in an acute-care hospital. But they can live for years, even decades. Like Clay, they have reached a stage that our health-care system does not recognize, what I came to think of as the In-Between Stage.

Where do people belong when they enter the In-Between Stage? At home? That's what more than 80 percent of Americans prefer. But who can afford the time and cost of watching round the clock over an adult who can't take responsibility for his or her own care and safety?

Our health-care system has no affordable solution for this stage. Only very short-term help is available for the chronically ill at home. Shuttling them in and out of acute-care hospitals at the sign of any new symptom or unrelieved pain is debilitating for the patient and defeating for the caregiver.

I always kept a set of clothes laid out on a chair and shoes in place on the floor, ready to jump up at a moment's notice. But every time Clay went into the hospital for a week or even less, he was set back a month in bodily strength and in his mental and emotional level. He was like a climber who's stayed too long near the summit and been deprived of oxygen. And I was out of breath, too.

Seeking Solace from My Daughter

I had only a few days to explore the hushed world of supervised dying before the hospital's discharge nurse would chase me down and out. I traveled to the north pole of the Bronx to see the gigantic Calvary Hospital, a name that struck fear in my heart. I took an hour's ride on the subway to the darkest end of Brooklyn to investigate a more intimate residential hospice facility. In both cases, the patients were almost all cancer victims in the final stage of wasting disease. None of them even moved. These were compassionate warehouses for the last weeks before death.

I fled to my daughter's house in the country and huddled on her couch, obsessing about the decision. Time and again, Maura had soothed my soul over earlier decisions, always offering an empathetic ear and smart suggestions. She was, after all, the professional therapist in the family. Indefatigably, she showed up at hospitals and rehab facilities, often trailing her husband and children. I leaned heavily on her. But this decision—hospice or hope—was too morbid and threatening for me to talk about rationally. I just wanted to run away from it.

Maura did her heroic best to talk it through with me. I wasn't sensitive to the burden I was offloading on her. Late on a Saturday night, after we had tucked the children in bed, she looked up from her knitting and said gravely, "Mom, this is my beloved stepfather and my mother's husband we're talking about. I just can't . . ." and she choked back sobs.

There is only so much one can ask of family.

The Magic Partnership: Caregiver and Care Manager

I needed a professional to help me walk through this turning. I found a care manager, a graduate of both Marymount Manhattan and Sarah Lawrence with a master's degree in health advocacy. Mary Tierney was short, solid, and indomitable, but with a coating of Irish charm. She could make things happen without making people mad. Her flaring red brows lit up the furrows in her perpetually worried face. Mary could sit with me over a glass of wine and help me think through the tough decisions.

She charged $125 an hour, but her experience in the Byzantine world of home care was always worth far more than her fee. Working many hours for which she didn't charge, Mary became my partner, my guide, my sanity saver, the kind of frontline buddy that soldiers talk about.

It is crucial that the patient and care manager like and trust each other, so Mary spent time with Clay until he got to know her and welcomed her help. Mary worshipped Clay. She would not allow me to choose anything that wasn't just right for him.

Together, Mary and I visited Cabrini Hospital's hospice unit. The intake nurse waited for us in the family room. With a dimpled smile, she extended her hand and enveloped us with warmth. "How can I help?" She led us into a womblike room and explained how they would care for Clay.

"An ambulance picks up your family member from the hospital and brings him here, where he doesn't enter the hospital. He's taken right up to the tenth floor and our unit—a smooth transition. All the paperwork is done in advance with a consent form. This would be covered by Medicare in full. We will finish out his course of antibiotics. Then it's up to our physician what to do next. But it would be nothing aggressive."

All I could think about was the six-month deadline under hospice.

The nurse wound up her standard introduction. "The purpose of our state-of-the-art inpatient unit is to offer short-term acute care when a patient needs it, until they can return home. Then he'd be visited at home by a hospice registered nurse, once or twice a week, to coordinate his care with you and manage pain or other symptoms. Our doctor would come every four to six weeks. But you can call our hospice nurses twenty-four hours a day."

"How soon do you think he could come home?" I asked.

Suddenly the nurse shifted emphasis. "Taking someone home in your husband's condition is emotionally draining because it's not like he's getting better—every day, he's getting worse. Even if you hire private nurses, he will have another lung infection."

The nurse then described how Clay would be treated as an inpatient. He would be weaned off antibiotics. His feedings would be gradually reduced, since, she said, he wouldn't be moving or using calories. He would gradually weaken. Ultimately, they would suspend hydration. It was a sentence to die.

"I'm afraid he won't accept hospice care," I said. "He's not ready to die." I told her we had beaten cancer four times.

The nurse raised her hands in a halt motion. "That's a problem!"

Mary Tierney and I looked dumbfounded. "Why?"

"Because then they get to thinking they'll beat it again and again and never die. He needs to witness his decline, day by day, in order for him to make the decision. As he feels his body shutting down, his thoughts will be clearer."

Shutting down.

It was then that I realized Clay would never come home. I made a feeble attempt at an alternative. "Your signs say you also offer palliative care. Could he have that?"

"I can use those words, if you prefer. It just means comfort care, no aggressive measures."

"Could you talk to my husband in the hospital?"

"Of course," said the nurse. "I'll see him tomorrow to do an assessment."

She came in the morning, kind and comforting. But she wore a badge that read "Hospice Intake Nurse." When Clay's eyes fell on those words, he stopped listening and looked away. The ambulance was scheduled to take him to the inpatient hospice unit the next day.

The Call woke me at home before midnight. It was Dr. Mina. The intensivist had just returned from vacation and read the latest lab report on Clay's culture.

"It's negative for pneumonia," he said. "Clay is not ready for hospice." It felt like a call from the warden granting a stay of execution. My heart soared.

But what about the next infection, and the next?

"He's a fighter," said Dr. Mina. "It would be great to give him another chance. And when it's all over, you'll be able to sleep at night knowing you did everything possible for him."

When it was all over? I couldn't allow myself to think that far ahead. I focused instead on just getting a good night's sleep so I could run across Central Park first thing in the morning and tell Clay. He took in the good news passively, having been *forced to forfeit any sense of control over his life's course. By now, he was numb in both legs and indifferent toward his survival.*

Leaving the hospital, I bumped into the intensivist in the elevator. "I can't keep him in the hospital over the weekend," he pleaded. "The business office calls about him every day."

Too soon for hospice. Too late for the hospital. Like so many of the chronically ill, we were medical refugees.

STRATEGIES

When Is It Time for Hospice?

Hospice is comfort care for people who are clearly dying. It is a wonderful program, available almost everywhere in the United States and Europe. It emphasizes comfort and relief from physical and emotional pain for both the patient and the family as they work through the dying process. A team, which includes a nurse practitioner, a social worker, a pastoral counselor, and possibly a grief counselor, coordinates with the patient's physician and is usually able to respond to questions or crises twenty-four hours a day.

Outside of big cities or major medical centers, hospice may be the only free service that offers comfort and support to relieve suffering that is often neglected—pain, fatigue, anxiety, agitation, depression—once doctors give up on treating a patient with aggressive medical interventions.

But what about people who are not yet at the end of their lives? What is offered for people at the In-Between Stage? People like Clay who are not actively dying and unwilling to agree to die on a government schedule. Even today, chronically ill patients and their caregivers are commonly presented with a draconian either-or choice. Either you accept a miserable half-life in one hospital bed after another or a nursing home, or you accept a speedy death on the hospice schedule. Six months to checkout.

"Most patients and their families do not accept hospice until the last couple of months of life, and many resist calling upon hospice until the last week or even the last day of life," says Dr. Diane Meier, a pioneering geriatric physician at Mount Sinai Medical Center in New York and director of the National Center to Advance Palliative Care.

Palliative care is appropriate for any age and at any point in an illness. The goal of palliative-care programs is to keep chronically ill people out of the hospital and seriously ill people from ending up in the ER at three in the morning because of a pain crisis. (Read more about palliative care in the Eighth Turning: The Long Good-bye section.)

Caregivers often receive the most cherished benefit of hospice care. They and other family members almost universally express gratitude for being guided and supported through the mysteries of the dying process. The common refrain is "We couldn't have done it alone."

Follow the Money

The most stressful part of the caregiver's journey is managing the transitions from hospital or rehab to who knows where. It reveals our fractured health-care system in stark terms. You may have been at the hospital day and night, and suddenly it's a Thursday and you're being told your loved one is ready to leave—tomorrow. Help! I'm not ready.

After experiencing dozens of traumatic transfers from home to ER to ICU to rehab and back home again, I needed to understand the rules of the game. Finally, two of Clay's attending physicians explained to me how the system works. It's really quite simple: just follow the money.

"There is no business case for keeping people from going to the hospital," Dr. Sean Morrison, a palliative medicine physician at Mount Sinai Medical Center's Palliative Care Institute in New York, later told me. "Quite the opposite. There is a business case, an incentive, for getting patients into the hospital, giving them more and more expensive high-tech tests, regardless of the benefit, and then getting them out quickly. The federal government set up a payment system, Medicare, and the health-care system aligned itself perfectly to take advantage of everything the payment system has to offer. If we really want to change the health-care system, we have to change the reimbursement system."

Hospitals get a lump-sum payment from Medicare for each hospital admission, based on the diagnosis for which the patient is admitted. The diagnosis is called the DRG—diagnostic-related group. "The insurance pays the hospital a predetermined, set rate for a fixed number of days assigned to that diagnosis, instead of paying to keep the patient until he gets better," explained the medical director of a large New York hospital.

For example, the DRG for uncomplicated pneumonia is usually three days. If the patient is discharged in three days, the hospital gets the full reimbursement. If the patient is released after only two days, the hospital makes half again as much money. But if you are held over for five days, because your lungs weren't cleared or other troubling symptoms needed investigation, the hospital will still be paid for only three days and will thus lose money. (A lab culture for complex pneumonia takes almost a week to produce accurate results.)

This is the crux: hospital staff have time to treat only the immediate acute episode, for which the hospital is paid the lump sum fixed for that diagnosis. All the incentives point toward releasing patients quicker and often sicker. Doctors are often caught in the middle between the protesting family and the hospital's business office together with a faceless insurance representative. The latter two have the last word—*discharge*.

Juxtapose this with the physician's incentives. Doctors are paid a fee for service for every day the person is in the hospital. All they have to do is pull aside the green curtain and ask, "How are you feeling today, Miss Jones?" and they get paid. Ordering costly procedures also improves the doctor's fee.

My physician informants spelled out their Hobson's choice. Most doctors are reluctant to release a patient too soon, but if they make a practice of waiting until the patient is actually well before discharging him, they risk retribution.

"The hospital tracks internally what the length of stay is per diagnosis," says the medical director. "A spreadsheet shows them how many days a given doctor extends his patients' stays beyond what the DRG allows. A review board is always trying to reduce the average length of stay. If a doctor exceeds his DRG for many months in a row, and his patients stay longer than other patients with a similar diagnosis, his privileges to practice at that hospital may be revoked."

Now I understood why, every time you call to report a medical problem in a chronically ill person, the doctor is primed to tell you to take the patient to the ER "for reevaluation." That is how financial incentives drive hospital behavior.

Healing Places

As an insular Manhattanite, I felt my palms sweating as I drove across the Henry Hudson Bridge and entered Riverdale, gateway to the mysterious Bronx. Looming on either side of the highway were tall stone nursing homes, stuffed with the halt and the lame, where I had long ago visited my great-grandmother. How could my brilliant husband be ready for this?

Clay was being ambulanced up to the Bronx—destination unknown—before I could get through holiday traffic to ride with him. "I'm riding with Clay, don't worry," Mary Tierney called to assure me. The nursing home had been preselected by the hospital.

The Schervier Nursing Care Center, as it was called, turned out to be an old redbrick Catholic establishment. Most floors housed long-stayers with some dementia who toured the place in wheelchairs. I found Clay in a large private room, cloudy-eyed, unshaven, slumped over half-mast in a wheelchair. My heart ached. The poor battered man desperately needed tenderness and loving presence. I leaned over to kiss him. I had wonderful news.

"Maura's pregnant!" He stirred slightly. "Her amnio shows a healthy baby girl. Now Eva will have her own baby sister."

His head rose slowly. The lights came on in his eyes. His clenched lips relaxed and spread into a slow half smile. What's love got to do with healing?

Everything.

Unlearning Helplessness

The next morning I was at Schervier by daybreak. Clay hadn't been fed. Every care transition is traumatic, I told myself, but I was on the verge of losing it. Just then the medical director appeared. Dr. Joseph Scarpa was a courtly gentleman with great compassion for the indignities of age and infirmity. He introduced Clay and me to his team of nurses and therapists, including Sister Sheila, doyenne of what they called "the spiritual department." Every one seemed bright, motivated, positive, and English-speaking.

At our first care meeting, the whole team, including Clay and me, were present. Each member gave an upbeat report and stressed Clay's eagerness to start active therapies, despite his lingering pneumonia. Afterward, I asked Dr. Scarpa, "You've seen many patients at this stage—can you tell me how long?"

"Given the best of care," he said, "he will hopefully last to the end of summer." With Dr. Scarpa's blessing, I gave instructions for no more antibiotics or emergency hospitalizations. Clay and nature would take their course. Meanwhile, we would lavish on him the best of care.

To me, best of care includes pleasurable experiences. The situation requires imagination and a little daring. It is essential to widen the circle of care, drawing in old friends, and if at all possible, a paid aide who fits well with the patient as a *companion and even a confidant. The impact of cheerful, supportive, fun-loving people around a chronically ill person can coax him or her out of resignation and revive the hope of recovering some capacities—above all, the capacity for joy.*

Clay needed a male companion. Through my contacts with private aides in other homes, I found Timothy, a spirited African-American man in his forties who loved to talk guy talk. Timothy came every morning to wash and shave Clay and take him out to the beautiful hill park overlooking the Hudson River, where they fed squirrels and read the sports pages. As Clay's health improved, Timothy used my car to smuggle Clay out of the nursing home to see the gorillas at the Bronx Zoo, downtown to look at the tall ships at South Street Seaport. Timothy made it look effortless to waltz Clay from wheelchair into car with a synchronized one, two, three. He sent me pictures all day from his cell phone. When I arrived for the late-afternoon shift, he would surprise us with a bootlegged DVD of a first-run movie. Timothy's gift to Clay was to allow him to break out of his mundane routine and even break rules, to be a man again.

Chris, an adorable, young, pint-sized physical therapist, made an instant hit with Clay when she suggested they set goals together. He wanted to walk in the worst way. With her head tucked under his arm, Chris faithfully walked him up and down the corridor twice a day, marking their progress with chalk until he was able to circle the whole floor.

Visitors from his former life began making the hegira to the Bronx. One afternoon I found Tom Wolfe sitting at Clay's bedside, all decked out in his signature white suit, white spatted shoes, and white leather watchband. His gray-blue eyes were still as quick as a lizard's blink. The two of them were talking over their escapades when Tom lived with Clay and they had no fear of challenging sacred cows like The New Yorker *and the Black Panthers. Clay's mood soared.*

Tom offered to drive me home. He opened the door to his new all-white Mercedes and ran his hand over the white leather seats and white suede interior roof. "I had it pimped up," he said with a sly smile. But on the long drive down the West Side Highway, he was nostalgic. "I remember Clay as a strapping six-foot, two-hundred-pound man, always full of ideas. Half the stories I wrote were his ideas. He was the greatest editor I've ever had. What really surprised me about Clay was his transformation after he lost New York *magazine. When Murdoch took over, I thought Clay would just spin out into the atmosphere. But not at all—the opposite. He's a real man."*

By the middle of that summer, Clay had unlearned helplessness. He was relearning how to walk. One day, in his old voice, he announced, "I want to go to the country!" He wanted to be in charge again.

We didn't have a country house anymore. I had put the house that Passages bought on the market and rented it out for the summer. Maura found us a simple cottage near her weekend house in upstate New York's Columbia County. It sat on a vast rolling farm. The moment I saw the covered porch, I imagined Clay sitting there, scanning the endless green fields humped with hay bales and watching the grandchildren kick a soccer ball.

Everyone in our care circle got excited about getting Clay out to the country. We rented an oversize SUV and packed it up with his wheelchair, his oxygen machine, and all his medicines. That morning everybody on his floor began chanting, "Clay's going out! Clay's going to the country!"

For many of the previous months, he had spoken only in monosyllables and communicated mainly with his eyes. But that morning, he remarked on the sun outside his window and joined in the chitchat of the nurses. It seemed to me Clay had come to a major turning point in recovery, emerging from the dark side and coming back into the light.

After a cookout at the cottage, Clay presided over the family's activities from the covered porch. Color literally rose in his ashen cheeks. The sun on his chest, the scents of hydrangea and chlorine, new-mown hay and cow dung, the squeals of delight from grandchildren—the whole concatenation of stimulants—revived his senses.

"Beautiful," he said. "I forgot what beautiful was."

———————————

twenty-four
COMING HOME

By September, Clay was doing leg lifts and walking up and down a few stairs, even making three laps around the floor on a walker. Dr. Scarpa triumphantly announced to the care team that Clay was free of lung infections and medically stable. He could go home after Labor Day.

Tellingly, Clay asked to stay another few weeks until his physical therapist left to get married. He wanted to work with Chris until they reached their highest goal. Since he was still making progress, Medicare would cover the full allotment of ninety days. We set the date of October 1 for his homecoming—the day before his birthday. I began planning a homecoming party.

My delight was tempered by a sudden sense that the lifeline I had prepared for Clay might also produce a noose around my neck. Where could I find the time and money needed to care for Clay at home? I gave Mary Tierney my own wish list. I wanted to return to my role as a wife, rather than nurse attendant. I already had a job. There was no way I could take my husband home and meet my writing deadline for a book already overdue—not while giving him breathing treatments, suctioning his tracheostomy, giving him feedings, checking vital signs, and following instructions to "turn him every two hours."

I was much more effective when I was able to touch Clay and talk to him in our own intimate language. I was the entertainer, a fount of fun ideas for outings. I was his gossip connoisseur, his spiritual companion, and the confidante who could listen to fears or woes without making fake promises to fix the unfixable. These are *the unique gifts on offer only from a spouse, son, or daughter; from a brother, sister, or grandchild. They are true wealth. Mary Tierney heartily agreed. Then I spilled my fears.*

What would happen the next time Clay bled from the opening in his throat? Or when his feeding tube pulled loose inside the stomach wall? How could I keep him out of the hospital when things went wrong? Mary Tierney gave me the quick and ugly facts behind the fantasy of supporting a chronically ill loved one at home for any length of time.

"Everyone thinks Medicare is going to pay for long-term care at home. It doesn't," she began. "If you want financial help, you have to make your husband eligible for Medicaid, the government benefit for the poor."

"Do they count the spouse's assets?" I asked dumbly. Mary's eyebrows flared. "Oh yes, the spouse is liable for her mate's medical debts. That can only be challenged if you file for 'spousal refusal.'"

"Does that release the spouse from legal responsibility?"

"No. There's a Look-back Period of five years, to detect whether or not the sick spouse has transferred assets to a mate. If a state can show the spouse has hidden assets, it can sue you to recover the costs of your mate's care."

"That could mean my whole life's work—forty years of savings— could go down the drain." I sighed. "How do wives survive this punishing system?"

Mary shrugged. "They don't. They do the caregiving for as long as they can, then the patient goes into a nursing home. The spouse spends down her savings until there's virtually nothing left, so they can get the husband on Medicaid." She shook her head in disgust. "That's the way the system works."

In disbelief, I consulted another care manager.

"Is there anything else people can do?" I persisted.

"Divorce."

"Excuse me?"

"Yes, divorce . . ."

"What kind of stone-hearted caregiver could abandon a sick husband at his most vulnerable point? That would kill him for sure."

"There may be ways smart lawyers can hide assets, but Medicaid can look back to see how you spent your money."

My head ached. "Does our medical system trump our marriage vows?"
The veteran care manager gave me the look of a teacher who has just
enlightened her student to one of the ironies of life.

STRATEGIES

What Kind of Home Care Do You Need?

Here is what Medicare will do for you when a patient comes out of the hospital or a rehab facility. The discharge planner will refer you to a Medicare-approved home-care agency. Typically, a visiting nurse comes to the home to evaluate the patient and consider the need for physical therapy, occupational therapy, and/or speech therapy. This visit is very brief, twenty minutes at most. While there, the visiting nurse will also check out the living situation. Is the house safe? Is it clean?

The nurse writes up a plan of care, which will be given to the private physician who signs off on it—or modifies it. Don't let the nurse out the door without asking her to describe the plan. Speak up. Call the doctor and voice your approval or objections. This is a written document with force. Not all doctors are up to speed on just how this system works. Even geriatric specialists like Dr. Scarpa have to stay on top of constant rule changes.

These Medicare services usually begin the third or fourth day after the patient comes home. Initially, the plan may call for two or three weeks of visits. Thereafter, the visiting nurse will reevaluate if there is further need and might extend some service for up to a limit of six weeks. If the patient's doctor authorizes skilled nursing care at home, which is rare, it may also be provided, but not for long. These short-term Medicare services allow for the family caregiver to learn the procedures and to bring in any other family member or privately hired aide to learn the techniques and develop a routine. But once the nurse determines that "the patient has plateaued," services are terminated. The patient is now labeled "custodial care" or "long-term care"—and the sole responsibility and cost rest on the family. However, if the patient needs the services to maintain his level of progress, a doctor may be able to argue for continuation.

Does Medicaid Cover Home Care?

States are only obliged to provide care for Medicaid patients in a nursing home, not at home. Some Medicaid waiver programs do provide limited home care, such as PACE (see Chapter 8). But eligibility is not easy, and availability is scarce, with long waiting lines. You will need a social worker, elder law attorney, or a volunteer from your local Area Agency on Aging to explain the rules.

To be eligible for Medicaid in most states, the patient can have only $2,000 per month of "countable assets." That does not include the family home, as long as the home is occupied by either the patient, their spouse, a minor, a blind child, or a disabled child.

Elder parents often transfer assets to their adult children hoping to qualify for Medicaid home care. If you are considering this option, beware! Most states will deny a Medicaid home care applicant if assets were transferred within the previous *five years* of the application. These five years are called the Look-back Period. Who can plan to voluntarily impoverish themselves five years in advance of a medical crisis? The best advice is to find out *now* if you or your loved one resides in a state that has a Look-back Period. You may be in luck. The state of New York is one of several states that has no Look-back Period for Medicaid home care.

I'm grateful to a woman who attended one of my lectures and told me how she escaped financial ruin when she moved her mother from Florida to New York and obtained Medicaid home care for her. To assure her privacy, I'll call her Judith.

Judith's mother is part of a mounting wave of "reverse migration" by retirees who moved to the Sun Belt, anticipating endless rounds of golf, bridge, and swimming. They often don't anticipate living beyond their spouses or even beyond their seventies, and needing help from their adult children. So, when their health deteriorates, they move back up north, near family or where there are better government benefits.

"My widowed mother was basically homeless," says Judith. "When she fell and broke her hip, she couldn't go back to the assisted-living home in her Florida community. I had to create a home for her, near me." This "call" came to the daughter at the fevered peak of the real estate boom, and Judith lived in a high-rent district in Manhattan. At that time, 2004, a semiprivate room in a nursing home on the island of Manhattan cost in the neighborhood of $13,000 a month.

"That's what I faced," moans Judith, remembering the feeling that she had died and gone to hell. "Fortunately, I found the way out: the no-look-back policy for Medicaid home care in New York State."

Below are several other solutions I discovered for New York residents facing a similar predicament. In New York State, Medicaid allows a maximum income of $767 per month (as of 2009). Income above this amount can be paid into a "pooled supplemental needs trust" that is then used for expenses of the at-home patient. One example is the NYSARC Trust and Trust Services (www.nyarc.org/family/nysarc-family-trust-services.asp#a).

Be forewarned: the application process is daunting. Judith describes herself as a Rottweiler and took charge of completing her mother's Medicaid application. "Tenacity paid off," she told me. "My mother is living in an apartment she loves, basically a care facility for one. For the last five years, my mother has had a home-care attendant 24/7 who is paid for by Medicaid." Not everyone is eligible for 24/7 home care. However, since the quantity of home care depends on proving medical need, the services of an elder law attorney or a geriatric care manager at this stage can be well worth their fees in later savings.

Since states differ in Medicaid restrictions, you may use this information to probe deeper with your social worker or elder law attorney to find a solution that works for you.

If you are not an adult child, but rather the spouse of a chronically ill person, you may be in a much more vulnerable financial position. The assets of the well spouse will be counted as belonging to the patient. A working spouse's middle-class income will disqualify the patient for Medicaid.

Any escapes? Yes, "spousal refusal." But this maneuver carries the risk of an administrative boomerang later on. In most states, the healthy spouse of a nursing home patient can keep only $109,560 total assets without being challenged (as of 2010 federal law). For example, the patient transfers all assets to the healthy partner. Then the healthy partner may invoke the right of "spousal refusal" and decline to provide further financial support for the partner in a nursing home. Medicaid then must foot the bill for the impoverished spouse.

But only a few states, including New York and Florida, honor "spousal refusal." And even these states can later claim that the "refusing" spouse has "sufficient ability to pay."

Finding an Elder-Care Attorney

Contact the National Academy of Elder Law Attorneys, Inc. (NAELA) at 703-942-5711. An elder-care attorney's services may include: Medicaid, Medicare, and Social Security claims and appeals; probate and estate planning; nursing home issues; long-term-care planning. To find elder-care attorneys near you, enter your zip code into the organization's searchable directory of members at http://www.naela.org/MemberDirectory/.

Does Your Insurance Cover Home Care?

Check out your own medical insurance policy. If you are on Medicare, you may have a supplemental policy. Familiarize yourself with terms such as "activities of daily living" (ADL). These can be qualifiers as to whether or not the policyholder is eligible for services in the home. ADLs include feeding, bathing, dressing, toileting, walking/transfers, and continence.

Ask your agent the following:

- Is home care listed as a benefit? If so, How many hours?
- Does the policy cover a licensed RN, LPN, or CNA?
- Does the policy cover a caregiving family member?
- Do you need to hire from a Medicare- or Medicaid-approved agency?

You Need a "Fixer"

Who would think that last question could reveal a Catch-22?

I thought my husband's secondary insurance policy, a high-option plan with Blue Cross Blue Shield of California, had us covered for home care. It spelled out that if a doctor specified that it was medically necessary for the patient to be visited at home by a trained nurse, the policy would pay for four hours a day, unlimited days, with reimbursement at Medicare rates: up to $10,000 per calendar year.

I consulted a distinguished attorney and pioneer in the field of elder law, Peter J. Strauss, an adjunct professor at New York University Law School. He told me our plan looked almost too good to be true.

There was one catch, but it was crucial. The nurse had to come from a Medicare-approved agency. When I called the Visiting Nurse Association (VNS), the gold standard of Medicare nursing agencies in New York City, they adamantly refused to provide a special-duty nurse. My elder-care attorney tried. No nurse. My accountant tried. Still no nurse. My office assistant called every Medicare-approved agency in the New York area. All refused to provide a medically trained nurse. I sought out the supervisor of the appeals department of Blue Cross and asked, "If our secondary insurance company refuses to pay for anything that Medicare won't pay for, then what good is it to have a secondary provider?" The supervisor was nonplussed. "If you want to look at it that way, your secondary policy is useless."

To deal with this Kafkaesque world, I had asked for a consult with a geriatric care manager months before. She had told me, "The insurance company will say they will pay for it, but they know the agencies in New York won't provide it. That's the Catch-22. You can pay the elder-care attorney his retainer but he won't get anywhere, either." I had refused to accept this harsh truth at the time.

I tried calling the VNS nurse supervisor herself. "Hello, Pam," I began. "I am trying to understand how to get some limited skilled nursing for my husband when he comes home from rehab in a few weeks. He has a permanent trach and a gastronomy tube."

"I know. I read his chart."

"He needs suctioning and nebulizer treatments several times a day, sometimes he bleeds or starts choking, and the feeding tube often gets clogged and even pulls out," I went on.

"You have to have someone at home to do that." The words sounded rote.

"I am willing to hire some aides but I have to be out at work and I travel, so I can't be around to supervise aides who aren't trained to respond to medical emergencies. I need a skilled nurse to supervise his care and to answer questions or—"

Pam cut me off. "VNS does not provide that type of care. You have to have somebody in place to do all those skills while you go to work."

"I'm trying to understand where the disconnect is here," I try again. "His insurance company designates—and I will read it to you—'If the special duty nurse is from a Blue Cross-approved agency, then Blue Cross will pay a hundred percent of the contracted rate, up to an amount of $10,000 per year.'"

Pam was unmoved. "We don't do what you are asking. You have to get a private-hire person who will do all the suctioning, the feeding, and the nursing when you are not there, the same as if he were in a nursing home."

"I can't afford to hire a private-duty nurse at $55 an hour, on top of aides around the clock."

"Then you can't take that man home." Pam's voice was triumphant. "It would be an unsafe discharge."

All I'd accomplished was to put us in reverse. Then I remembered Mary Tierney telling me that when it comes to maneuvering for the patient in a jam, the doctor is in the driver's seat. I asked for a meeting with Dr. Scarpa. He agreed to make the case, but admitted that one has to know the magic words to use when approaching VNS. "I'll say that we need a nurse to go in for evaluation and then come by on a regular basis for—and here is the word they like—monitoring."

I was scribbling the magic words when Dr. Scarpa held up his hand. "Every six months they change the rules on you, so you always have to stay ahead of the game and figure out the new rules. I struggle with it every day—how do I get services for my patients? I do this because I care for the elderly."

With his permission, I listened in on the doctor's bargaining strategy. Nurse Pam began by asserting that this would be an unsafe discharge.

"Mr. Felker is my patient; if I thought it would be an unsafe discharge, I wouldn't be having this conversation with you," the doctor countered. "But he does require monitoring periodically."

"You're right," Pam said, suddenly cooperative.

Dr. Scarpa now spelled it out. "He needs to be assessed and evaluated to make sure that complications from his illness do not occur, such as bleeding from the trach or aspirations." Once Pam agreed to that, Dr. Scarpa had the upper hand. "That's why we need a skilled nurse to come in, monitor his breathing, monitor his blood pressure, his vital signs, do an assessment, and, if required, do suctioning."

Pam mumbled a grudging assent. Now Dr. Scarpa went for broke. "The family and I will all be happy if you could do that seven days a week."

"Seven days is out of the question," she snapped. "We've never given that to anyone."

"Then five days a week?"

"That's a bit much. The most I could probably do is three."

"Can we settle on four?"

"Four is doable."

"Then that's what you should do," the doctor said firmly, "because that's what Medicare is paying you to do."

Nurse Pam was suddenly agreeable. "Oh, right, absolutely!"

Now I knew how the system really worked. Imagine yourself in the old Soviet Union trying to squeeze help from bureaucrats. Agencies pay little attention to mere family caregivers. To milk your loved one's rightful services from stone hearts, you need a fixer. The best candidate is your medical quarterback.

STRATEGIES

Can You Afford a Geriatric Care Manager?

In recent years, an entire industry of geriatric care management (GCM) has grown up, creating home-care agencies in the process. This new industry serves people who live longer but don't want to spend years in nursing homes. The one constant is that Medicare doesn't pay for long-term care. Geriatric care managers come from backgrounds of nursing, social work, and psychology. Professionally accredited GCMs are increasingly available for private hire nationwide. Fees range from $80 to $250 an hour depending on where you live, the services you need, and the manager's experience. Although their fees are not covered by Medicare or Medicaid, some employers offer GCM help through their Human Resources departments. Certain large insurance companies subsidize or cover these services for employees or policyholders. Some state Medicaid programs offer GCM to people of low income.

Let's say your loved one has expended the few weeks of post-hospital therapy or limited nursing that Medicare offers free. He or she may now need some daily-living help, temporary medical care, or just a sense of not being home alone. If you can't be sufficiently available, call a home-care agency and ask about services and costs. Be warned—it's expensive.

What Can a Home Health Aide Do?

Don't expect a home health aide to turn up with a little white cap and sit watching 1940s movies over a home-cooked meal with your loved one. Be realistic about what you can expect. Home health aides are limited to providing personal care: bathing, toileting, dressing, light housekeeping, shopping, and taking vital signs like temperature and blood pressure. Their hands are tied by state laws in many ways that can seem comical if not inhuman. They cannot do anything remotely medical, such as give injections or oxygen or touch a feeding tube. They can hand a patient pills or remind her to take medication, but they can't prepare medication. They can clean a dry wound but can't touch an open wound. An aide can make a meal for the patient, but not for the caregiver, and cannot sit down to eat with them.

The problem in dealing with many private agencies is a lack of process in matching the needs of the patient and the family with the skills and personality of the home health aide. Normally, you get the next aide who is available.

"The training required to become a home health aide is often shockingly minimal," says Carol Levine, who has turned her own seventeen-year vigil as a caregiver for her husband into a tell-it-like-it-is book, *Always on Call,* and an excellent website resource, www.nextstepincare.org.

Medicare does not actually operate as a national system. Its rules are established state by state, and locality by locality. Licensing of aides is also up to the individual state. A few states like New York require a significant number of hours of training. Many other states, including Florida, despite its senior citizenry, have almost no requirements or regulations for home health aides.

California requires only twelve hours of continuing education every two years. Agencies generally charge $18/hour for a home health aide and pay the person only $10 or less.

"The level of an aide's credentialing is not as important as their ability to cope with the patient and fit in with the family," advises Levine. "You want somebody who is reliable, of course, but who also isn't mean, somebody you like having around." It's also vital that an aide is flexible and can deal with moods and volatility in a patient. That makes it easier to maintain boundaries and make compromises.

Recommended Agencies

HOME INSTEAD is one example of the national home-care agencies that have sprung up lately. It is a private, in-home senior-care agency. Each agency is an independently owned franchise. Services include companionship, home help, and personal assistance, including bathing, toileting, and meal preparation—most everything but medical care itself. The franchises usually screen, train, and supervise the aides they employ. They are typically licensed, insured, and bonded. Clients pay them directly.

To find Home Instead in your area, call the national number, 888-484-5759, or visit http://www.homeinstead.com/home.aspx and type in your zip code. Local agency names and fees vary.

I called Home Instead Senior Services, 212-614-8057, in New York City. Their fee (in 2009) is $21/hour, plus time and a half for holidays. Full daily rate is $260.00. If the client has long-term-care insurance and qualifies for in-home care, Home Instead Senior Services will bill your insurance company.

What if you leave the hospital needing home care but have no caregiver or family?

SENIORBRIDGE is another agency with offices throughout the United States. Using a team approach, they are able to assist you with the difficult transitions from hospital to home. The care manager goes to the hospital, reviews medications, talks to attending physicians and nurses, determines medical follow-up, keeps the patient informed, and gets prescriptions filled. The care manager also inspects the patient's home, gets it cleaned, fills the larder, then escorts the patient home.

The care manager advocates with Medicare for home services, briefs the health aide on medications, then makes sure the patient is safe and in touch with family or friends. Service includes doctor's appointments with nurse escorts.

SeniorBridge charges $22/hour for home-care aides and $180/hour for geriatric care management services. Monthly cost could be $3,000 to $5,000, with round-the-clock care as high as $20,000. To find the closest SeniorBridge, call 866-506-1212 or visit the website at www.seniorbridge.com.

Do You Need to Hire a Nurse?

The next level of care available from an agency is a licensed practical nurse. An LPN can give injections, operate a feeding pump, administer oxygen, clean an open wound, and prepare and administer medication. She cannot set up an IV. An LPN can also be an informed conduit to a physician when a new symptom or an emergency arises. The usual LPN fee is $35/hour.

The highest level is a registered nurse (RN) at $45/hour. You don't need an RN.

Compare the Cost of Alternatives

Assisted living in New York City costs a minimum $4,000 a month for room and board. If the person needs help with daily living, the help must be hired and paid separately. A nursing home in New York City in 2009 costs about $15,000 a month, unless you qualify for Medicaid.

You Have an Advocate

If you have any questions about Medicare, call the Medicare Rights Center, a nonprofit consumer group with legal and medical volunteers ready to respond with accurate information. Your tax dollars pay for this service. Primed to help patients and caregivers, the volunteers decipher laws, regulations, and insurance speak. Consult them about what Medicare covers, your care complaints or payment hassles, and where to appeal your case. I've found them to be very receptive and extremely knowledgeable. Visit their website at www.medicarerights.org or call the Medicare Rights Center (800-333-4114).

Go to the Gray Market

To avoid high cost, low competence, and maddening bureaucracy, many care seekers find home aides through word of mouth—commonly referred to as the "gray market." If you bypass private agencies, you can skip fees and use the money to attract a better home aide. Working outside Medicare rules also allows you to train the person to handle medical procedures relevant to your case. Private working relations also tend to become warmer, longer, and more effective.

Privately hired home aides are usually immigrant women. Though not bonded or insured, they can be more skilled and flexible than aides sent by agencies, which often demand a minimum of eight-hour days at $18 to $22/hour. Their aides usually receive a lot less. The key to finding people who can be trusted and trained, we found, was to save the phone numbers of all carepersons we met and liked along the way. They always had a sister or a cousin in the gray market.

Ask friends, neighbors, doctors, social workers for recommendations. Look for caregiver candidates with health skills, of course, but above all with personalities most likely to be right at home with your loved one and yourself.

Look for well-trained foreign nurses and even doctors happy to work as caregivers while studying to become credentialed in the United States. I happened to luck into networks of Gambian, Polish, and Ecuadorian health workers. Friends report great success with Irish, East Germans, and exiles from the former Soviet Union. Scan classified ads in a good ethnic newspaper like the *Irish Echo*. Place your own ad. The going rate for gray-market health aides is $20/hour plus overtime.

Our Team

Mary Tierney, my care manager, helped me search the "gray market." The captain of our team was Isatou Sawahnee, the tall, turbaned Gambian woman who had been through the wars with Clay and me, from California to New York, from hospitals to rehabs. She invented his superhealth diet and tag-teamed with me in standing vigilant against potential medical errors by the pros. Isatou, a Muslim, had the courage to reinvent herself after being demoted to "second wife" by her African diplomat husband. Clay taught her to respect herself as an Americanized professional woman. They developed a deep bond. Isatou's father passed while she was working for us. When she returned from the observances in Africa, she told me that God had called her to see Clay through this life; he was her second father.

Among Isatou's many gifts were her soaring height and her warrior's tongue. To see her steaming down a hospital corridor when someone had neglected Clay was a fearsome thing. Taxi drivers who took one look at Clay's wheelchair and tried to refuse us could be reduced by a few words from Isatou to quivering obedience. When Isatou was out of the country, she steered us to a Senegalese woman, Safoura Tall. Elegant, reserved, and even taller than Isatou, she brought a spiritual intelligence into the mix that soothed Clay and grounded our whole team. We had one of the best little nursing homes on the West Side of Manhattan.

Mornings would begin with a "Hi, honey!" and light kiss from Yolanda, a petite Ecuadorian woman who brought Clay the paper and breakfast. She would help Isatou change the bed and dress Clay while I went out to exercise; then two of us would take him for the first walk of the day. At night, a sweet Filipino man named Florenz would bring his guitar and sing Clay to sleep. Then he'd slip in and out of our bedroom, hunched and poised on tiny silent feet, to respond to the alarm on the feeding pump or a ding-a-ling from Clay's bell to summon help to get to the bathroom. Florenz never called attention to Clay's dependency on him. His addition to the care circle allowed me to take Clay out to a show or a concert or free rehearsals of the Philharmonic, knowing there was another pair of arms and a wheelchair at the ready if we had a repeat of Clay's fainting scene offstage at Lincoln Center.

The VNS nurse who Dr. Scarpa had obtained for us came faithfully, two or three times a week. She trained all of us on dozens of procedures, from taking Clay's blood pressure to changing the curved plastic "noodle" that was inserted in his throat to help him breathe. Called a canula, it had one collar that protected his airway against aspiration of saliva, and another, with perforations, that allowed enough air through to let him speak. Changing to the "speaking noodle" was a painstaking procedure, since everything had to be sterile. If the noodles were inserted incorrectly, he could not breathe. But it was essential that Clay be able to continue to communicate. So we learned.

I had to find an office nearby, since I could no longer work at home. Serendipitously, a sublet became available in the building next door. That allowed me to run home several times a day to have lunch with Clay and be present for the changing of the guard among aides.

As winter progressed, we grew into a powerful chain of caring that encircled Clay day and night. In addition, Clay's colleagues turned up frequently with fresh gossip. My sister, Trish, stopped in twice a week to read to Clay from Noël Coward's hilarious letters. My playwriting coach, Milan Stitt, read plays to him. His Berkeley students were especially faithful in stopping by to get his blessing on their career moves or kick around an idea for a magazine or a book.

The cost of a 24/7 home-care team is exorbitant. I paid my aides $18 to $25 *an hour. They were worth every penny. It was the only way I could keep Clay at home and still keep my career alive enough to support us. When I traveled on assignment, I knew my husband was safe under watchful eyes. The system also allowed ample time for me to be just present with him, the greatest need for anyone suffering. At night I insisted on our private hour together, before he went to sleep and brought on the patter of Florenz's feet.*

Most nights I felt blessed that I still had him. But I must be honest. As often as I thought, I'm afraid he won't live, *I sometimes thought,* I'm afraid he won't die.

STRATEGIES

Managing Home Care

Full-time home care is like managing a small business. It requires many interviews to staff it with people you and your loved one trust and like having around. You need to establish a timely payroll system and parcel out responsibilities clearly and fairly. Our care manager worked with me to encourage cooperation among the staff. It was essential to be secure that they would arrive an hour before their shift to glean input from the previous aide.

I would not have been able to manage without my geriatric care manager, Mary Tierney. Mary helped to train and manage our care team, talked to doctors when I was not available, and took Clay to appointments, giving me feedback on all of the above. If you have to travel, as I did, you can authorize your care manager to take emergency calls concerning your loved one. If something dire happens at 3:00 A.M. in your mom's condo in Florida, and you live in New York, you can call your care manager in Florida to make a quick check on Mom's condition and organize an ambulance if needed.

We had a weekly team meeting around the dining room table to air problems and invite suggestions for new strategies. Mary Tierney was moderator. We tried using a website calendar on the computer to post notes and update the schedule, but practically speaking, most aides are not computer savvy and not entirely comfortable with written English. Everyone preferred writing a log of their shift in a big ring binder. Those care notes were enormously helpful to the visiting nurse and any queries we made to doctors. The meetings helped to cement loyalty among the aides who then didn't want to let one another down.

When your little business begins to run smoothly, it frees the caregiver to get back to some work and friends and respite. But unlike any normal business, it is all loss, no profit, in monetary terms. I couldn't bear to look at my checkbook. Even more troubling was the loss of privacy. Our apartment was transformed into a nursing home, with the whir and grind of oxygen and suction and feeding machines in the bedroom, the indiscriminate drone of CNN on TV, and the comings and goings in three shifts of four full-time aides and one backup, to cover weekends. Despite the lack of privacy, it was a comfort to know a caring person was always there. The aides and I would pass in the day or night and share a late snack or wakeup yogurt and a joke or the latest bulletins from the presidential campaigns. But I must be honest. I also felt sometimes like a displaced person, alienated in my own home.

How to Find a Geriatric Care Manager

To repeat, visit the website of the National Association of Professional Geriatric Care Managers at www.caremanager.org. Enter your zip code to locate the geriatric care managers in your area. Or call 520-881-8008.

Social workers at hospitals, senior centers, and charitable organizations such as the Alzheimer's Association may have recommendations of people they know to be skilled and trustworthy. Carry a caregiving notebook and constantly fill it with addresses and numbers for everything from doctors to dog walkers, from insurance policies to massage therapists for yourself.

Last Trip to the Hospital

"He's bleeding from the trach."

"How much?" Dr. Orsher asked me.

"Not a lot, but it's plugging up the noodle in his throat. I woke up several times last night hearing him choking on it—trying to breathe. It was new. And scary."

"Let's get him into the ER right away," he said. "I'll order a CT scan."

Hadn't we pledged not to go to the hospital again? We were caught without a Plan B. The intake nurse in the ER had that dried corn-husk look I associate with people who spend their lives under artificial light in windowless hospitals. She asked if Mr. Felker could talk. I prompted him to say hello—he wasn't feeling any friendlier than I was.

She asked him to take off his coat. Safoura started to help.

"No, I want to see if he's alert," warned the nurse.

Clay struggled to crook his elbow.

"We have to speed up now," scolded the nurse.

She stared at her computer screen and fired off questions about his history as if Clay had never been there before. I said, "You must have a book on him in your computer, he's been admitted here dozens of times in the last year and a half."

"I know, but the computer program asks the questions, and I input, so you need to give me the answers."

Safoura pulled out the pocket medical history we had prepared for such situations. The nurse waved it away and continued to input. "I have to follow the program."

Seconds bled away, dripping time, but it's always like this. Hospital people are prisoners of computer programs. How many inputters does it take to ask the same questions before the answers register on some website in the sky? Why can't a hospital immediately pull up a file showing all previous admissions, diagnoses, doctors, tests and procedures, findings, and final status on discharge? Every admission is like trying to enter an unfriendly foreign country without a visa.

Six hours later, the test still hadn't been done. I told the charge nurse my husband was faint from lack of food; we needed to go home. "Don't worry, Dr. Orsher has put in for a bed for your husband," he said.

"No! We don't want him admitted," I protested. "He'll pick up a virus and be in here for weeks."

Clay asked for his speaking noodle: "No more hospitals!" Safoura and I covered him with our coats and calmly wheeled him out the front door with the IV needles still stuck in his wrists. Clay was smiling. It would be our last time around the revolving door. Just taking back that little bit of power felt like a triumph.

————————

BUT THAT NIGHT THE *choking sounds were more frequent. There was more blood in the noodle. Were his lungs being torn up by all the suctioning? This is why a nurse or doctor has to be available to monitor such emergencies, which could then probably be treated at home.*

In the morning I sat on the floor in the dark and prayed. "I'm willing to surrender my will to you, God. I'm lost. Please show me the way. Thy will, not mine, be done."

————————

twenty-five

THE NEW LATINA MODEL

"Traditional Latino families tend to be multigenerational households, so it's automatic for the daughter to switch roles once you see that Mom is not able to take care of herself," says Eva Martinez.

Eva is a modern working mother, divorced with grown children, and accustomed to planning ahead. She is fifty-seven and works full-time as executive director of a nonprofit community organization, Acción Latina. She loves her work.

Eva is also an integral part of a traditional Latino family in San Francisco. Her grandmother devoted her adult life to being the support system for the women of the family—all of whom were working wives—moving from household to household to help care for children and elders.

When Eva's mother became old and sick, no conversation was possible with Eva's only sibling, a brother. She describes him as stoic and uncommunicative. "It's hard for Latino men to express their feelings. I think my brother was really saddened to see what was happening to my mother. He chose to clam up and not deal with it. I just naturally took her in."

Eva's lifestyle before her mother moved in was "a pristine home, a little salad maybe at ten at night, or grab something to go." The bachelorette could invite the person she describes as her "nonresidential boyfriend" to stay over, as she pleased. After her Mom moved into her home, Eva's lifestyle changed. Now it's not so different from when Eva nurtured a young child.

She makes her mother breakfast, leaves something for lunch, and makes sure there is dinner in the fridge in case she is late getting home.

Toddlers are tough to keep on track, their favorite word being "No!" But a sick and dependent mother—especially one fiercely independent all her previous life—is likely to be even less cooperative than a Terrible Two. Eva's mom was widowed at an early age, and she was used to working and calling the shots in the family. "The fact that she had to live with me, that she needed me to take care of her—she fought me on that every day, every day," said Eva. She had to coax and cajole for a year and a half before being allowed to close down her mother's apartment. Her mother had her own version. She told the world, even strangers on the street, "I'm just staying with my daughter for a while because I hurt my knee. Then I'm going back to my own apartment."

A scathing argument between Eva's mom and her brother alerted Eva that the volatile woman wasn't thinking quite right. Subsequent tests showed she was in second-stage Alzheimer's. She refused to take her medicines and told far-fetched stories. Eva had to make sure she changed her mother's clothes every day. Luckily, the organization Eva works for was open to her taking one or two days a week to work from home. "It's almost like another family. Our values—creating a community that's good for families—flow over into how we function as staff."

In her community, Eva notes with concern, a lot of Latina caregivers become isolated. "They're caring for children at home—teens—but also for their elderly parents. The husband usually works and the wife gives up her work. If they're poor, they have less access to preventive health care, and the parents may take sick earlier than usual. Then of course there is a language barrier."

Eva was able to plan ahead and anticipate crises because she sought out local resources. Among her prize finds is On Lok, a San Francisco community organization that has been a pioneer in keeping seniors out of nursing homes by surrounding them with care in their own homes.

On Lok, a multicultural and multilingual organization, began in San Francisco's Chinese community but expanded care to the city's Spanish-speaking areas. Workshops for caregivers include need-to-know practicalities,

such as "How to Get Financial Matters in Order" and "How to Work with
People with Alzheimer's." On Lok offers full medical care and support services for eligible seniors living in San Francisco, Fremont, Newark, Union
City, or Santa Clara County (not including Gilroy, Morgan Hill, or San Martin). For more On Lok information, call 415-292-8888 or visit the website at
www.onlok.org.

The On Lok program proved that a community-based model not only
delivered quality care but was more efficient, reliable, and cost-effective than
nursing homes. That made an impression on Medicare and Medicaid. A
more recent community-based program of comprehensive day care for seniors, called PACE (Program of All-Inclusive Care for the Elderly), has since
been introduced in fifty states. PACE is a Medicaid waiver program for
Medicaid-eligible patients. It consolidates all medical visits and social stimulation for the elderly in one agency and one place. (PACE is discussed more
in depth in chapter 8.)

Eva overcame her cultural resistance to sharing her family secret (Mom's
Alzheimer's) when she joined a support group for caregivers of people with
dementia, covered by her Kaiser Permanente health insurance. "I was surprised," she said. "It was only me and a couple of other women. But it was really useful for me. I can deal with things if I know what's coming, and the
other women were at a later stage. We're all becoming little experts with this
illness."

I asked Eva about respite—when did she get a break? Her reply was not
laced with resentment. "My sister-in-law took Mom for one weekend a month.
That's the only free time I had."

Did she feel appreciated?

She laughed. "No. But you don't go into this for appreciation."

Would Eva's children do the same for her? Again, she laughed. Her son is
thirty-four. He teasingly told her he would put her out on the corner and
wave to her as he drove past. But the truth is very different. "He's very close
to his grandmother, and I mean a lot to him. So I feel secure he will come
through for me."

And indeed, more men are stepping up to help with family caregiving.
Eva's son resigned from his job in Chicago and moved back home to help his
mother during the last months of his grandmother's life. "He was such a

great help with my mom. He'd sit with her at night and tell me, 'You go out, Mom.'" Eva's boyfriend, too, was put to the test and came through with flying colors.

Eva's mom died in her daughter's home after five months of tender care by hospice. She went into a light coma and passed away gently the next day. Eva was so glad they were together for her last three years. "It really helps me, the memory of that time."

With no regrets, Eva is looking forward to rejoining the Freedom Fifties. She says "I have so much time now. Before, I was always rushing home and the weekends were filled." She is beginning to feel a throb of exhilaration. "It's time now to move on."

EIGHTH TURNING:
THE LONG GOOD-BYE

twenty-six

THE CRUCIAL CHOICE

When a loved one enters the evening of life, family caregivers face wrenching paradoxes. We all yearn to prolong life, and we all fear losing it. For years, we rely on denial. Deep down, we know that death is inevitable, but mainly for other people. If it ever happens to us, it will be in some unimaginable future.

Suddenly death is real and present, lying in wait to seize a person so close to us as to be part of us. We often resist with all known medical weapons, some potentially as toxic as they are curative. What if those efforts cause needless suffering? Throughout this last battle, family caregivers deal with crises that may peak every few weeks, or days. We yearn for answers to the least answerable questions: When will he die? How will she die? How can we comfort them?

DECIDING ON HOW AND WHEN TO LET GO

The most sensitive negotiation in any family surrounds the question of when to let go. How do we divine the patient's real wishes? How do we resolve our own contradictory beliefs? Many of us pray on it. Others seek professional counseling with a psychotherapist or grief counselor. How do we settle family disputes between members who insist upon extraordinary medical procedures and others who argue for refusing further invasive treatments?

In many families there is at least one Toxic Thomas—the contrarian who assumes he or she knows best. If this agitator impedes family decisions that must be made under great pressure, set boundaries. Keep your Toxic Thomas in the loop, but only as long as he or she avoids intimidating others.

When is enough enough?

This is the universal mystery. When Senator Ted Kennedy finally succumbed to brain cancer on August 25, 2009, after a long and heroic fight, the family issued a statement that rings true to many of us: "He was ready to go, we weren't ready to let him go." But the patriarch of his family had not spent his last year dying; he had lived intensely, focusing his energies on continuing his long work on health-care reform, completing a memoir, and sharing profound moments with his family.

It took me a long time and many false starts before I found a way to move through this long turning at the end of the labyrinth, and I hope our story will introduce some ideas that may be new and useful to you, dear caregivers. But before we get to that, I want to share with you the story of a family that had every good intention of shepherding their beloved father through his slow dying at home. They kept thinking, "Why can't we make this better? What are we doing wrong?" Because the gaps in America's ways of caring for terminally ill patients are so wide and discouraging, family caregivers often begin to blame themselves. It must be their fault. It isn't.

THE CONTINI* FAMILY CRISIS

"Look at Dad, he's not swallowing."

Maria Contini consistently brought up her husband's trouble in swallowing at the family's Sunday dinners. Her husband, Anthony, always managed to change the subject. By the time he gave in and saw a doctor, in August, Anthony came home with a devastating diagnosis: advanced esophageal (throat) cancer.

In his midseventies, Anthony was still a kick-butt athlete. He kept his legs rock-hard with constant biking and was known for his deep, resonant cello of a voice. A born politician, he knew everybody in his semirural home-

---

*Pseudonym.

town, where he had been reelected mayor for several terms. He all but ignored the implications of the doctor's words.

"Dad was fatally ill from the day he was diagnosed," I learned from his daughter Camilla, a fact-based epidemiologist married to a physician. "All three of my siblings and their spouses agreed to tag-team the care."

As a seasoned emergency room nurse, Anthony's wife knew that hospitals can be nasty places—cold, loud, airless, congested, with no privacy for a family needing precious time together. After absorbing the shock of her husband's illness, Maria easily convinced everyone that they could care for Anthony at home. "This is the only way to preserve the sanctity of family," she told her four children. "I can keep him comfortable in the beautiful heirloom bed your grandparents slept in." She retrofitted it with a wedge and a cascade of pillows; she bought the softest sheets and kept them beautifully scented. The bed was high and looked out on trees and grass. Maria continued working full-time as a nurse to maintain the father's health insurance. They prayed they could keep him alive at least until his favorite holiday, Thanksgiving.

The family's instincts couldn't have been more humane and generous. There was only one problem—a widespread misunderstanding about the rules surrounding end-of-life care.

The Continis needed professional help in caring for Anthony's painful symptoms and counseling for their own anxieties and grieving. The first social worker who visited to assess the family's needs challenged their choices. She was surprised to learn that Anthony was receiving chemotherapy. Taking an extremely rigid position, she said he couldn't be treated by hospice as he insisted on medical care.

The family was puzzled. They wanted comfort care for Anthony. Camilla argued that the chemo treatments had provided some comfort from day one. "We didn't know the difference between hospice and palliative care," says Camilla. She points out the irony: "And I do research on caregiving and healthy aging!"

Three months passed, with Anthony continuing trips to the hospital to keep up his chemo treatments and his wife fighting to get the social agency to help keep him comfortable at home. No success. Here was a family up against the torturous either-or choices so common in the In-Between Stage.

Either continue exhausting trips to the ER and readmissions to the hospital or surrender to rigid hospice rules and give up all hope of extending life beyond six months. The social worker did offer to order a hospital bed for Anthony. If and when hospice did take his case, she said, a hospital bed would be the only kind he would be allowed, "to keep him safe."

During his first night in the hospital bed, Anthony woke up in a panic. He was lying flat on his back and could barely breathe. "Maria, call an ambulance," he cried hoarsely. "I need to go to the hospital." Maria crawled into the hospital bed and coiled around her husband's trembling body. "Tony, I want to keep you here where we can make you comfortable," she said. "At the hospital they'll just put you on a stretcher and ignore you. Whatever's coming, we can do it. Our family, all together."

Then, for the first time ever, Maria dispatched orders to her grown children: "Get that hospital bed out of here and get your father back into our bed before I come home from work."

From then on, the whole family suffered the constant eruptions of anxiety felt by Anthony over the most terrifying question of all: *How am I going to die?* "Am I going to bleed? Choke to death?" he constantly asked. The family had no answers. He was in pain and they were powerless to help. Over and over, Anthony whispered, "I'm so sorry you have to see all this suffering."

Shortly before Thanksgiving, the social worker visited again. "She asked my father, 'Do you want to forgo all further treatment now?'" recalls Camilla. "He said, 'No, I'd like to keep my next hospital appointment and see if they want to do more chemo.'" Camilla appealed: "The chemo holds out some hope for my father, and yes, for us, too, that it might slow the progress of the tumor growing in his throat and ease the horrible sense of choking."

Camilla remembers the chilling scene. "The social worker looked at the IV connected to my father. It was just fluids, to keep him alive—he could no longer swallow. She turned her back on my father and looked exasperated. 'This IV is inappropriate,' she said. 'This could make it more difficult for him to die.' She told us in no uncertain terms that if he were to choose hospice, he would have to forgo all treatment, including food and fluids."

The family was appalled. Determined to do whatever it took to allow Anthony to enjoy his last Thanksgiving, God willing, they called upon the

Dominican Sisters. "A visiting nurse was the first person, including my father's doctor, to indicate unequivocally that my father's passing was imminent, and to counsel us," says Camilla. She also remembers how tenderly the nurse sat beside her five-year-old son on a swing and told him that Papa would soon join the angels.

The visiting nurse strongly encouraged the family to initiate hospice. "We later had a positive experience with East End Hospice, including several days of intensive nursing and social support," says Camilla. The family's regret was that human comfort took so long in coming—only three days before Anthony expired.

Camilla describes the state of mind that overcomes many families when they are ill-equipped to comfort a dying loved one because they cannot answer the deepest end-of-life questions: "Our family was so frayed, and afraid, we took on all the professional care that used to be done by nurses, and at the same time we were grieving as a family. We're all competent people. But we became incompetent to think straight."

STRATEGIES

Palliative Care Versus Hospice

All creatures share the instinct for self-preservation, but humans, being conscious, spend much of our lives trying to deny death, the one certainty we face. Accordingly, the drive for continued life is our prime motive. It shapes our behavior from the first scream for air out of the womb to the last gasp for breath on a deathbed.

The best we can hope for in preparing a loved one for a good death, if there is such a thing, is to strengthen whatever sense of control he or she can retain over this most personal of passages. We caregivers need help in this process from trained professionals or volunteers familiar with the ebb and flow of this phase of life. They can offer support and reassurance to help us avoid becoming engulfed in anxieties and obsessed with the unknowns.

The most emotionally wrenching task for each family member is to find one's own way to let go. This process can be guided, if we allow it, by the signs and signals sent by our loved one. Most of us also need to interpret those signals. We may be so caught up in our own feelings of loss, we hold on too tightly. *We* are the ones who must give up control.

Can you imagine a more demanding passage?

Dying takes work. And time. It's a process, one that involves the whole family. It requires everybody's honest recognition that the patient's former powers, skills, and independence are ebbing; that all this is natural and inevitable, not unjust. Caregivers must also provide the patient with time and opportunity to question, to defy, to find a new spiritual centering. The most important medicine during this time is honest conversation, guided by professionals and spiritual support.

How do caregivers mollify the existential terror brought on for a patient like Anthony, accustomed to being a town leader and family patriarch? The more he became aware of the impossibility of satisfying his most fundamental instinct of self-preservation, the more helpless the family became to absorb his fears. Families need help in responding to the questions that almost certainly arise as the final passage into the unknown approaches.

The Continis' story of panic and despair might have been different if the family had not run up against the rare social worker who adheres blindly to the rules. Hospice is a federal government benefit program, and because it is paid for by Medicare, it holds people to government rules. The primary doctor must warrant that the patient is expected to die within six months. The other rule specifies that the patient agree that medical care, hospitalization, or life-prolonging treatments such as surgery or chemotherapy are no longer beneficial. So all medical care must be stopped, including artificial feeding. This is the way the government rations care for the elderly who are seriously ill.

"Some hospices, like the one the Continis experienced, are very rigid," says Carolyn Cassin, president and CEO of the National Hospice Work Group (NHWG). "Many others have expanded their services to embrace the ambivalence the patient and family feel when they are facing a life-threatening illness. They understand and support the patient's and family's need and desire to continue with chemotherapy, radiation, or feeding options that may provide comfort and improve the quantity and quality of life."

The National Hospice Work Group is a voluntary coalition of hospice CEOs who seek to break down the barriers to hospice care. These twenty-six innovative nonprofit, community-based programs do not require that patients and families make the "terrible choice" between receiving treatment and hospice care. They do not require their patients give up anything.

When to Ask for Palliative Care

No one could blame the Contini family for confusing hospice and palliative care. Many doctors are unaware of the difference. Palliative care is the opposite of imposing a deadline on patients who are not responding to acute medical treatment, yet who are still eager to live. Such a program could have kept Anthony Contini more comfortable from the day he was diagnosed.

Palliative care is appropriate from the time one is given a life-threatening diagnosis. Most chronically ill people, unlike Anthony, are not actively dying. Palliative care allows any medication—even chemotherapy or radiation—if it is helpful in subduing symptoms. In the later stages, hospice is often called in, and the combined team is committed to respecting the patient's values until the moment of passing on.

Everybody on hospice is entitled to palliative care in its most basic definition—comfort care. But in recent years, palliative care has been evolving as a much broader philosophy. The big shift in moving from acute care to palliative care is this: doctor, patient, and caregiver all stop focusing exclusively on the illness and concentrate on how to manage the best quality of life for the chronically ill person. It is a philosophy that returns control to the patient, based on his or her value system.

"Palliative care focuses on finding out who the patient is, what they care about, and what they are hoping for—then doing everything we can to help the patient and family to achieve their goals," explains Dr. Diane Meier, director of Mt. Sinai's Center to Advance Palliative Care and winner of a MacArthur Genius Award. She gives examples.

"For a patient who will live for a long time with a chronic illness such as heart disease, the goals might be the maximum possible prolongation of life along with treatment of depression; support for an exhausted spouse; and physical therapy for improved mobility. For a patient with dementia who is suffering repeated bouts of pneumonia and revolving-door hospitalizations, palliative care goals might be to give the family a picture of the future, and to help them to make decisions as their loved one would, if it were possible. The family might want continued antibiotics for infections, expert treatment for shortness of breath and agitation, but choose to avoid any future hospital stays. We call this 'nonhospice palliative care' because it is for patients who are seriously or chronically ill but not yet dying.

"In contrast, hospice is quality of care for the dying," explains Dr. Meier. "At this last stage of illness, hospice helps patients and families retain some control over the dying process—how to manage symptoms and how to think about spiritual and emotional aspects of dying."

Most hospitals negate all this. What people at this turning need is fairly simple—an informed advocate who can speak up for them to anyone who panics and wants to call 911 in a crisis that might be resolved at home with a call to a medically trained nurse or geriatrician.

Solid studies tell us that at least 20 percent of hospitalizations of older adults are preventable. Even a two- or three-day hospitalization contributes further to the health decline of many adults. But as previously explained, hospitals and doctors have a financial incentive to run people in and out of repeated short-term stays.

In 2009, the American Academy of Hospice and Palliative Medicine began for the first time to credential physicians in the new subspecialty of medical palliative care. They may be employed in hospices, hospitals, long-term-care facilities, palliative-care clinics, or managed-care organizations.

What to Ask For

Here are the critical questions to ask before choosing a hospital or a doctor for your chronically ill family member: *Do you have a palliative-care team who will work with our primary doctor?* If you are fortunate to find a medical palliative-care physician or a geriatrician, or to "educate" your own doctor to partner with you, the caregiver, then you can work together to return the power of decision making to the patient. That initiates the process of weaning the patient off learned helplessness. Other members of the team may be a nurse practitioner who makes regular visits, a social worker who counsels the family, a chaplain, and possibly a grief counselor.

- Will your hospice program allow chemotherapy or radiation if it will help make the patient more comfortable or reduce symptom pain?
- Will your program require that we give up all treatment, including tube feeding?

- What if the patient lives beyond six months? (The right answer is "We do not discharge patients just because they live beyond six months." In fact, good hospice and palliative care has been shown to extend life beyond expected prognosis.)

Where to Find It

Of all U.S. hospitals with more than four hundred beds, roughly half now offer some form of palliative care. Unfortunately, you still have to be a very informed caregiver to find palliative care and insist on it. Most doctors and hospitals are paid for practicing acute-care medicine, not palliative care. To get palliative care at home is still limited. But as demand grows, along with studies showing the huge cost savings it offers to Medicare and Medicaid, more and more families are likely to be served.

Visit the website www.getpalliativecare.org. To find out which hospitals in your area have a palliative-care program, search the Provider Directory.

See Resources at the end of the book for a list of the most progressive palliative care programs in the U.S.

twenty-seven

FINDING THE "WHY?" TO LIVE

What if we could call an "811" number before hitting 911 to summon the screaming ambulance? I actually made such a call, and it wasn't fictional. I cold-called a number I had saved for Sean Morrison, a geriatrician at Mount Sinai Hospital Palliative Care Center in New York. I had only heard vaguely about palliative care; it was my last hope.

To my surprise, Dr. Morrison himself answered. I gave him a capsule history of Clay's condition and asked for an appointment. Clay was running a high fever and choking on blood in his tracheostomy, but he refused to go back to the ER.

"Good," the geriatrician said. "Our whole goal is to keep people with chronic illnesses out of the hospital."

"Where do we go, then?"

"I think it's best if I make a house call," he said.

I almost dropped the phone.

Shortly after noon, a surprisingly young man turned up at our apartment. Sean Morrison had a curly thatch of brown hair and a fleshy handshake and a warm, direct manner. He went straight into the bedroom and sat knee to knee with Clay and began a conversation that lasted almost an hour. He treated Clay with the utmost respect. He kept asking what he wanted. Clay spoke up more clearly than he had for the past year. I was fully included in the conversation.

"Do you know what's wrong with you?" Dr. M asked.

Startled, Clay blurted, "No!"

It was a brilliant opener. Clay looked at this bright young doctor with a plea in his eyes to put the story together so it made sense. Like most people who have been up and down the roller coaster of chronic illness—endlessly tested, burned, cut, probed, poisoned—Clay had lost track of cause and effect. At this point, he was cancer free. Why couldn't he walk like he used to, talk like he used to, eat like he used to?

With only a few questions, Dr. Morrison was able to construct a clear narrative of Clay's journey to his present state of frail health. "It sounds to me like the best thing is to start you on antibiotics," he wound up. "Even if you don't have a full-blown pneumonia, the medicine will help reduce some of the inflammation from the infection and make you feel a lot better."

Then Dr. M asked the necessary questions to understand Clay's life story, his values, and how he wanted to spend this precious period of his life.

Astonishingly, this doctor listened.

Dr. M: *How's your mood?*

Clay: *All right.*

Dr. M: *Do you feel depressed?*

Clay: *No.*

Dr. M: *Sad?*

Clay: *I want to get back to walking.*

Dr. M: *Does it worry you that you might not?*

Clay: *Yes.*

Dr. M: *Have you thought about what that would be like?*

Clay: *I know what it's like! I haven't been able to walk for almost a year.*

Dr. M: *Tell me, is it frustrating, or is it more than that? Some people who feel they'll never walk again find a way to make peace with it. Others I've taken care of feel that if they can't walk again, it's not worth living. I wonder where you fall.*

Clay: *I don't feel that life is not worth living.*

Dr. M: *How about on the other end?*

Clay: *I'm frustrated.*

Dr. M: *Does that get in the way of your enjoyment of things?*

Clay: *Not really.*

Dr. M: *Would you give me a different answer if your wife were out of the room?*

Clay: *No (emphatically), not for me.*

Dr. M: *Are you afraid of dying?*

         Clay nodded yes.

Dr. M: *What is your biggest fear?*

Clay: *Being alone.*

         We assured him that would not happen. Dr. M asked what else worried him.

Clay: *Dying in a hospital.*

         Again, we reassured him that wouldn't happen.

Dr. M: *Some people worry about what it's going to feel like, the process, the symptoms.*

         Clay grunted in vigorous assent.

Dr. M: *I'd be lying to you if I said you and I are in complete control of this process. If you have any physical symptoms, let me or Gail know and I can make sure they don't bother you. The second thing is, we make decisions together, okay? I'll make recommendations, but the final choice is always yours.*

Dr. M emphasized that we were entering a partnership, the three of us. He asked us to continue talking about the questions he had raised and to write out a statement of our values and our goals for care. "I find that much more helpful than the standard living will," he said. "It's your wishes in your own words." We agreed to do our part.

It was the most honest exchange that Clay and I had ever had with a physician. Our only regret was that we hadn't had this conversation a year or two before. Dr. M. agreed that the ideal time to reach out for a home-based palliative-care team was when it became clear that Clay would continue to aspirate and infect himself with pneumonia. We could have set realistic goals and avoided the trauma of repeated hospitalizations. Clay might have gotten better at home. Certainly he would have enjoyed a better quality of life.

Privately, I admitted to Dr. M, "I have never been so doubtful of my ability to rise to a challenge. I don't know how to walk Clay through this."

*"Nobody does," he said. "We'll walk it together." He gave me permission to
e-mail him whenever I had a question or to call his cell if things suddenly took a
turn that I didn't know how to deal with. "Even if I'm traveling, I'll get back to you
as soon as I land."*

*Our "811" call and initiation into the palliative-care philosophy developed into
a series of conversations over the next seven months. Each one was more revealing
and reassuring than the last. Just as grieving has its stages, dying has its signs and
phases. We felt blessed to find a holistic solution and a practitioner willing to take
us by the hand, break down the process for us, and guide us through each step of
this final passage.*

When to Push the Body, When to Nourish the Spirit

*I had finally come to accept that Clay might get a little better but would never
get well and would inevitably pass on. That realization helped me adjust my
expectations and set more realistic goals. I stopped pushing Clay to do as much. I
shifted my focus from striving to cure his body to doing whatever I could to nourish
his spirit.*

*But it's rare that caregiver and patient reach acceptance at the same time.
Death is a fickle dance partner. Just as you think your loved one is taking the final
dip, the music starts up again, and you're back to circling round and round in a
limbo of unanswered questions—How? What? When? Clay's resistance to acceptance
seemed virtually infinite. He had made that clear in our conversation with Dr.
Morrison.*

*"I just don't know if he will ever accept the reality that he's moving toward
the end," I told the doctor. He assured me that Clay would eventually get to that
point.*

*"Our goal together," he said, "is to help Clay find meaning and purpose even
as he is losing his independence." What dying people cling to, he explained, is the
hope of somehow regaining their accustomed abilities. This being impossible, Dr.
Morrison sought to replace Clay's lost satisfactions with others that he might
appreciate. His purpose in asking "the hard questions" was to understand what
made life worth living for Clay. That would guide his recommendations for*

medical treatment and also guide me in when to push Clay and when to back off. In time, Clay could master realistic achievements tailored to his current abilities. New satisfaction would follow. This philosophy is at the heart of palliative care.

Walking was the first test. Once the antibiotics kicked in, Clay regained some of his capacity to stand and walk on the street with a walker. He showed off for me, ambulating for two blocks, executing a swift turn, and covering the full distance back to the apartment. We were both thrilled. The next day he was drained. I called Dr. M. "Sometimes, when people feel better, they overexert themselves and burn out," he explained.

To compensate for Clay's loss of independence in ambulation, I shifted to his other wishes. One was to stay active in the world, another to satisfy his legendary curiosity as a journalist. I made a game of wheeling him helter-skelter through the crowds of Times Square to see a show. I asked strangers for help in shimmying his wheelchair down a spiral staircase to a jazz club, and I maneuvered him around museum exhibits. We had awkward moments, but these expeditions were exciting, full of unexpected sights and sounds, a little risky, but they definitely helped Clay feel reconnected to New York culture.

When I took him to Hillsdale one weekend, Maura piled us and the grandchildren into a roomy SUV and off we went to a Saturday night salsa funk party at the Opera House in Ancram. A wild jam session by a dozen musicians ignited the crowd. Scores leaped to their feet, dancing and stomping up a storm. Clay rocked his wheelchair to the beat, and we improvised a kind of swing dance. The grandchildren gave him an ovation. Beauty can be found in spontaneity.

Clay was also eager for visitors, especially his former students. He loved advising rising stars on ideas for magazines, reading their books to offer blurbs, and discussing how to adapt their personal views and voices to the burgeoning new forms of Web-based journalism. In turn, they kept him in the loop on new media, updating his knowledge and sense of still being in the game. His students' constant visits touched him deeply.

Over the next few months, Clay's attachment to his public character faded, and he became more alive to the deeper personal convictions and commitments that had sustained him through the struggles of his long life.

———————————

STRATEGIES

Asking the Right Questions

First, ask your loved one whether he or she is ready to stop running to hospitals just to treat symptoms. As you know by now, that's no way to cure chronic or serious illness. On the contrary, hospitalizations at this point usually multiply ailments. Hospitals don't fix the muscle weakness or the combined assaults of previous invasive surgeries and treatments that lead to overall frailty. And emergency rooms are magnets for invisible bacteria that can't wait to move into warm compromised bodies for a nice long vacation.

According to palliative-care doctors I have interviewed, the key question to ask the patient is this: *What is your goal in care?* You can change the whole dynamic of this phase by talking to your loved one, not about physical symptoms but about how to find meaning in his or her life story. How might he or she pass on this well-earned wisdom to family, friends, students? This is a form of inherited wealth potentially far more enriching than material goods.

Returning Power to the Patient

- What does he or she want to accomplish? Physically? Spiritually? Financially?
- Are there to-do items awaiting action?
- Amends to be made?
- Beloved people and places to revisit?
- Grandchildren who should hear his or her story?
- Estranged family members open to overtures?
- Leadership successors awaiting approval?
- Unfinished touches on the will? Gifts to pass on? Letters to leave?
- What kind of service or memorial would he or she like?

Some people want to select a cherished place or clothing that makes a statement about their identity. Such discussions can even turn into something like planning a grand party.

Palliative Care for the Caregiver

- Are you seeing your doctors to maintain your own health?
- Are you taking time out to exercise, to prolong your own life?
- Are you resisting isolation, finding ways to get respite, keeping in touch with friends?
- Are you sleeping? If not, ask for help.
- What are the lifelines, the sources of meaning and joy in your life, that you may have given up? Ask the palliative-care team or a grief counselor to help you reconnect with those lifelines. Use them to help find your way back to life after your loved one has passed on. You must avoid clinging to a person no longer alive. Neither of you can possibly benefit from your hanging on. Go forth and seize life on your own separate path.

A Call to Action

How does a geriatrician like Dr. Morrison get paid? Medicare reimburses him for home visits. Because he is attached to an academic medical center and performs research, he is also compensated from private grants. Geriatricians are among the scarcest of medical resources, since their expected income is among the lowest of medical specialties. Thus, most palliative-care teams are based in hospitals. They take over the care of a patient who asks for it, combining medical and comfort care, usually in a dedicated section of the hospital. The team's real contribution is to patch together services the patient and caregiver will need for help at home.

Dr. Morrison negotiated with VNS to send a visiting nurse to monitor and treat Clay at home, as needed, and to be his conduit, for which Medicare paid. He also had a grant to provide a pastoral counselor. In Clay's last months, Dr. M called in hospice to supplement his team's care. The hospice social worker, Evelyn Tuchs, guided me tenderly through an understanding of the ebbs and flows of Clay's energy and moods, when to cheerlead and when to back off.

Palliative care is an idea whose time has come. Doctors in your community may still consider the idea impractical or too time-consuming to maintain their bottom line. Hospitals will resist because it would cut down their readmissions in the later years of people's lives. But economic analysts warn that we cannot make any serious dent in our exploding health-care costs until we find ways to reduce the ballooning of expense in the last two years of life. These are the hospital patients whose care swallows up over 70 percent of the Medicare budget.

Such patients may soon include your own loved ones. An ounce of publicity about palliative care may undo a pound of resistance. Ask your doctor what he or she thinks. Bring this book with you.

Resisting

"A hospital bed? No way!"

Clay's reaction to this suggestion by Dr. M was totally negative. I wasn't happy about the idea, either. One way Clay and I could still be together, close and intimate, was sleeping in the same bed together. At the end of a long day, we had our hour of privacy with no aides around. I was the last touch he felt before surrendering to sleep, soothing his fear of shortness of breath or choking. He was the first thing I touched on awakening, a reminder that I had at least one compelling reason to tackle another day.

For me, the hospital bed implied not just one more degree of separation, but a sentence to solitary confinement. Sleeping in separate beds, in separate rooms? Each of us would now be forced to rehearse an afterlife—in short, being alone.

What would this mean for Clay? He had told Dr. M that his quality of life depended heavily on the presence of his wife. I was his translator when his words tangled, his eyes when the stroke made newspapers too taxing to read, his pipeline to aliveness in our outings, his constant rejuvenator. Now he would be physically separated, day and night.

But the doctor recommended it because it made it easier for Clay and for his caregivers to move him in and out of bed. Then I remembered. I had lost it late one night as the aide and I struggled to move Clay out of the wheelchair. His body was limp as a rag doll, but heavier. I climbed up onto our bed to pull him in while Barbara lifted him from behind. Suddenly my frustration exploded:

"Oh, Clay, how long do you want to go on like this?"

His eyes widened. I berated myself: How could I say something so unthinkable? He said nothing. But I saw the fear in his eyes: How did you read my thoughts?

I fell into a circle of confusion. With no time to work, I stopped thinking about the issues of the day. With no thinking, I stopped writing. Soon I was a victim of identity theft—my own. As I saw it, my life was now meaningless beyond ministering to my husband and paying minimal attention to my children and grandchildren.

Discipline vanished. I couldn't make the simplest decisions, whether to wear pants or a skirt, wash my hair or leave it limp. I put off calling friends or planning dinners. All my remaining energy went into running the medical home we had made for Clay and occasionally writing proposals for magazine stories that were never accepted. I ate only perfunctorily. Ten pounds dropped away, and for a naturally skinny chick, that was not pleasing. Mounds of junk mail and unread magazines piled up in the apartment like stalagmites in some icy cave. I was frozen in place.

"You're not the same the person I met six weeks ago," Dr. M confirmed. "These are classic symptoms of depression."

I confessed that I had a recurring fantasy of running away. Since I no longer had the energy or reason to fight, the prolonged stress was pushing me in the other direction—toward flight. I considered dispatching Clay to a hospice residence and asked Dr. M if he could recommend one. He was sympathetic and named one very small residence on the Upper East Side. But it could be weeks or more before a room opened up.

I prayed and debated. Hadn't Clay done everything that I and rehab teams had asked him to do in preparation for coming home? He was still trying. How could I run away and leave him to face the hardest stretch alone? It wasn't right for either of us. He would teach me something about dying.

STRATEGIES

Rehearse Physical Separation

The arrival of a hospital bed is a momentous change. For the patient it spells "invalid," for the caregiver "invasion." To everybody else, it implies that helplessness has come to stay.

Apart from death itself, hardly anything is more difficult for loving spouses than accepting physical separation as the new, permanent fact of life. In the beginning, it's like being dropped off at boot camp or a strange college town, cut loose from your parents' protection. For spouses, it's the beginning of an end you you don't want to face.

The best course is to use physical separation as rehearsal for the emotional loss ahead. Begin accustoming yourself to living without your missing piece. Try meditating or listening to soft music before you drift off to sleep. On the plus side, a bed of your own ensures much-needed rest. But do provide your loved one with an effective bell or other emergency signal.

This is all very good advice, but I refused it even after the hospital bed arrived.

The caregiver needs his or her own emergency protection. I found mine in the writings of the Austrian psychiatrist Viktor E.

Frankl, author of *Man's Search for Meaning*. After surviving several Nazi concentration camps, Frankl concluded that one human freedom outlasts all others. It's the ability to "choose one's attitude" in any situation, however hellish. Frankl's message is the need for humans to find meaning in their lives, a purpose strong enough to overcome suffering. Frankl often quotes Nietzsche: "He who has a *why* to live can bear with almost any *how*."

Recognize Caregiver Burnout

Much later, I understood my condition as classic caregiver burnout. This is not the same as short-term fatigue. Short rest periods can renew an exhausted caregiver, and they should happen often. Burnout is deeper and more insidious. Here are questions that help indicate whether you have reached burnout:

- Think back to the last time you saw a doctor when you felt sick. Do you have trouble remembering?
- How many new pains or persistent aches, irregular heart rhythms, suspicious skin lesions have you ignored?
- When was your last visit to the dentist or eye doctor? Your last mammogram or prostate exam?
- Have you put all future plans on hold?
- Do you have a vacation to look forward to—even just a full day's break?
- Have you noticed bruising under your skin or welts under your eyes or sprays of burst capillaries in your face or legs?
- Do you look at the clock at 9:00 P.M. and wish it were later so you can justify crawling into bed? Or do you go to bed early but can't sleep?
- Are you turning to food or alcohol as your nightly companion, or using heavy drugs to induce sleep?
- Have you lost your delight in things you used to love to do?

If you answer yes more often than no, you must reach out for help. This is anticipatory grief: we don't hold back our sadness until the final separation. The sense of loss saturates many of the days of The Long Good-bye. Any caregiver in this state of depressive grieving needs a doctor of his or her own, a familiar religious guide or a pastoral counselor, a psychotherapist or a grief counselor, or a twelve-step group—a sanctuary where he or she can speak with shameless honesty and in turn receive warmth, clarity, hope for the future, and stern reminders to care for him- or herself. When you're running on empty, all you can expect yourself to do is to put one foot in front of the other and show up for what absolutely needs to be done.

If ever there was a time that caregivers need respite, this is it. In marathoner's parlance, you have hit the wall. It's the nineteenth mile, but you won't get a second wind by continuing to run. Your endorphins have gone missing. Many devoted caregivers I have interviewed had an uncanny sense of when the end was approaching, and they chose that point to take a vacation.

Heartless? No! Intuitively, they were replenishing their bodies and spirit in preparation for finishing the race.

You will probably need somebody to *make* you get away— another family member or your doctor. Find a facility that will take your loved one for at least a week. It could be a hospice inpatient unit. Some nursing homes that offer rehab also have an accommodation for a short-term stay by a patient whose caregiver has to be away. It is billed like a hotel room but has the added benefit of a nursing staff and possibly hospice or palliative care to attend to the patient's needs and comfort.

Curing Codependency

I had to answer yes to most of the questions in the preceding list. I often woke up at four in the morning with eight hundred volts of anxiety, heart pounding, skin clammy, head flooded with nightmarish visions of my husband's face severed into jagged Picasso-like pieces. I would run into the next room to see for myself, only to find him sleeping peacefully. When dawn finally arrived, I felt no anticipation. Just dread. For the first time in my life, I pulled a mask over my eyes, shutting out every new day.

I had stopped practicing meditation and prayer to help control anger. I slid into a classic funk. I was angry at being trapped and guilty over feeling inadequate—at doing too much yet not doing enough. I had to be reminded that keeping Clay alive was not within my powers. I had to give myself permission to fail.

As I saw it then, I was suffering from a spiritual thirst. To me, the goal of spirituality is to decipher God's will for us and quiet our own self-centeredness. I would try to reopen my mind and heart to my higher power and await an insight or inspiration suggesting the next right step.

It was Dr. M who insisted that I get away for at least a week and get back to work. This would allow Clay and me to practice physical separation and reconnect me with the world outside of a sickroom. The doctor also saw an opportunity in my absence. He offered Clay a time trial.

"Let's try you in the hospital bed for a week, while your wife's away [thus absolving me of any guilt]. See if it makes it easier for you to breathe and move in and out of bed. If it isn't acceptable, we'll send the bed away. Deal?" It was a deal.

Serendipitously, Vanity Fair *asked me to cover Hillary Clinton's presidential primary campaign. It was early March 2008. Here was a chance to replug into the central circuitry of a society being electrified by the most highly charged election in my memory. I asked Clay's opinion. "It could be over in a month or two, or it could go on until June," I warned him. "I'll be away a few days almost every week."*

"Go," Clay commanded. "Just call and fill me in."

Dr. Morrison saw it as a necessity for me and an opportunity for Clay. "You must go," he urged. "You're a writer. Be yourself."

I could feel despair lifting from the moment I hoisted my bag into the trunk of a cab and said, "LaGuardia, please."

"ARE YOU HERE FOR *the death watch?*"

That was how my friends in the traveling press corps welcomed me into the bubble of the Clinton campaign plane. A month before, on February 5, Super Tuesday, the campaign had slammed into a wall when Hillary failed to live up to her prediction that she would pocket most of the twenty-four states and force Barack Obama to fold. She had fallen disastrously behind in pledged delegates, behind in the popular vote, behind in the number of captured states.

But Hillary was no quitter. She was surprisingly radiant in an electric-blue jacket as she welcomed me and a few other journalists to cross the line from the quarantined section for the press into her forward cabin. She did not appear to be the least discouraged.

As the author of a mostly sympathetic biography, Hillary's Choice, I might have received easy access in return. But the revelations in that book had put me on ice with the Clintons for several years. So I was surprised to get her signature wide-angle smile and full five-knuckle handshake.

"Hi, Gail. I'm so glad to see you out here!"

I asked how confident she felt about Ohio; only two weeks before, she had enjoyed a commanding eighteen-point lead over Obama. But it was now down to a mere four or five points. "Ohio is America, so I feel good that we're doing well there," she said. "Just keep working at it."

"Will you keep going right down the road to the last superdelegate?" I asked.

"Absolutely, absolutely," she insisted.

Right then, I knew I would be reporting until June. No matter how often she was counted out, Hillary would never throw in the towel until the last possible moment. Her mantra remained what it had always been: "We go on."

Once Hillary's campaign revved up to position her as the Comeback Kid, reporters worked twelve to fourteen hours a day, sleeping briefly in Best Western beds before another day geared up at 5:00 A.M. I welcomed the whirlwind. The plunge into breaking news—tense presidential debates, rushed speeches in high *school gyms, spot interviews with fiercely divided mothers and daughters all over Texas and Ohio—yanked me out of depression in no time. I felt reborn.*

After my first four days on the road, I rushed back to New York. Outside our apartment door, I took a deep breath, envisioning Clay immobilized in a hospital bed in the small dark sitting room. I wanted to be elsewhere. Finally, I put on a smile and turned the key.

To my surprise, I found Clay sitting up, eager and grinning, arms outstretched for a hug. He savored all the political gossip and personal messages I brought from old colleagues. Before I knew it, he pushed himself up and out of the high bed and onto the walker and sailed smoothly into the living room.

He was literally on a roll. "It's still light out, let's take a walk," he suggested. We ended up seeing a movie. It was a fine night.

Dr. M was pleased to hear my report. It confirmed that the hospital bed had not worsened Clay's dependence. On the contrary, it made him more independent. Dr. M saw an even more important sign. "I called Clay a few days after you left, worried that he might be furious with me about the bed. He was perfectly happy with it! He wouldn't have accepted it so readily if there wasn't a recognition, at both the unconscious and now the conscious levels, that this is where he is. This is the first sign that he is beginning to accept."

"It feels like we're moving into a different phase," I mused. "There's a big difference between running away and a caregiver who goes away to revitalize herself, right?"

Dr. M murmured full assent. "I have to be honest: your being busy at work is one of the best things that's happened. It erases all that feeling of codependency. There is life here, and it's not all about his illness. The idea that things are okay enough that you feel comfortable taking off—and you should—is a return to normalcy."

———————————

STRATEGIES

Pick Up Your Former Passion

In hindsight, this is what I learned from The Long Good-bye: it is crucial for the long-term caregiver to reenter the outside world and recover or rediscover what could offer you meaning. Whatever you have done in your life that awakened your passion or made you feel worthwhile, pick it up again. This is the key to breaking the dangerous lock of codependence.

By the time it is clear that your loved one has only months to live, you should have hospice. Medicare or Medicaid will pay for a home health aide to stay with your loved one. That frees you to take a class at the local Y or community college. To join a baseball or bowling league. To take a part-time position at the town hall or in the public library. To join a book club.

You might start a class at home, teaching what you know best—knitting, cooking, accounting, computer techniques, bridge, journal writing—as a way of recovering your confidence and enjoying social interaction.

I know, I know, you're too tired. But even if the activity does not feel like a respite at first, keep it up. Meeting and greeting new people is a natural antidote to the solitary confinement of late-stage caregiving. And you will need these new people as a bridge to your new life. Go out for coffee or a movie or bowling or a wine-tasting with them.

This is the time to save yourself.

twenty-eight
MOMENTS OF PRESENCE

While looking over my old journals, I had the idea of inviting Clay to recall our most memorable times. I dug out all our photo albums to supply the visuals. Added to this, I took off the shelves the dozens of bound volumes of his seven years as editor of New York *magazine, his earlier years at* Esquire, *and even his original Sunday supplements of* New York *in the* Herald Tribune. *Dr. M fully endorsed the idea of a life review. "It's a perfect way to ease him, and yourself, through this next phase."*

Clay murmured over and over, "I'm so glad we had our time together. It's been the most beautiful time in my life."

We talked about his bonus life, the ten years he was given after the cancer wars began, to teach at a first-rate university. He recalled his fascination with probing his students' personalities, teasing out each person's unique point of view and endorsing it. Editing is a kind of teaching, and Clay's last decade had carried that idea to a whole new level of service and satisfaction.

It was surprisingly easy to bring up the question of where he would like to be put to rest. We loved the village of Sag Harbor, filled with writers, editors, and artist friends of ours. A few already inhabited the historic nineteenth-century whaling-era cemetery, Oaklawn, and others had reserved their resting places. I found a sylvan area with side-by-side plots for us, beneath a canopy of tall oaks, and showed the photos to Clay. He was pleased. Raw nature was the closest he felt to the divine. We decided to have a harpist friend strum the guests into our natural sanctuary. Tom and Sheila Wolfe graciously offered to welcome guests to a lawn luncheon to follow. Later, I would plan a memorial, a celebration with a jazz band.

But a certain rift had opened between Clay and me. I believe in God and wanted to talk to my husband about death and the afterlife. Although Clay had grown up in a family of Missouri Protestants, his journalist's skepticism had erased any religiosity in his character, much less any interest in churchgoing. He cut my overtures short. But I sensed that at this stage he suffered from his lack of faith. I felt he needed help in blessing his life and finding a sense of peace. I told Dr. M that I was searching for a spiritual companion for Clay. He eagerly suggested we meet with the palliative-care team's young chaplain. We made an appointment.

A lovely round-faced, bright-eyed woman barely past thirty appeared at our door and gave me her name. "I happen to be Jewish, I'm a rabbi, but I visit with patients of all different faiths and backgrounds," she said. Within minutes I could tell that Chaplain E was wise beyond her years, serene and grounded. She asked, "What can you tell me about Clay?" He's a teacher, I said, but not a believer.

She knew instinctively how to approach him, kneeling beside his hospital bed. "Hi, Clay. One great thing about having a Jewish chaplain is I won't try to convert you."

Clay appreciated her candor. He turned fully toward the chaplain and gave her a big smile. "I'm glad you came." As they talked, Clay's words became clearer, then came faster, and soon he was more voluble than he'd been for months, probably a whole year.

The chaplain asked him if he felt locked inside a body that was betraying him. He knew right away she understood. "But everything upstairs is intact?" He gave an enthusiastic "Yes."

"Then let's think about identifying some moments of presence in your life," she suggested quietly. Clay nodded. Then the young rabbi struggled to find the words that would express the meaning of "moments of presence." Clay helped her with the words. He became animated. Once again, he was the teacher-editor. Between the two of them, they worked out that it meant those rare times when the past and future seem to fuse and one is totally in the present moment, feeling broadly connected to all of life. "Can you think of some?" Chaplain E asked.

Clay remembered the moment with his first cancer surgeon, the eighty-year-old John Conley, when we sought him out for a second consult. Clay was able to express his own fears of surgery. In response, Dr. Conley had demonstrated his steadiness as an elderly surgeon. He had silently held out his hands for a full minute, keeping them as still as gloves lying on a table.

Clay told us, "I'd never confessed fear to another man. He didn't make me feel small. And I was surprised when the doctor asked me to assure him that he would do a splendid operation. He had fears, too. I had a feeling of shared humanity with him."

Clay then recalled how he and I walked out of Dr. Conley's office—it was early April—and found ourselves across the street from Central Park. I remembered the sun splashing over the waxy green leaves and how we could almost see them opening, like baby's fists. It was spring and life throbbed all around us.

"I grabbed Gail in my arms. And I remember that feeling, having hope again." Clay's face was luminous as he looked at me. "Love and hope. I kissed you, I remember."

The chaplain smiled. "You shared a moment of presence that day. And that moment is seared into eternity. It will forever exist."

Letting Go

Well-meaning friends kept saying, "You have to let go." I was ready, or thought I was, but the caregiver is not in charge of that decision. The patient is. Dr. M told me Clay would eventually show signs.

One Sunday night, I felt Clay's will go slack for the first time. He didn't want to leave his home hospital bed. Pushing the wheelchair against a stiff wind, we were late joining my sister and brother-in-law for dinner at Josephina's, a nearby Broadway restaurant that Clay had always liked. The three of us talked animatedly about movies and books and food and the state of the world. Clay never said a word. In a cab going home, I asked Clay if he'd enjoyed the outing. "No," he said, bleakly. "Why?" He shrugged. "Who knows?"

I said, "You don't want to stay in a little room for the rest of your life, do you?" With a grimace, he said, "Yes."

Next morning, Lynn Fisher, RN, the perceptive hospice nurse who had joined our team, spotted another sign. For the first time, Clay refused to get out of bed and go to the computer for his daily reading of The New York Times. *When I tried to read the paper version to him aloud, he waved it away. "Hard to believe," I told*

Lynn. *"Ever since he was eight years old, he's been running to the door every morning to grab the newspaper and devour it."*

"Disengagement from the world," Lynn explained, *"is the most important sign that a person is ready to die."*

When he slept most of the next two days, I called Dr. M. He offered to come over and talk to Clay. He knew all the right questions: *"Was going out to dinner just too much effort?"* Clay nodded: yes. *"Was it hard to focus on the conversation, and be 'on'?"* Clay nodded again: yes.

"Are you struggling with wanting to stop trying so hard?"

Clay's head snapped up. His eyes scanned the doctor's face, as if trying to understand how this man could see into his soul. He had been "caught" thinking the unthinkable. The choice of giving up.

Clay whispered, *"Yes."*

"Are you worried about other people's opinions?"

Clay shook his head emphatically: no.

"Are you worried about what you will think of yourself?"

Clay's immediate response: *"Yes."*

The choice he faced was whether to surrender the very life force that made him a man of action—the survivor of a hundred setbacks; the editor who picked himself up every time the horse of fortune threw him off; the cancer patient who shared his magazine savvy with upcoming journalists, even when the disease stole most of his voice; the grandfather who could barely walk but climbed steep icy stairs to hear his six-year-old grandson play a piano recital.

Dr. M took me aside. *"He wants to want to go on, but when it comes down to it, he just doesn't have the energy to work at living. It has to be monumentally hard for him to give up, to want to stop fighting, he's been doing it for fifteen years. It's hard for both of you to let go of fighting."* I nodded. *"Let him know you're not going to make him feel guilty for not exerting the energy to get up or go out."*

It was time to decide on whether or not to treat the next aspiration, which would inevitably stir up another episode of pneumonia. Dr. M spoke with Clay, one-on-one, about how comfortable he would be with delegating that decision to the doctor and me. Clay gave his grateful blessing. It was his way of avoiding personal responsibility for giving up.

Shortly thereafter, signs of pneumonia reappeared. Clay sent us all a message without speaking it. He pulled out his feeding tube. When Safoura tried to reconnect it, he pushed it aside. She sensed it was intentional. But when I later asked Clay if he meant to disconnect it, he insisted it was just an accident.

"Don't keep asking him!" Dr. M chided me. "Look, a husband can't admit to his wife, 'I don't want to fight anymore.' That would be abandoning you. That's not what a good husband does in this society. Leave that role to me. Your role is to keep him living as long as he's alive."

We agreed not to give him antibiotics and not to reconnect the feeding tube. Wait and see.

"Sweetheart, you've been in and out of pneumonia for two years now, what keeps you going?" I asked him.

"I don't know," he said.

"Are you doing it for me?" There was a long pause.

"Yes."

The secret was out at last. I had to let him know I was ready.

Is It Time?

Inevitably, a few days later, it looked for all the world as though Clay was ready to go. I couldn't wake him. The visiting nurse came early and recorded a high temperature, rattling in the chest, and short periods of no breathing. She called it apnea. Infectious pneumonia was coursing through his body with no sentry on duty to call out his warrior cells.

I called my sister, Trish; she and my brother-in-law would skip work and be right over. Maura pulled Declan out of school and soon arrived with all three children and her husband, Tim, filling the apartment with the welcome clatter of toddlers' feet climbing and falling in a clutter of toys. Declan, about to turn seven, was unusually solemn. His mother had told him that Grandpa Clay was dying. That was the way in our family. Everything was named and discussed. When Maura gave birth to Declan's first baby sister, at home with a midwife, he skipped school. We had asked him if he would like to go into the bedroom and see the birth. He hesitated.

"Next time."

And there was a next time. When his second baby sister was born at home, he did look in moments after she was born. It wasn't scary at all. He was invited into the bed to touch the newborn, as much a part of him as his parents.

Now, Declan watched as his baby sister was plopped down on his grandfather's chest, grabbing for his chin and touching his nose. To baby Mairead, Clay's sleeping face was just another fascinating live object to finger and see what reaction she got. She woke him up. She drew forth a smile. Then the stories we all wanted to retell spilled forth, and Clay became animated. This is the beginning of closure. In the face of death's omnipotence, we can settle for at least keeping our loved one's identity alive.

For the next ten hours the children ran in and out of the room, insisting the grown-ups cripple ourselves playing Twister, bouncing balls off the walls, coaxing everybody else out to the park, and coming back to eat while the baby pulled stuffing out of a torn pillow.

Declan asked me to get out the paints. He'd had a "vision" driving over from Brooklyn and he wanted to do a picture for Grandpa Clay. He bent over the coffee table, intent on depicting for himself what this dying business was all about. A half hour later he produced a painting of three bright red gumdrop mountains under a smiling sun and blue sky. Planted atop the center mountain was the figure of his grandfather, with a tablet beside him reading "Rest in Peace." It was signed "For Grandpa from Declan, with love forever."

When he showed it to Clay, they exchanged a look of sweet innocence. This is the way it is: childhood to elderhood, birth to death. It was as natural as waiting for his mother to give birth at home. Now he was watching his grandfather give way to death at home. Two of the most potentially frightening episodes of the human condition were already becoming part of this child's everyday experience.

That day, for once, there were no agendas. No expectations. No holiday meals to produce or planes to catch or emergency calls to be made to a doctor. We could all just be with one another and savor the moments of lucidity with Clay. Declan summed it up when he announced: "I like this day."

I felt a layer of calm settle over the sadness, like clouds that sometimes lighten a night sky after a thunderstorm. There is a point at which each of us seems to surrender. It strikes me as an intervention of grace. Once we have some spiritual understanding of what is happening, the naturalness of it brings release. Our grandchild brought us that release.

The next morning, I was surprised to see his eyes open. I touched his cheek. It was not hot. His breathing was not labored. The nurse listened to his chest. "It's not rattling anymore." Without any medicine at all, beyond the medicinal properties of love and touch, laughter and foot massage, children and storytelling, Clay had fought off the infection on his own. Dr. M was not as surprised as we were.

"When you remove all the stress of hospital and you make someone feel loved and comfortable, in their own surroundings, they often get better," he said. "I've seen it again and again."

It wasn't the gentle denouement we had all expected. But it was a giant step for us all toward resolving the final passage.

———————————

twenty-nine

CROSSING THE RUBICON

Our birthdays are always marked by ceremony, so I suppose it is natural to wait for the right ceremonial moment to mark the end of our lives. We all know elders who waited for the last holiday that would bring the whole family together. Some wait for a cherished person to come and say good-bye. I know of one husband who couldn't die until his vigilant wife was finally persuaded to leave the house on a shopping trip, wanting to spare her the final agony of losing her fight to save him. Wives often hang on to life until the husband gives up the ghost, and she dies a few weeks or months later. Some people wait for a beloved parent or child who has already passed on to "come for me."

Professionals in hospice work have told me they believe the mind recognizes, on the soul level, that one is making a momentous transition. And during that transition, one has some choice about going sooner or later.

None of us knew exactly why Clay was hanging on. I was bedeviled by what-ifs. What if we had recognized two years before that he would suffer from recurrent pneumonias? What if we had known there was another choice and saved all the trauma and money squandered on circling the hell of hospitalworld? What if we had asked for palliative care when he first entered the "cycle of slow dying"?

We might be at peace by now.

A part of me was dying, too. But our chaplain had to remind me of the reality: "You're still alive. This is his death. It's not your death. Everybody gets their own death. It's essential to make that distinction."

I could still go to the gym and after twenty minutes on a treadmill I would feel my heart rate pump up. But my heartsong was still dying. I was in suspended animation and it was not healthy. Dr. Morrison intervened. In late April, he ordered me to go back out and catch up with the Clinton campaign.

Catching Up with Hillary

The May 5 Indiana primary was Hillary's last best hope to prove herself the Comeback Kid by scoring a knockout with Indiana's blue-collar voters. We were on the Clinton campaign plane shortly after 1:00 A.M., following her confident election-night "I've got it in my pocket" speech, when NBC correspondent Andrea Mitchell looked up from her BlackBerry and called out, "[Tim] Russert just reported it's over."

The faces of Clinton's advisers blanched. Obama's muscular victory by fourteen points over Clinton in North Carolina, the same night, obliterated the bare two-point margin Hillary held in Indiana. "A win is a win!" shouted her sunny-in-hell campaign chairman, Terry McAuliffe. In a hasty confab among Hillary, Bill, Chelsea, and aides, Hillary said decisively, "I want to be out there tomorrow, as early as possible, to show my commitment."

When we landed in Washington at 2:00 A.M., every BlackBerry aboard was blinking red with the AP alert from 1:10 A.M. Russert had indeed pronounced on MSNBC, "We now know who the Democratic nominee is going to be, and no one is going to dispute it." It was Barack Obama.

On June 7, after two years of running for president and four days of internalizing the shock of her defeat, Hillary Clinton conceded in the finest speech of her career. She acknowledged that whenever she was asked what it meant to run as a woman, she said she was running because she believed she would be the best president. "But I am a woman," she finally declared, without qualification, "and like millions of women I know there are still barriers and biases out there, often unconscious. Although we weren't able to shatter that highest, hardest glass ceiling this time, thanks to you it's got about eighteen million cracks in it."

Her supporters broke into deafening applause, many of their faces swamped with tears and lips tightened in commiseration. But Hillary Clinton would not allow herself or her heartbroken supporters to dwell on the what-ifs. "Please don't

go there," she urged. "Life is too short, time is too precious. . . . We have to work
together for what still can be."

Like millions of other women, I took that message to heart. I had to work for
what still could be—for our country with its first black president, for Clay's best
last days, for me after Clay.

How Am I Going to Die?

I came home to find a pale man swallowed in the vast whiteness of a hospital
bed, a surrealistic blur that seemed to swell beyond the walls of
the little sitting room like a Magritte painting. The walls held enlarged
photographs, depicting the man in the bed at his prime—larger than life. Boyishly
eager reporter walking the beach with John F. Kennedy. In-a-hurry publisher
striding impatiently past Big Ben. Cocky feet-up-on-the-desk editor as he worked
his spell over the phone. Proud husband in black tie as he escorted me up the steps
to an honors dinner at the New York Public Library.

Dr. M and I began to understand. Clay could not reconcile the conflicting
images of himself. Was he the famous editor with the booming voice that once
penetrated walls? Or was he the invalid now barely able to speak, much less stand
on his own feet? *Who am I now?* his eyes seemed to implore.

"The only way to find out what his fears are is to ask," Dr. M told me.

And so, in June, the doctor came by and knelt on a footstool at Clay's bedside,
ready to ask him the hardest question of all. I was grateful, I couldn't have done it
myself. Kneeling allowed the doctor to be on the same eye level as Clay, an
intentional equalizing of the power balance.

"Are you afraid of dying?"

Clay nodded yes.

"What is your biggest fear?"

"Being alone."

Again, we assured him that would not happen. Dr. M would alert me and I
would be there. So would Safoura or Isatou. Dr. M asked what else worried him.

"Dying in a hospital," Clay said. We could reassure him that wouldn't happen
(although most Americans will not have a choice).

"Some people worry about what it's going to feel like, the process, the
symptoms," Dr. M said. "The other thing I find that people worry about is the

feeling that things are moving without any control. Is this something you worry about?"

Clay grunted in vigorous assent.

"I'd be lying to you if I said you and I are in complete control of this process," the doctor began. *"But there are a couple of things we can do to take control. One is to make sure that you're really comfortable and you don't have trouble breathing. If you have any physical symptoms, let me or Gail know and I can make sure they don't bother you. The second thing is, we make decisions together, okay? I'll make recommendations, but the final choice is always yours."*

Early on, Clay had told Dr. M that he feared being stalled between living and dying, unable to move either way. "I can make sure that doesn't happen," Dr. M assured him. "At any time when you think this is not how you would want to live, I can stop things. Some people, as the process unfolds, want to just sleep. They don't want to be aware of what's going on. I can then use medication to help you go to sleep."

Clay shook his head furiously, indicating that was not what he wanted.

"Good. For people like you, it's the opportunity to live in the moment. To enjoy the spontaneity of 'Oh, I feel good today. I'm going to go outside. Maybe I'll have an ice-cream cone.' Or, 'I'm going to go to a concert.' That's fine. At some point, the body begins to shut down."

Clay's brows pinched. He told the doctor he was afraid to close his eyes and go to sleep now, for fear he'd never wake up.

"In my experience, it doesn't happen like that," said Dr. M. "It's only when the brain begins to shut down. When that point comes, people feel ready. It doesn't come as a surprise, and it doesn't feel frightening. It's a gradual transition. And because it's gradual, people feel in control of what's happening. So if you're tired, you should rest. And we'll be here when you open your eyes."

Clay's worried frown relaxed.

Dr. M explained that the time when people feel most worried and anxious is *"right now, when you're looking ahead and thinking about what's going to happen, rather than when it's actually happening. This is the hardest part. Do you want me to go on?"*

Clay indicated yes.

"You've told me that you've said good-bye to the people you want to say good-bye to." Yes. "And I'll bet you've thought through your life by now, right?" Clay nodded yes. "Many people don't have the opportunity to do that. Now it's a

question of setting some small goals over the next days, or weeks. Things you may want to read or have read to you."

I asked if he'd like me to read poetry or Shakespeare. Clay said it was just hearing my voice that made him feel good. And music. That squared with Dr. M's private instructions to me: The last sense to go is hearing, so don't say anything in front of the dying that you don't want them to hear. But do keep talking or singing or soothing with music; it can be received even through a coma.

Finding Myself Again

What was going to become of me when he was gone? That was now Clay's number one concern. Dr. M. had told me that the chief worry he hears from people with serious illness is not about themselves, it's about the well-being of the loved ones they will leave behind.

I assured Clay that I had wonderful support from our family and our friends. "What you're leaving me is a world of people who have been part of our lives," I said. "You've left a part of you in each of them. I'll feel it when I'm with them. That's what I'll hold on to."

But what about your writing? he wanted to know.

I fell silent. That question opened up my own greatest fear. When I tried to sit down and compose a coherent narrative out of the four months of reporting on the dazzling presidential campaign, I froze. My mind was splintered between the twenty-four-hour cable news-squawk cycle and our own twenty-four-hour life-or-death vigil. I had one week to capture the whys and wherefores in a ten-thousand-word story for Vanity Fair. I also had to plan a funeral. My powers of concentration deserted me. I was fighting a fear that pierced to the core of my being: Could I still write?

My sister, Trish, was the only one to whom I could confide such a shattering possibility. She passed it on to Dr. M. Trish told him that she and Maura didn't recognize me anymore. I had lost myself. And they couldn't bear to lose both Clay and me.

Dr. M called a family summit meeting at Clay's bedside. He told Clay that he was ordering me to go to the country for a week, to do nothing but write and rest. It was a prescription I must follow. And he wanted Clay's endorsement.

Clay gave an enthusiastic thumbs-up. He would wait for me to finish the story.

In my week's getaway to the farm in Hillsdale, blanketed by the simplicity of the buzzing and greening and mooing of early June, I began to find myself again. An early bike ride, freshly laid eggs deposited on my porch, a day of writing, a dusk for walking to the song of turtles, and a night for a second burst of writing was the best medicine anyone could have prescribed.

Clay couldn't wait to hear me read my first draft when I returned. We reverted to mentor and disciple. He commented. I listened. I felt a frisson of his old intellectual force. More important, he felt it, too. One night, after I came home from closing the story at the magazine, I found Clay sitting up with a broad smile.

"I'm feeling so happy," he said.

I looked at this man propped up in a hospital bed with a special valve that permitted him to speak, and I could barely ask the question: "Why are you feeling happy?"

"Because they liked your story."

The Crisis of Impermanence

A parade of Clay's colleagues and friends brightened the apartment all through June. Milton Glaser, the famous graphic artist and Clay's partner in starting New York magazine, and the art director Walter Bernard and his wife, Bina, brought their latest artwork and shoptalk. Tom Wolfe came to read to Clay the essay he had spent a month composing for an upcoming anthology of four decades of New York magazine writing, "New York Stories." The editor and portrait artist Byron Dobell told him that the American Portrait Gallery of the Smithsonian Museum wanted to acquire the oil painting he had done of Clay. As word spread, distant friends from California to Maine to Florida made visits to bid good-bye to a treasured part of their own past.

I kept racking my brain for how to help Clay in his ultimate existential struggle. It is not the caregiver's responsibility to prepare the spiritual pathway that will allow a dying loved one to let go. But when a powerful ego cannot surrender his or her will to God, or some reasonable facsimile, the dread of oblivion can become the source of immense suffering. Granted, if we accepted the brevity of our life span early on, we would not live with the vanity and vehemence we normally do until some time in sobering middle age. But once the signs of our mortality become unmistakable, it is well to begin our negotiation with the Crisis of Impermanence.

For Clay, and for me as his enabler, the fight for perpetual life had gone on too long. He was stuck in limbo. It was wearing everybody down. I was glad when he asked to see our chaplain again.

For this visit, he insisted on getting dressed and coming into the living room to meet her, a sign of respect. She kneeled beside his wheelchair and asked, "Why do you think so many people have been going out of their way to find out where you are and to come and see you?"

"Because Gail asks them," he said.

"No, Clay. They call me," I said.

"In the short time I've known you, I've come to understand the gift you have of connecting with other people and appreciating their uniqueness," Chaplain E said. She was unusually articulate that day; the words fell easily as she laid her hand on his. "Directly and indirectly, so many people have been touched, influenced, provoked, changed, by ideas you have expressed in your many publications, right?"

Clay looked away.

"That's so special."

I asked, "Why can't you feel loved and valued by the hundreds of people you have known and worked with and published?"

He didn't answer. Chaplain E probed. "What is it about accepting love that is so difficult for you?"

"I don't deserve it."

At last it had surfaced, the bottomless doubt of self-worth that keeps so many of us from allowing love to flow freely, in and out of us.

"What makes you think that?" the chaplain asked.

"I was using them."

"For what?"

"For my purposes, for my publications."

I couldn't hold back. "Clay, you have always been able to reach into writers and artists and apprehend their essence, their idiosyncratic way of viewing the world. You are able to illuminate people to themselves."

His eyebrows shot up. Something had reached him.

"*That's the unique gift of creativity that God gave you,*" I said. "*It's what we as writers and artists all yearn for. You've extended it to hundreds of the people you've worked with over the years.*"

Chaplain E chimed in. "*That includes me.*" *Clay looked surprised.* "*I've learned about your history as one of the great editors of the last half of the twentieth century,*" *she said.* "*Your soul has been implanted in many thousands of people, through your publications. But I have to tell you how you have impacted me, myself.*" *She revealed that she had a documented learning disability—a problem with word retrieval.* "*Being heard and understood is really important to me. Clay, you have helped me find my words.*"

A look of pleasure softened Clay's stoic face. "*Really?*"

"*Really.*" *The young rabbi told him that she herself had experienced his gift as a teacher.* "*And that will help me say what I need to express, to comfort people in my work.*"

Then Clay asked if he could have a private talk with the rabbi. She followed him into his room with a hand-lettered alphabet that would allow Clay to point to letters if he couldn't form all the words he wanted. When she emerged twenty minutes later, she looked very satisfied. Without spilling any beans, she told me, "*He said he was able to communicate with me something he wouldn't communicate to anyone else in the world. He said he found it very helpful.*"

"*You are the spiritual confidante we were looking for, another godsend,*" I said. "*Thank you.*"

That was the day Clay found the peace to die.

———————

IN THE MIDDLE OF *June, Clay's body began to shut down. But as he approached his final deadline, his life force returned with gusto. He asked Dr. M,* "*How long?*"

"*Not long,*" *the doctor said.* "*A week to a month.*" *Clay accepted the news without surprise.*

Then I said, "*Do you want to do one great thing, darling? Something wonderful?*"

He nodded vigorously.

"*How about we go out and hear some jazz?*"

"*Tonight?*"

"Tonight."

He shook his head up and down.

I ran to the computer and googled Dizzy's Club Coca-Cola. It occupies a high floor in the nearby Jazz at Lincoln Center building in Columbus Circle. It had a show that night. I ran back to Clay: "The show starts in two hours—think we can make it?"

He wheeled himself to his closet and picked out a linen jacket, a deep blue shirt, and a suede cap. He allowed me to touch up his face with tinted sunscreen and wheel him in front of the full-length mirror.

"How's that for handsome?" I asked. He looked pleasantly surprised to see a picture of normalcy.

Dizzy's was the quintessence of New York. A giant window wall opened to a sweeping view across Central Park and the jeweled lights of Fifth Avenue. A nearly full moon was rising over the city of fables, his beloved city. We watched its course. Clay's attention locked on the jazz pianist. Mike Melvoin was a man of Clay's vintage with a perfect-pitch philosophy, right in tune with Clay's.

"There's a lot of pessimism out there," the pianist said. "Feelings of futility. It's the job of music to dispel those feelings." Then he played an original composition called "Life Is What You Make It."

When the drums kick-started an up-tempo piece, Clay's fingers drummed on the table. He was a drummer as a boy. For the next hour and a half, Clay sat tall and straight in his wheelchair and drank in the music as his sustenance.

We were back in our apartment shortly before midnight. But Clay was not the least bit tired. He wanted to talk.

He gripped my hands and said clearly: "That was a magical evening."

Two days later, on the morning of July 1, 2008, I rushed back from a morning TV interview and slipped my hand over Clay's. I felt a slight movement. His eyes did not open. His lips formed the words . . . thank . . . you.

Safoura wrapped the blood pressure cuff around his arm. The needle slowly but steadily dipped. I climbed into bed beside him. The needle hit zero.

Twenty minutes later the phone roused me from my weeping reverie. It was a reporter from The New York Times obituary page, wanting to confirm the time and cause of death.

"He died at 8:22 A.M.," I said. "Of natural causes."

"We never use that."

"You've never known anyone to die of natural causes?"

"It's not Times *style."*

"But it is the style in which some people go out."

"Didn't Mr. Felker have cancer?"

"Yes, four times," I said. "We beat it four times. He hadn't had cancer for the last two and a half years. And he wouldn't want anyone to think he died suffering."

The reporter persisted. "Well then, what did he die from?"

A cascade of emotions silenced me for a moment. Then I came to rest on an inner smile. "He stopped breathing."

EPILOGUE:
WHO WILL TAKE CARE OF US?

William Sloane Coffin Jr., the famously Radical Yale University chaplain in the 1960s, expressed an enviable goal before he died at home, under the care of hospice, at the ripe age of eighty-two: "The art of living is to die young as late as possible."

It's a mantra that matches the mind-set of many boomers. Asked in an AARP survey at what age they would become "old," the majority said seventy-nine. They may be right. But despite the longevity revolution wrought by astonishing changes in medical technology over the last fifty years, one thing will never change. Ultimately, our bodies weaken, our sight dims, our limbs creak, and the hunger for human connection on the physical, emotional, and spiritual levels expands in proportion to our isolation.

We don't want to grow old alone.

Where does this leave boomers as they tip over into the new Medicare generation? We are not going to find anything like holistic caring in our hospitals or nursing homes. And we can't expect our overscheduled adult children to drop their lives and come to our rescue when we can no longer live safely alone.

Some of us would rather die than call a daughter in the middle of the night to take us to the emergency room. Clare Harmon, a widowed gourmet cookie baker in Manhattan, is a case in point. She remembers the night shortly after her husband passed on. She felt strong heart palpitations.

Accustomed to being the caregiver, she didn't know what to do *with herself.* She took her poodle out for a walk. Then she walked down the street and checked herself into an emergency room. She didn't want to wake her daughter, who lives four blocks away.

In an ideal world, we would all be cared for in our last years at home. Home—the very word conjures warmth, safety, familiarity, and loving family members with the skills, time, money, and compassion to sacrifice themselves to tend to us. But that romanticized world, with deeply connected "till-death-do-us-part" families, doesn't exist anymore. Western societies are increasingly transient. Families are smaller, which means fewer adult children are available to share the burden of elder care. Women are no longer a free labor pool—they work outside the home. Seniors live longer, much longer, and develop complex medical ills or severe chronic conditions, often requiring decades more of care than in the past.

Even for the most loving and dutiful family members, the financial and emotional burdens of long-term caregiving can be unbearable. The only way families are going to be able to afford the shift from institutional care to home care for seniors is if government helps to support family caregivers. This book is a call to action.

But as the stories in this book illustrate in painful detail, the very subject of elder care is politically taboo. It was yanked off the congressional tables early in the yearlong shouting match over health-care reform. "Too sensitive," I was told by then Democratic Senate leader Christopher Dodd. So the opponents of reform were able to disrupt and distract with hysterical lies about government "death panels" that could supposedly decide when to pull the plug on Grandma. That scared the socks off the oldest seniors. They didn't want anyone to mess with the socialized medicine they know and love—Medicare. Many resisted reform at any cost.

So, who will take care of us? The answer is—us.

SUSTAINABLE AGING

The "village movement" is an increasingly popular grassroots response of leading-edge boomers who don't intend to grow old the way their parents have. They don't want to be a drag on their children. And many reject what could be called "elder islands," those retirement communities built on mountains or near golf courses that have traditionally segregated older people, or the continual care campuses where the last stop is the nursing home.

A bold cadre of healthy, high-powered, mostly professional boomer women is determined to change the experience of aging by empowering adults to remain in their own homes or apartments to the end of their lives. It is a goal shared by almost nine in ten Americans, according to AARP.

"The high concept is to change the way older adults are viewed in our culture," says Mary Moore Gaines, the guiding spirit behind the birth of San Francisco Village (SFV) in January 2009. A fireball who earned her degree in divinity studies in her fifties, Rev. Gaines is rector emeritus of St. James Episcopal Church, where SFV was born.

The practical concept is what I call *sustainable aging*, meaning no new real estate, no traumatic transitions, no more putting the full burden of long-term care on a single primary caregiver. The concept of aging in community attracts people over fifty who are passionate about wanting to remain engaged in all three rings of the circus of life, not hidden in retirement homes waiting for the escalator to heaven. This approach is also the foundation of other new community-based models, such as shared equity housing and naturally occurring retirement communities, known by the jaw-crunching acronym NORCs.

But how? By reinventing the spirit of the village: people helping people, connecting with their neighbors, volunteering to walk the dog, water the plants, share intellectual stimulation, bring a casserole and eat it with a convalescent, or advocating for a newly diagnosed cancer patient on his or her first frightening consult with the surgeon.

Members of community-based villages have a one-stop number to call, like a concierge, to ask for the professional services they need. Members also invite each other for informal gatherings in their homes, to show off their Chinese cooking, to read a part in a play, to learn mindful yoga, or to head off together to a show or museum or concert or an adult education class. By sharing with the group their many life skills, as gifts, members feel valued.

The pioneer of the movement is Boston's Beacon Hill Village (BHV), which opened in 2002 (www.beaconhillvillage.org). The name called up an image of affluent Brahmins living in their town houses in close proximity, easily able to afford memberships of $600 per year for an individual and $890 per year for a household, plus à la carte fees—in exchange for the security of knowing that a prescreened carpenter, chef, computer expert, or discounted home health aide is one phone call away.

Today, Beacon Hill Village also serves central downtown Boston. Thirty percent of its members, who have an annual income below $45,000 or $50,000, are given vastly reduced membership rates for the same services.

"The explosion of the movement has been phenomenal," says Judy Willett, executive director of Beacon Hill Village for seven years. "It's a commonsense idea that is quite revolutionary." Their 450 members span a half century of ages, from fifty-one to one hundred and one. The most popular programs offer intellectual stimulation, friendship, and travel. Aging in community means meeting new friends and getting discounts—from hairdressers to personal trainers to massage therapy, all the way to home care, meal deliveries, and Lifelines.

Forty-eight villages are already operative, another eighty-plus are in development. Massachusetts has six villages; Washington, D.C., has five; Connecticut has four. They are mostly membership organizations, self-governing, consumer driven, and compared with any sort of assisted living, cheap! Memberships usually run around $600 a year for an individual and $750 to $900 for a couple.

The database is the key. These organizations vet service providers of all kinds. "You tell us what you need and we'll get it for you" is the promise. A roster of home health aides and care manager is often offered at a discount through partnerships with agencies.

I think of it as a resurgence of the commune spirit of the 1960s. Instead of isolation, aging boomers want to belong to communal families, networked as part of a virtual community, with a spicy variety of ages, sexes, cultural backgrounds, and life experiences.

What's new is that these villages are cropping up in the middle of big tough cities like New York and Chicago and San Francisco. I traveled to the Bay Area to meet with members of San Francisco Village (www.sfvillage .org).

AFTERLIFE OF A CAREGIVER

Cresting the highest hill in San Francisco, Jeanne Lacy gasps as she pitches her car down Divisadero Street at a breathtaking 180-degree angle. It's not a gasp of fear, but one of pure pleasure. Suddenly the vast bay of San Francisco has spread below us. The billowing sails of Big Boat racers slice the metallic blue of the water.

"I love this drive," breathes Jeanne.

Sailing her thirty-six-foot sloop on the bay was the one pleasure she allowed herself, weekly, during the ten-year stretch as the sole caregiver for her husband through a series of his strokes. Her beautiful face is crinkled like the water on a gusty day. "When my husband died, I just kept on sailing," she says, bringing her fist down on the steering wheel. "I won't ever give it up."

Jeanne is tall and regal, with a slight bend. "I used to be very erect," she tells me. "I rode horses and played tennis for years, and those are hard on your spine. Mine has been compressing." The only other sign of aging she noticed in her seventies was a pleasant surprise. When her hair turned white, her eyes turned bluer. They are riveting.

But after seventy-seven years of being a healthy outdoorswoman, Jeanne was completely upended by her first serious illness. It was nothing that she could have predicted or prevented. All she knew was that she flew home from London, and the next day awoke with a high fever and excruciating pain in her right leg. One of her three daughters happened to be visiting and insisted on driving Jeanne to the doctor. He called a surgeon, who recognized a rare streptococcus infection under the skin that rapidly devours soft tissue around muscles. Without immediate surgery, it can be fatal.

"It was very frightening," Jeanne says, lifting a trouser leg to show the skin grafts that saved her leg. It took multiple operations and six weeks of lying on her back. She had wonderful care at California Pacific Medical Center but was discharged from rehabilitation with no provisions for home care.

"I was extremely weak, and my foot had been raised so long that I couldn't get my heel down," she recalls. As the mother of three children, accustomed to helping her husband with their brick business, the widow didn't know how to ask for help. It meant facing the fact that there were things she could no longer do. "My girls all took turns flying in, one from Texas, one from Oregon, and my daughter farther north in California—they were fran-tic," she says. "They had no idea who to call or where to look to find somebody to care for me, drive me to doctor's appointments, shop, make some meals. . . ." Her voice trails off as she relives the shame of being such a burden.

They got through the immediate crisis with the help of Jeanne's church and family sacrifices. But her daughters were left worried about the next time, wondering "Would Mom have called 911 if she were alone? She might not have realized how sick she was."

The episode taught this hardy sailor a tough lesson: "Being independent is fine, but being too independent can be detrimental." When Jeanne Lacy finally accepted that she was "getting older," she and her daughters scouted around the Bay Area looking at three-stage retirement facilities. Jeanne hated them.

"I'd walk down a hall and see all these closed doors, and I realized I could be as lonely here as in my own house."

She was one of the first to join San Francisco Village, for the social con-nection. "Isolation is frightening to me," she admits. "As you get older, you need to have people to call to drive you, or help you with your computer, or organize a garage sale, or just come over and talk to you. If I can meet more people in the village who I feel comfortable with, it's healthy."

FOR BETTER OR WORSE

In seven years, the village movement has substantially changed the way many seniors think about preserving their independence and replenishing their sense of belonging as they move past sixty-five into their seventies and eighties. Thirty percent of Beacon Hill Village members are couples who may still be able to care for each other at home. Only 5 percent of members use home-care services.

But members who do have health crises or chronic conditions get much more than hand-holding. "Instead of being dependent on a sole caregiver, a village in your neighborhood allows you to continue to be independent and in control of your own life as you grow older," says Willett, executive direc-tor of BHV. "Members are pledged to neighbor helping neighbor through good times and bad times, instead of some institutional stranger doing it for them or telling them what to do."

Imagine this: Three of the office staff at Beacon Hill are social workers with master's degrees. They offer geriatric care management free. "We spend a lot of time on the phone talking to hospital discharge planners, to ensure a smooth and effective transition to home," says Willett. If the case becomes complex or ongoing, BHV has vetted an outside provider of professional geriatric care managers. The village also has a strategic partnership with a home-care agency that offers its members flexibility in care, ranging from one hour to 24/7. All these services come with a 10 percent discount.

Prevention is key in all the villages. Some offer exercise classes, checkup calls, and respite care for the caregiver. Beacon Hill Village has a roster of $20/hour helpers who can deliver prescriptions and meals, give rides to doctors, and offer coverage when the family caregiver needs a vacation.

True to its egalitarian spirit, San Francisco wanted to adapt the village movement to its heterogeneous neighborhoods. The first hub is in the Richmond District, just across Golden Gate Bridge on the city side. An upwardly mobile middle and lower-middle-class neighborhood, it's a mix of Asians, Irish, and Russian families who migrated when the Soviet Union broke up.

In my interviews, I heard story after story of robust seventy-somethings, accustomed to climbing the hills of their city until the day they "stepped off the cliff," meaning the day of their first fall or emergency hospitalization, or the day they could no longer pretend that their memory blanks weren't just senior moments.

"The idea of having a community of people we can socialize with and depend upon as we grow older had a lot of appeal to us, as a couple," says Judy Spain, the older partner in a lesbian relationship with a physical therapist. Judy is sixty-eight and still wears ankle and knee braces from a car accident decades ago. "I walk with a cane, so that automatically ruled me out for long-term care," she says. "We have each other, but that doesn't last forever. We need a backup." She and her partner took immediately to the village concept. "Gays and lesbians don't usually have children and are often ostracized by their families. Relying on a community to take care of each other has been our survival."

The experience of Don and Judy Langley broadened the vision of the SFV board. "We had planned to spend the rest of our lives in our big Victorian house in Pacific Heights," says Don, a trim, well-barbered retiree. But then he was bed-bound on painkillers for several months following hospital-ization. His wife, Judy, a gerontologist, hovered over him constantly moni-toring his drugs—not too many, not too few. Once Don recovered, he woke up to a new reality.

"We have no children and no dependable family nearby," he realized. It began to sink in that he couldn't keep up with the gardening and house re-pair. "We knew we had to take care of ourselves, and we were looking for a way to get services." They joined San Francisco Village in the nearby Rich-mond District. This would be their backup.

But just as they were about to move into a retirement condo project, the economy tanked, bankrupting the project and forcing the Langleys to sell their home of forty years into a down market. Their Realtor found them an-other condo, but it was far across the city in Mission Bay, a construction zone near the new AT&T ballpark on the water. To their surprise, it was ideal. "The big change energized us," says Don. "We loved making new friends and meeting all the dogs." Soon after they moved in, Judy broke her elbow. She was helpless. People in their new building, people she hardly knew, be-gan bringing her food.

"I thought, why can't I start our own village over here?" Judy put out a flyer in the neighborhood in November of 2008, inviting neighbors to help neighbors as they aged. Houseboat people came; they had never met the land people. Numbers grew. Younger people joined in. Groups began doing a weekly walk together, biking to find new restaurants.

Board members Gayle Geary, Susan Poor, and Mary Moore Gaines got excited about seeding "pods" of new villages throughout the city's diverse neighborhoods. Why not the Mission District, Chinatown, the Marina, Pa-cific Heights? Still, the biggest barrier is people's reluctance to admit they are getting older. Potential members who hear Rev. Gaines pitch the concept most often say, "Great idea, but I'm not ready."

Dawn Ming, a petite Asian painter, wasn't ready, either, until she fell and broke her femur. More than a year later, at seventy-nine, she is still using a cane. She is rallying other Asians to think ahead about their long-term care. "A friend told me she's already bought into an assisted-living home, but she's waiting 'for later.' Her husband has Parkinson's and is in pain. I said, 'How long are you waiting?'"

Don Langley bristles when he hears such procrastination. "You don't wait until your house is on fire before you get fire insurance."

NEW YORK, NEW YORK, IF YOU CAN AGE HERE . . .

. . . you can age anywhere. It might seem daunting to imagine dodging kamikaze cabbies and texting speed-walkers; being subjected to the noise of jackhammers, sirens, and screeching subways. Not to mention the prospect of being stranded in your high-rise apartment when the elevators go out.

But New Yorkers are getting older, too. And many of us think the city is the best of all places to grow older. We like our sloped sidewalks and snug apartments and dazzling street life and theater in the park. We wish we had time to catch all the free entertainment and classes and rehearsals of the Philharmonic. Our transportation as seniors is virtually free—a buck and change on any bus or subway will get you almost anywhere. And our buses kneel—that's right, they whoosh right down to the curb to allow wheel-chairs to board and be locked in and unloaded at their stop.

The only question is: Can we live solo as we age without any hedges against loneliness, inactivity, or the middle-of-the-night health crises?

Charlotte Frank didn't miss a beat after retiring from her career in publishing as a senior vice-president at McGraw-Hill. In 2000, she cofounded The Transition Network (TTN) (www.thetransitionnetwork.org). It is a virtual community of women over fifty pledged to help one another reinvent themselves for a second and third act that has proliferated into forty-four states with a total of forty-five hundred members. Frank is seen as a polestar to women of her generation, pioneers of the women's movement who poked the first holes in the glass ceilings of medicine, law, finance, academia, journalism, politics, and so on.

TTN members are culturally and racially diverse. They are accustomed to being productive and authoritative and, on the proper occasions, pushy.

"Turning into a little old lady would not be a graceful transition for us." Dr. Diana Killip, a retired internist typical of TTN members, laughs. "We don't have the proper humility." Dr. Killip shifted into advocating for children by grappling with the city's bureaucracies.

But as the earliest TTN members are moving into their sixties and seventies, many find themselves living alone. Charlotte Frank is among those who chose to stay in New York City. She would depend on the same fierce self-reliance that had always protected her—until it almost killed her.

In the summer of 2006, Ms. Frank braved successful surgery to remove her thyroid gland. Just seventy, she took a taxi back to the midtown apartment she had occupied for twenty years, expecting a rapid recovery. But she couldn't talk. Her vocal cords had been paralyzed, and she wouldn't be allowed to replace her thyroid functions with medication for several months, until a scan could show if all the cancer was gone.

"In addition to not being able to speak, I had no energy," she recalls. "I had no interest in food. They talked about putting in a feeding tube. It was terrifying."

Several friends found out about her plight and began bringing soup and smoothies and stashing casseroles in her freezer. "I would never have asked them," she admits, "but they knew I needed help."

Rather than give in to fear and frustration over those months, Charlotte Frank gathered a core group of retired and working doctors, nursing professors, lawyers, and journalists who belonged to The Transition Network. They, too, were a little older now. How could they tap into the sustainable aging concept in the big brawling city they loved? They wanted to extend the role of caregiver into a broader community, to give the family caregiver a break and take the pressure off adult children.

This was how the village concept awakened in Manhattan. On an island of 1,634,000 people, the group came up with a new model called the Caring Collaborative. After two years of focus groups and a $144,000 grant, they have trained more than a hundred members to act as a "service corps" of volunteers in five neighborhoods. One woman might escort another to a medical appointment, take notes, and help sort out the instructions and medications, relieving the patient from hiring a geriatric care manager at $100 to $250 an hour. Or the service might be walking the dog, paying bills, or reorganizing a closet.

How does this model override the habitual resistance to asking for help? "By giving help," replied Laura Traynor, project manager of the Collaborative. The beauty at the center of the Caring Collaborative is a time bank for depositing and withdrawing mutual help. The hours each member gives to help others are recorded. If one woman spends two hours on the phone with another, sharing her experience in caring for a spouse with Alzheimer's, she can redeem those hours when she needs an escort after an outpatient procedure, or when she needs a prescription filled, a drop-by visit, or just an evening call to see if she's okay.

"This way, a value is placed on caregiving," says Traynor.

Newcomers fill out a questionnaire recording any medical history they are willing to discuss, from arthritis to cancer to depression. They're encouraged to share any outstanding experiences they have had with medical professionals or hospitals. A database records this rich store of consumer information, enabling the Collaborative to share it with members seeking advice.

There is already a substantial and growing demand by active seniors to participate directly in their own health maintenance and healing. But people don't want to have to run all over town to see different doctors; it's tiring and expensive.

Martha Stewart to the rescue! As a trusted innovator in improving quality of living, Stewart has expanded her vision to attract older residents of the Big Apple into a unique environment for comprehensive health care, healing, and activities. The Martha Stewart Center for Living is part of Mt. Sinai Hospital on the upper east side of Manhattan. It's an aesthetically soothing ground-floor environment designed by I. M. Pei and decorated with Stewart's knowing eye.

The care team includes a physician specializing in geriatric medicine and palliative care, nurse practitioners, registered nurses, social workers, and medical assistants who work together to deliver comprehensive care. Consultations are arranged with on-site specialists such as cardiologists, rheumatologists, gastroenterologists, endocrinologists, and psychiatrists. The interdisciplinary team also provides spiritual and emotional support and palliative care consults for patients with active or advanced illness.

COMMUNITY CARE COMES TO YOU

Residential senior-care campuses are beginning to see the light. Why wait until seniors in their community are too old and enfeebled to remain in their own homes? Considering the staggering number of boomers who will be moving into the Medicare generation, how can institutions afford the brick-and-mortar facilities to warehouse them without breaking their budgets?

One of the most enlightened models of integrated senior health and caregiver support in the country is the Motion Picture & Television Fund. Originally founded almost ninety years ago, MPTF is dedicated to taking care of over sixty thousand members of the entertainment industry in Southern California. The organization has six outpatient health-care centers and a beautiful forty-eight-acre campus in Woodland Hills offering multiple levels of senior care, including independent and assisted living.

Ken Scherer, executive director of the MPTF Foundation, realized the Fund needed a new vision. "We had frustrated people waiting for seven or eight years to get onto the campus because of the explosion in seniors. That meant the residents were not coming in until age eighty-six or eighty-seven. You don't become old and dependent overnight. The people coming in shocked us. They were very frail and their end-of-life care was complicated and very demanding for families as well as our staff."

Scherer had a similarly traumatic experience with his own mother six years ago. "My mother was eighty-four and in a rehab hospital," he remembers. "She refused to eat or talk to me. I flew from California to see her in Bethlehem, Pennsylvania. She said, 'Let me go.' My mother chose to die, but she didn't have to." As his mother's sole caregiver, he had no one to talk to. "I needed to tell someone, I don't know what to do. I'm lost."

He went back to MPTF thinking he'd had a revelation. He learned that their geriatrician and social workers were having those kinds of crisis conversations with caregivers all the time. The Fund was ideally set up to create a network of support, beginning with an intensive evaluation of people referred by their clinics. It was also plain to the MPTF board that given the multitude of boomers moving into Medicare age, the nonprofit couldn't possibly serve them with long-term, full-service nursing care in their hospital. The hospital was losing in excess of $10 million annually. It would have to be closed in order to meet the growing and changing needs of its community of seniors.

Many of their contemporary seventy-five-year-old retirees were resistant to residential living, protesting, "No, no. I'm not ready yet, but I do have some needs. Can you help me with my diabetes?" MPTF's response was to build a state-of-the-art Health and Wellness Center, and to launch an Age Well Program of preventive care. Their mission needed to shift to helping greater numbers of members remain safely at home and independent. As the issues of aging become more complicated and emotional for everyone involved, the Fund also wanted to offer support and counseling.

Fund members can now come to the center for a full physical and cognitive assessment by the geriatrician. Family and any potential caregivers are invited to join in. The doctor doesn't just ask about aches and pains but delves into individuals' needs. What, for them, constitutes quality of life? Who are the family members, neighbors, friends, and church members who could be involved in expanding that quality? How can seniors be encouraged to be more actively engaged?

Seniors are invited into the center's state-of-the-art gym. Once a geriatric trainer programs their exercises, they are given a personal "smart key," which reproduces the sequence and monitors their progress or decline (many YMCAs now offer similar equipment programming). Veteran actors and screenwriters offer classes in various forms of creative expression. There are opportunities for civic engagement. Probably the greatest benefit for people who frequent the Saban Health and Wellness Center, while they are still well, is the new friends they make.

This is community-based care. This is the future. Programs like these treat the family, not just the individual. The ultimate objective is to develop a life management plan and the support to pursue it.

FINAL WORDS . . .

We are not meant to travel the labyrinth of caregiving alone. In this book you and I together have learned how to empower ourselves to fulfill the role of family caregiver confidently and effectively, without losing our own health or capacity for joy. Over and over again, we have seen that successful caregivers seek out and enlist people who are able to partner with them in a collaborative team: doctors who are willing to be your medical quarterback; care managers who can direct you through the minefield of muddled choices; palliative-care teams that can help you restore control to your loved one and support a good quality of life through the In-Between

Stage. Just as important is learning to let your family members and friends know what help you need, and building a circle of care that will share the responsibility.

Now you know to start having The Conversation early with your parents and your loved ones. You know to begin broaching the subject with your siblings before a crisis about how you can pool your strengths when it comes time to help Mom and Dad.

Most important of all, I urge you to remember to take care of yourself. Remember, there is life after caregiving. And having done the work of angels, you deserve to be alive to enjoy every moment of it.

What follows is a list of mantras—reminders of actions that will take you around each turning—and keep you on the right path to the end of the labyrinth. Tear out the page and stick it on your refrigerator. Think Serenity!

FROM CRISIS TO CLOSURE

1. Shock and Mobilization: **Advocate with Authority**
2. New Normal: **Turn Illness into Opportunity**
3. Boomerang: **Summon a Family Meeting**
4. Playing God: **Accept What You Cannot Change**
5. I Can't Do This Anymore! **Create a Circle of Care**
6. Coming Back: **Replenish Your Lifelines**
7. The In-Between Stage: **Prepare Your Own Path to Comeback**
8. The Long Good-bye: **Love Is Letting Go, Together**

RESOURCES
HOTLINES FOR CAREGIVERS

National disease organizations are excellent resources, primed to answer your first questions about the diagnosis you or your loved one has just received. Most have tools to help you decide among treatment recommendations. They also have local chapters that can steer you to telephone support groups.

CANCER

American Cancer Society: www.cancer.org. Hotline: (24/7) 800-227-2345. Cancer information specialists answer myriad questions about any kind of cancer, insurance, and employment rights after diagnosis.

Cancer Care: www.cancercare.org. Hotline: 800-813-4673. The website provides free counseling for cancer patients and caregivers. Oncology-trained social workers field queries about your disease, treatments, financial assistance, insurance. The hotline provides direct conversation and telephone support groups.

People Living with Cancer: www.plwc.org or www.cancer.net. 888-651-3038. The website provides detailed information on eighty-five types of cancer, articles on coping with the disease, and a national database of oncologists you can use to find those in your local area. No hotline. A service of American Society of Clinical Oncologists.

HEART DISEASE

American Heart Association: www.americanheart.org. Hotline: 800-242-8721. The website provides useful facts about most heart diseases, plus an online treatment decision tool. At the twenty-four-hour hotline, trained operators can amplify website information, but they cannot refer to doctors in your area or offer mental health support.

STROKE

American Stroke Association: www.strokeassociation.org. 888-478-7653. The website provides medical information and a database of doctors, hospitals, and rehabilitation centers known for quality care of stroke patients.

LUNG DISEASE

American Lung Association: www.lungusa.org. Helpline: 800-548-8252. The website gives general information about lung cancer, emphysema, and chronic obstructive pulmonary disease (COPD), and includes online deci-sion treatment tools for various conditions. Registered nurses answer ques-tions about your disease, refer to a doctor in your area, counsel you on insurance, medication, and case management.

ALZHEIMER'S DISEASE

Alzheimer's Association: www.alz.org. Hotline: 800-272-3900. The website contains information about the disease, including treatments, statistics, and help for caregivers. It also includes information on Medicare and Medicaid insurance, and a list of clinical trials. The trained hotline operators handle general questions about the disease, treatment, insurance, and financial is-sues. They can transfer you to a clinician for help with decision-making tools, personalized advice, and caregivers' questions.

MULTIPLE SCLEROSIS

National Multiple Sclerosis Society: www.nationalmssociety.org. (800-344-4867). A fifty-state network of chapters offers job counseling, family pro-grams, and volunteer opportunities. The national office's easy-to-use website has information about the disease, treatments, and affiliated treatment fa-cilities.

PARKINSON'S DISEASE

National Parkinson's Foundation: www.parkinson.org. (800-327-4545). American Parkinson Disease Association: www.apdaparkinson.org. (800-223-2732). Both websites provide general information on Parkinson's and its treatment. The National Parkinson's Foundation site has an online library of articles that can be downloaded free. Neither national organization offers medical advice, mental health counseling, or doctor referrals. But each web-site has contact information for local chapters that may help you find some of these services.

ALS

Amyotrophic Lateral Sclerosis Association: www.alsa.org. Hotline: 800-782-4747. ALS hotline operators guide callers to website information and offer doctor referrals in your area. The site can also clarify your Medicare eligibility.

DIABETES

American Diabetes Association: www.diabetes.org. (800-342-2383). The easy-to-use website is packed with information. Click on Newly Diagnosed, and the site will walk you through the disease and its management in a straightforward and practical way.

AIDS

National Association of People with AIDS: www.napwa.org. (866–846–9366). NAPWA is the oldest national AIDS organization, as well as the world's first network of people living with HIV/AIDS in the world.

Centers for Disease Control and Prevention: www.cdc.gov. (800-CDC-INFO [800-232-4636]). CDC'S twenty-four-hour operators can refer you to local hotlines, clinics, counseling, and support groups. They don't offer mental health counseling or specific doctor referrals.

OTHER SERVICES

Veterans Administration: www1.va.gov/health/HealthWellness.asp. (800-827-1000, VA Benefits; or 877-222-8387, VA Health Care Benefits). The VA has a wealth of health information and programs available to veterans throughout the country. Use their website or hotline for insurance and financial assistance, chaplain and social services, and special programs for cancer, HIV/AIDS, diabetes, blindness, kidney disease, and service injuries.

HOSPICE PROGRAMS

The Hospice of the Florida Suncoast
5771 Roosevelt Blvd.
Clearwater, FL 33760
Mary Labyak, MSW
www.thehospice.org

National Hospice Work Group
217 Lakeshore Drive
Grosse Pointe Farms, MI 48236
Carolyn Cassin, MPA
www.nhwg.org

National Hospice Work Group
314 Loudonville Road
Loudonville, NY 12211
Amber Jones, M.Ed., BA
www.nhwg.org

Hope Hospice & Community Services
9470 Health Park Circle
Fort Myers, FL 33908-3617
Samira Beckwith, LCSW, FACHE
www.hopehospice.org

Hospice of Michigan
400 Mack Avenue
Detroit, MI 48201
Dottie Deremo, MSN, MHSA, RN, CNAA, CHE
www.hom.org

The Center for Hospice & Palliative Care, Inc.
225 Como Park Blvd.
Cheektowaga, NY 14227

Bill Finn, MBA
www.hospicebuffalo.com

Valley Hospice, Inc.
10686 State Route 150
Rayland, OH 43943
Cynthia Bougher, MSN, RN, CHPN
www.valleyhospice.org

Hospice of the Bluegrass
2312 Alexandria Drive
Lexington, KY 40504-3277
Gretchen Brown, MSW
www.hospicebg.com

San Diego Hospice and The Institute for Palliative Medicine
4311 Third Avenue
San Diego, CA 92103-1407
Jan Cetti, BSN, MS
www.sdhospice.org

Four Seasons Hospice & Palliative Care
571 South Allen Road
Flat Rock, NC 28731
Christopher Comeaux, CPA
www.fourseasonscfl.org

Hospice of Dayton, Inc.
324 Wilmington Avenue
Dayton, OH 45420
Deborah Dailey, MBA
www.hospiceofdayton.org

Capital Hospice
6565 Arlington Blvd., #501
Falls Church, VA 22042

Malene Davis, MSN, CHPN, MBA
www.capitalhospice.org

Hospice of Palm Beach County
5300 East Avenue
West Palm Beach, FL 33407-2387
David Fielding, BA, MS
www.hpbc.com

Good Shepherd Hospice
245 Old Country Road
Melville, NY 11747
Marianne Gillan, RN, BSN
www.goodshepherdhospice.org

Community Hospice of Texas
6100 Western Place
Fort Worth, TX 76107
Andrea Green
www.chot.org

Alive Hospice, Inc.
1718 Patterson Street
Nashville, TN 37203
Jan Jones, RN, BSN, FAAMA
www.alivehospice.org

Covenant Hospice
5041 N. 12th Avenue
Pensacola, FL 32504
Dale Knee
www.covenanthospice.org

University of Colorado at Denver and Health Sciences Center (UCDHSC)
Academic Office 1
PO Box 6511
Aurora, CO 80045
Jean Kutner, MD, MSPH
www.uccc.info

The Corridor Group
2515 Ocean Avenue, Suite 3
San Francisco, CA 94132
Jeannee Parker Martin
www.corridorgroup.com

The Watershed Group
5745 SW 75th Street, #323
Gainesville, FL 32608
Patti Moore, RN, MSN
www.thewatershedgroup.com

Hospice Austin
4107 Spicewood Springs Road, #100
Austin, TX 78759
Marjorie Mulanax, MBA
www.hospiceaustin.org

Arent Fox LLP
1675 Broadway, 32nd Floor
New York, NY 10019
Connie A. Raffa, J.D., LL.M
www.arentfox.com

Hospice and Palliative Care of Cape Cod
765 Attucks Lane
Hyannis, MA 02601

David Rehm, MSW
www.hospicecapecod.org

Sutter VNA & Hospice
4830 Business Center Drive, #140
Fairfield, CA 94534
Marcia P. Reissig, RN, MS
www.suttervnaandhospice.org

National Hospice & Palliative Care Organization
1731 King Street, Suite 100
Alexandria, VA 22314
Don Schumacher, Psy.D.
www.nhpco.org

Midwest Palliative & Hospice
CareCenter
2050 Claire Court
Glenview, IL 60025
Mary Sheehan, RN, MSN, MBA
www.midwestpalliativeandhospicecarecenter.org

Hospice of the Western Reserve
300 E. 185th Street
Cleveland, OH 44119
David Simpson, MA, MSW
www.hospicewr.org

The Denver Hospice
501 S. Cherry Street, Suite 700
Denver, CO 80246
Bev Sloan, BS, MPH
www.thedenverhospice.org

The Community Hospice
295 Valley View Blvd.
Rensselaer, NY 12144
Ron Watson
www.communityhospice.org

Hospice and Palliative Care of Western Colorado
2754 Compass Drive, Suite 377
Grand Junction, CO 81506
Christy Whitney, RN, MSN
www.hospicewco.com

PALLIATIVE CARE PROGRAMS

San Diego Hospice and The Institute for Palliative Medicine, San Diego, California

San Diego Hospice and the Institute for Palliative Medicine is one of the ten largest community-owned, not-for-profit hospice programs in the nation, caring for a thousand patients daily in their homes or other facilities in San Diego County. Services include hospital-based consult services, dedicated inpatient units, outpatient clinics, home hospice, and home health services. The program is led by Charles von Gunten, M.D., Ph.D., E-mail: cvongunten@sdhospice.org. Their website is www.sdhospice.org.

Fairview Health System, Minneapolis, Minnesota

Fairview is a health-system-based palliative care program with interdisciplinary consult teams, an outpatient clinic, and a strong focus on community hospitals and home care. The program is led by Lyn Ceronsky, MS, GNP, BC, and Sandra Gordon-Kolb, M.D., CPE, MMM. E-mail: lcerons1@fairview.org.

Palliative Care Center of the Bluegrass, Lexington, Kentucky

Palliative Care Center is a wholly owned subsidiary of Hospice of the Bluegrass. It provides palliative care consultation to multiple community hospitals and academic medical centers. Program elements include outpatient clinic and consultation in long-term-care settings. The center is led by Gretchen M. Brown, MSW, President/CEO. E-mail: gretchen@hospicebg. com.

University of Alabama at Birmingham, Birmingham, Alabama

UAB provides clinical palliative care and supportive care services through inpatient consult services, home hospice coordination, and outpatient clinics. It is affiliated with the Birmingham VA Medical Center and is led by Christine S. Ritchie, M.D., MSPH; Rodney Tucker, M.D.; and Amos Bailey, M.D. E-mail: CRitchie@aging.uab.edu.

VCU Massey Cancer Center, Richmond, Virginia

VCU is an academic safety-net hospital and NCI-designated cancer center. It includes a consult service, dedicated inpatient unit, and rural outreach and active outpatient care programs. The center is led by Thomas J. Smith, M.D., and Patrick J. Coyne, MSN, APRN, BC. E-mail: tsmith@hsc.vcu.edu.

Akron Children's Hospital, Akron, Ohio

This is an academic children's hospital that maintains 24/7 inpatient and outpatient consult services. The hospital works closely with community hospice and long-term and homecare programs. The program is led by Sarah Friebert, M.D. E-mail: sfriebert@chmca.org.

ACKNOWLEDGMENTS

I began writing this work as I lived it—in journals. I was merely trying to make sense of what I was experiencing. There was no idea of a book, not until I published an article in *Parade*, titled "Are You Ready to Be a Caregiver?" Barraged with heartfelt e-mails from fellow caregivers, I called them up. We all felt alone and scared. We shared our stories. We needed one another.

It was Richard Pine, my agent at Inkwell Management and a family caregiver himself, who spurred me on to write the book that we all needed. We found the ideal editor in Mary Ellen O'Neill, another family caregiver and senior vice president at HarperCollins and executive editor of the William Morrow imprint. Mary Ellen was constant in her encouragement and a brilliant interlocutor, always asking me on behalf of all kinds of caregivers to find more answers and better help. Her editorial assistant, Mac Mackie, was enormously helpful through the editing and proofreading crunch.

Hugh Delehanty, editor in chief of AARP Publications, approached me with the idea of writing a first draft of my book on the new AARP website for caregivers. Ken Scherer, executive director of the Motion Picture & Television Foundation Fund, and another family caregiver, enthusiastically supported this year-long project. He provided a talented producer, Marijane Miller, and a multitalented director of photography/editor, Jeffrey Kaufer, to travel the country with me to search out creative caregivers and film their stories.

I was honored to be named AARP Ambassador of Caregiving. Through 2009 I wrote dozens of journal entries to accompany the videos on the website and answer questions. Nancy Luscombe, another fellow caregiver, became my indefatigable and ever-resourceful research assistant on both the website and the book. Kobi Carter, yet another member of the caregiver tribe, joined our team as a super-organized executive assistant. My brilliant website designers, Dave Campbell and Patrick Curran from 3 Rings Media, created my online questionnaire. Robert Shnayerson read the book as it developed.

I could not have completed this journey as a caregiver and a writer without the unfailing support of my daughter, Maura Sheehy, and my sister, Pat Klein, both of whom are writers themselves and discerning readers of this book-in-progress. I want also to thank: my soul sister, Dr. Pat Allen; my long time personal assistant, Ella Council; my resourceful care manager, Mary Tierney; and Dr. Sean Morrison, a visionary geriatrician; each of whom cradled my troubled soul at critical moments.

I am indebted to the professional caregivers who taught me and sustained Clay with extraordinary empathy: Isatou Sawahnee, Safoura Tall, Barbara Balazy, Florenz Loquias, Yvonne Morris, Jackie Joseph, and hospice nurse Lynn Fisher. Yolanda Ormaza was the perpetually-charged battery who kept this complex caregiving machine functioning smoothly.

Peter J. Strauss, a distinguished elder care attorney at Epstein, Becker & Greene and author of the definitive text on elder law, was an invaluable research guide and translator of arcane and inconsistent legal barriers. His colleague, Amy Trotter, and his counterpart in Boston, Harry Margolis at Margolis & Assoc., were also very helpful.

When it came to publishing, I was fortunate to have the full support of the skilled William Morrow/HarperCollins team: Liate Stehlik, publisher, SVP; Lynn Grady, deputy publisher, SVP; Dee Dee Debartlo, senior director of publicity; Seale Ballenger, director of publicity, VP; Andrea Rosen, special markets, SVP; Jean Marie Kelly, senior director of marketing; Shawn Nicholls, director of online marketing; Kim Lewis, senior executive managing Editor; Joyce Wong, senior production editor; Kim Chocolaad, marketing associate; Mary Schuck, art director; and Lisa Stokes, senior interior designer.

Many good people began dedicating themselves to building awareness and support for family caregivers long before I became involved. For their guidance I want to thank especially Lynne Friss Feinberg, who founded the Family Caregiver Alliance in San Francisco over thirty years ago as a grassroots program to improve the quality of life for caregivers of loved ones with cognitive impairments. Her senior social worker, Donna Schempp, was an excellent resource.

Another breakthrough program, Powerful Tools for Caregivers, developed by Kathy Shannon and Leslie Congleton in Portland, Oregon, for Legacy Health System, taught me a great deal and led me to interview inspiring graduates of their program.

Gregory L. Johnson, director of community outreach for EmblemHealth and co-chair of the New York Family Caregiver Coalition, introduced me to the many fine programs under the umbrella of the New York City coalition that he helped found.

I am grateful to leaders of the national movement who have established a knowledge base and freely shared it with me: Gail Gibson Hunt, president and CEO of the National Alliance for Caregiving is a tower of research; Suzanne Mintz, president and cofounder of National Family Caregivers Association, is also author of *Love, Honor & Value—a Family Caregiver Speaks Out About the Choices and Challenges of Caregiving* (Capitol Books, 2002); Carol Levine, another indefatigable researcher, directs the Families and Health Care Project out of the United Hospital Fund. The Fund provides an excellent free website where Levine has created booklets to help with all stages of patient transitions, www.nextstepincare.org. Levine is also a veteran caregiver and author of *Always on Call*. Carolyn Cassin is president and CEO of the National Hospice Work Group and a pioneer in advancement of hospice and palliative care.

INDEX